SAMUEL E. PAIR

Le Yankee Noir

The Power of Acceptance

Contents

Preface

I began writing this book two and a half years after retiring from jet engine producer Pratt and Whitney. Upon departing the company in October 2006, I was a thirty-eight-year employee (aerospace engineer) who had spent the last twelve of those years as an industrial specialist and manager of propulsion systems manufacturing—working with counterparts of aircraft manufacturer Airbus and other European aerospace companies. As I scanned a journal I had scribed while serving Pratt and Airbus and interacting with locals in France, I reflected on memorable experiences, reliving the feeling of acceptance, its influence on inspiring me, and my ability to build relational bridges.

Perhaps it was an April 2009 e-mail from Bernard, an Airbus Quality Department manager, that rekindled reminiscences of my time working with Airbus and the joy I felt from the accommodation in the south of France. In the prior two springs of my retirement, Bernard had sent e-mails at this time of the year to share his thoughts about controlling the frog population in the koi pond in my backyard in Connecticut. Although I accepted little of his advice, there was shared amusement in his recommendations to mitigate the frog propagation and likewise with my counter proposals. Nonetheless, during these repartees, there was mutual acceptance and respect, as it had been while collaborating on solving aircraft and engine problems in Toulouse.

While writing this book, I hoped to share an account of my sudden summoning to France in 1994 to oversee recovery of a floundering new propulsion program for intensely anticipated jetliners—noting key events, significant setbacks, and the impact of acceptance that fostered my perseverance to overcome them. More importantly, I wanted to impart a sense of what it was like being an African-American aerospace engineer plunged into a critical, highly visible assignment, in a working environment of cultural uncertainty, contention, and mistrust.

Additional stimulation to tell this personal story came from events that occurred decades prior to and during the writing. Admittedly, it was a struggle to get the words on the page, but my recollection of a crushing second rejection, earlier in my career, to a quest to enter a management development program in the company, remained vivid years later. Also, the election of the first black U.S. president in 2008 and the open resentment of his ascendancy to the nation's highest office broadcast a reflection of what many in the U.S. thought a United States president and occupants of important positions shouldn't look like.

Finally, I wanted to share a story that will inspire students of every ethnicity to consider rewarding STEM careers and persevere to succeed. When growing up, my mom and dad drilled college and "stick-to-it-ness" into me. They often recited, "We are Black, but a part of the same human race."

This book is for people, young and old, who are facing cultural chasms, as I had, and want to see intercultural acceptance in a new way that promotes building relational bridges. Furthermore, my desire is to convey a unique story to students, young professionals, and the aerospace industry that is intended to explore the benefits of acceptance and illuminate the rewards of STEM-related fields (science, technology, engineering, and mathematics). Hopefully this book stimulates an interest in standing in the shoes of people unlike ourselves, pursuing careers in aerospace and creating fond memories like mine.

July 17, 2023

1

The Premiere Jour - First Day

"I don't see why we need a Frenchman to come over here and tell us how to play American Music, I wouldn't think of going to France and telling him how to jump on a grape." *Eddie Condon, jazz musician.*

How do you gain acceptance and success in the new world when viewed with suspicion as the outsider? I wondered after listening to Norm's offer.

I was summoned to Norman's office on a quiet April morning in 1994, baffled by his urgency to see me. As I peered in bewilderment through the doorway of my boss's office, his furrowed brow and steely gaze told me it was serious. "Come on in," said Norm when he saw me, waving his hand in a welcoming motion. Seemingly edgy, searching frantically for notes of a prior conversation, Norm uttered a withering "Hi" and leaped into a demand he had just received from Toulouse, France.

Apparently, during a meeting that Norm's boss, Rick, the Vice President of our product delivery center, had attended in Toulouse, a vice president of European aircraft maker Airbus SE had demanded that an industrial specialist from our company be sent over.

"Rick needs an industrial manager in France right away," said Norm, looking me straight in the eyes. "Specifically," Norm continued, "he's looking for someone to oversee and take charge of the on-site recovery of our floundering new propulsion system program for the air-framer's intensely anticipated A330 jetliners." Intrigued, I listened closely as Norm explained the issues concerning Airbus, wondering why he was telling me this. I imagined the challenges of introducing a new commercial aircraft. As Norm spoke about the urgent call, my mind became tangled in who he and Rick had in mind to send over.

Following an hour of expounding about the urgent appeal, Norm asked the question I sensed he was leading to. With his eyes locked on mine, he repeated the demand of the Airbus vice president: to assign a point person to take on-site ownership of our new propulsion system program. From the beginning of Norm's explanation, it was clear that the introduction of our engines, developed for the A330 aircraft and their composite carbon fiber nacelles, weren't meeting the air-framer's expectations.

"Well, are you interested?" Norm asked with a persuasive smile.

Reluctant to say an immediate "Yes," I expressed an interest in the task and asked for time to think it over.

"Who do you think should go over?" Norm asked with a stern tone.

"I don't know. How long would the assignment be for?" I asked.

"No more than three months," Norm answered, scratching his head. "Any other thoughts about a candidate for the assignment?" he inquired.

Hearing my "No," Norm blared, "Well, I do."

"Who?" I asked, anticipating the inevitable.

Thrusting his index finger at me, Norman uttered a soft, "You!"

My throat swelled upon hearing his suggestion. "When do you need my decision?"

"Where will you be at this time tomorrow?" Norm queried.

"I'll be visiting my daughter's college in North Carolina," I replied.

At this time, I was totally in the dark about the complexity of the task and the issues of concern in Toulouse. Would prior knowledge of the problems affect my decision to accept the duty? It's easy to say "No," but after chewing on the proposal for a day, I gave Norm a guarded "Yes." Assignments like these are offered to favored sons and fair-haired boys, I considered before making my decision.

"Great. You're the right guy. See you soon," Norm said.

When I left Norm's office, I thought that this was a big undertaking with much at stake, but the prospect of an assignment in the south of France was alluring. Plus, according to Norm, the task would be just three months. The day after I met with Norm, I started a one-week vacation in North Carolina, where I continually thought about the assignment.

At the time, I was a forty-eight-year-old African-American manager of Manufacturing Engineering for the engine assembly and testing organization of Pratt and Whitney, headquartered in East Hartford, Connecticut. The company produced aircraft engines and propulsion systems (jet engines integrated with cowling and other aerostructures) in Middletown, Connecticut, and delivered them to aircraft manufacturers like Airbus in Toulouse, France, Boeing in Seattle, Washington, and McDonnell Douglas in Long Beach, California. I reported to Norm, the plant manager of engine assembly and testing, who absorbed the additional responsibility of delivering the entire propulsion system a year before selecting me for this assignment. After an inter-departmental reorganization, Norm became accountable for deliveries of major components of propulsion systems, including thrust reversers, cowling (items shrouding engines installed on aircraft), and the engines he had already been producing .

Since the beginning of 1994, I had been buried in managing restructuring projects associated with merging two engine assembly facilities (East Hartford and Middletown) located twenty-five miles apart. In addition, I was tasked with overseeing modifications to the consolidated assembly facility, its production fixtures and overhead support systems, and an array of commercial and military aircraft engines. It was an onerous task. Concurrently, I was immersed in launching the engine assembly introduction of three new commercial aircraft engine models and a new military engine for the F22 military fighter aircraft. Although my plate had been full since the beginning of the year, I imagined a greater task after hearing Norm's briefing.

During my eighteen months working directly for Norm, I thought we had a great boss-subordinate relationship. His affinity for aircraft engines was admirable, but his devotion to the organization that produced them made him highly respected and renowned throughout the company. No department in the company escaped his scrutiny when it came to providing parts needed to assemble his engines. As a boss, Norm relied heavily on me, showing trust in my ability to complete tasks on time. The mutual trust between Norm and myself was undeniable. We accepted one another, which, I thought, contributed to our great rapport.

Heeding the urgent need to fulfill the request of Airbus, I shortened my vacation by a few days. Upon returning to my home in Bloomfield, a small town near Hartford, I rushed to reduce the burden on my family, including my wife, Loretta, and our two college-age daughters. When I discussed Norm's offer with Loretta, she considered her aging mother living alone and felt it would be best for her to stay closer to her mother. Thus, we mutually decided that I would go to France alone. Optimistic about the task, I left the States full of hope that I would meet the expectations of the air-framer, those who tasked me and our company's senior management.

Among aviation and aerospace industry employees, there is a collective recognition of the importance of the task they perform and a common acknowledgment of the consequences of failure. It's the nature of work in this industry, as I learned during my three decades in the industrial trenches. When facing a critical task, anxiety juxtaposed with competence tends to elevate one's mindfulness of what they are doing. There is no entitlement to success. It's earned through hard work, perseverance, and trust. When the task is finished, those involved in executing it should be held accountable for the outcome because, in this industry, the lives of airline passengers are affected by incompetence and failures to succeed.

A week after accepting the assignment, I departed for France, carrying a ton of uncertainty about the work ahead. "Are the French wary of English-speaking people, or just Americans, Canadians, and anyone pretending to speak their language?" I wondered. "How will my Airbus counterparts, our veteran local on-site employees and the Americans working for our company receive me and accept my presence in their work environment?"

Upon embarking on this journey, I knew little about the issues of the new propulsion system program that had aroused the Airbus vice president to summon me to France. At this time, all I knew was what others had said about the people I would meet, and that France is renowned for its exquisite cuisine, wines, labor strikes, and cheek-kissing greetings of friends and colleagues.

Jacques, the Vice President of Industrial Programs at Airbus, was often mentioned and seemingly feared by engine manufacturers and other suppliers visiting the aircraft manufacturer. It appeared that Jacques was the man who had requested my presence during his meeting with Rick. Knowing that Jacques was going to be at a meeting would make people cringe, I was told. Jacques was portrayed as a smart and insightful leader who was highly respected. But some attendees of Jacques's meetings presented a view of him as emotionally charged with a short fuse. As they shared memories of prior industrial reviews, some colleagues advised, "Presenting nice words about best efforts could make Jacques explode. Particularly if he had qualms about the validity of the information." These depictions of Jacques and those under him made me apprehensive about my recent decision.

As the flight continued to Paris, my mind drifted to other comments and advice given to me prior to departing the States. A melange of suggestions, like "You better study French history because the French like their history," and thoughts about my ability to adapt to the language and culture swirled in my head. Remarks from some well-wishers saying, "You're nuts to accept the assignment," elevated my misgivings.

Comments like "Don't trust the Frogs" and "The French don't like Americans" weren't helpful. Speaking with a grimace, Joe Fine, a technical manager in the nacelle group and victim of Jacques's fury, lamented, "The assignment will be instant death." Stated by several people, "Watch your back" warnings also resonated. After marinating in this maddening counsel several days before leaving Connecticut, neither the voluble passenger seated next to me nor the cigarette smoke from the rear could erase my disquietude about the murky terrain to come.

As the plane approached the Toulouse–Blagnac Airport terminal, it appeared a damp, gray day was greeting me. It wasn't what I was expecting for springtime in the south of France. Nonetheless, when the aircraft reached the gate and the cabin door opened, the reality of the assignment hit me. *What have I done?* While walking up the jet way, I realized that I was in uncharted waters.

As I entered the terminal, advertisements for local wines and regional foods caught my drowsy eyes. A giant picture of a bottle of wine from the Cahors region excited me to discover more. A shop selling *cassoulet* (a white bean stew) and *foie gras* (duck and goose liver pâté) under a blue, white, and red canopy offered a glimpse of the region's cuisine.

As I made my way to the baggage claim area, I was watchful of the travelers I passed. Along the main aisle, people ambled in an unhurried fashion. A deeply tanned woman wearing a pale blue uniform strutted gleefully while removing trash and cigarette butts from sand-filled receptacles. The air was heavy with a faint scent of cigarette smoke. Looking at the sober expressions of the people walking by, I wondered, *is this what the French are like? What about the gaiety I had imagined?*

Grabbing my suitcase from the carousel for people arriving from outside of Europe, I joined a procession of travelers heading to the *douane* (customs officials). Near the exit sign was a statuesque man wearing a blue military-type uniform, his feet together in a saluting position.

"D'ou' venez vous?" he asked, stopping me abruptly.

I looked at him with a blank gaze.

"Where do you come from?" he repeated with a slight grin.

"I'm coming from Paris," I replied.

"Where do you come from before *Paree?*" the officer asked.

As I told him my journey had begun at New York's Kennedy Airport, his rigid facade transformed, and he smiled.

When stepping outside the terminal, I found that the downpour that greeted me on arrival had slowed to a fine mist. The air had a freshness of spring. As I walked to the taxi stand, thoughts of the question raised by the customs officer lingered. Suddenly, a greater reality whacked me like a slap upside the head from Dad. "I'm all alone. Don't know nobody, nor the language." At this time, my French was confined to two words: *Bonjour* (good day) and *merci* (thank you).

Before long, a yellow Mercedes pulled up to where I was waiting. A compact, olive-tinged man bounced out of the taxi with a broad smile. Speaking heavily accented English, he opened the door and asked where I wanted to go.

"Where are you from?" the gray-haired man inquired with a raised voice as he peered at me in the rear-view mirror.

"From America, New York," I replied.

"I've never been there, but I dream of going someday," he responded.

Curious about his complexion, I asked the driver about his origin.

"Well, I was born in Morocco and came to France when young," he said.

I was pleased that the taxi ride was just 10 minutes long but bewildered when I heard the whining sound of jet engines at the entrance to the hotel. Noticing my confusion, the driver pointed a finger at an airport barrier beyond the trees bordering the hotel.

Sleepily, I checked into the hotel, entered my room, plonked down on the bed, and conked out. The six-hour time difference and weight of uncertainty had taken their toll.

Awakening a few hours later, I opened the window and took a deep breath of spring in *Blagnac*, a small town adjacent to Toulouse. The sun had come out, the air was warmer, and signs of the season were present. The red and yellow flowers bordering the modest grounds of the hotel were in full bloom. Above them were bulbous trees showing new leaves. The air smelled clean and herbal.

After surveying my surroundings for several minutes, I called the local office of our company to advise them of my arrival. Within minutes, Cary, the head of our local office, was calling me from the hotel lobby. Stocky with sandy blond hair, the fiftyish-looking Cary greeted me with a jovial,

"Welcome to France." According to his bulging stomach, it seemed he liked the local cuisine, and lots of it. Following a brisk introduction, we walked to Cary's office, discussing the weather and how soon it had changed.

"It's the Pyrenees effect," said Cary, referring to the southern mountain range bordering France and Spain. We walked into a rose-colored building behind the hotel. At his office, Cary opened the door, revealing a middle-aged woman seated at a desk facing the doorway. Immediately, Cary introduced me. "This is the guy we were expecting from the States," he said to the sharp eyed woman.

"*Bonjour*, I am Crease," she replied with a glowing smile. Chris, Cary's secretary, appeared to be the eyes and ears of the office. Besides Cary and Chris, two other people were working in this office. Both of them were American, I was told. Following curt "hellos" from Roland and Matthew, Cary escorted me to an office at the end of the hallway. The smallest office among those in Cary's group, the space was just big enough to fit a desk and a two-drawer file cabinet. The view from the window revealed a level panorama of the motorway below, Airbus offices beyond the highway, and a glimpse of the tops of buildings in Toulouse on the horizon.

As I looked through the window at the adjacent pale-brick buildings, Cary returned, bringing a chair with him. He sat down and began briefing me about the status of our new propulsion system program and the airplane manufacturer's perception of the introduction of it.

"At this time, delayed deliveries and the need to upgrade delivered units on-site are affecting our image and relationships with people in Airbus. Put simply, they aren't happy with our delivery performance or control of the supply chain," Cary advised.

Still weary from the trip across the Atlantic, I sat through Cary's explanation in a daze. What he described was a seemingly monumental chore, and it appeared unlikely that the task would be completed in the three months Norm had described when offering me the assignment. While listening to Cary, I thought about what I had gotten myself into, second-guessing my decision to accept. Proceeding deeper into the delivery issues, Cary quoted what he had heard from the airplane manufacturer.

"These issues are disrupting the F.A.L. (final assembly line)," he mentioned, stating the most common complaint. "Also unsettling to them is the need to replace parts and components of propulsion systems after they are installed on aircraft," Cary continued. "In addition to the complaints of units requiring retrofits after arriving in Toulouse, the managers of Airbus are unhappy about some of our presenters at industrial review meetings—presenting excuses for persistent issues rather than solutions for the problems."

Reading between the lines, it appeared Airbus management wanted to see actions taken that would give them confidence that the program was recovering, as opposed to statements of best efforts. Most customers would expect nothing less from their suppliers. As I listened closely to Cary's summary, I realized that the more prevalent issues in our propulsion systems appeared to be with the engine cowling and thrust reversers. Key components of what is commonly called the nacelle, they are the parts encasing aircraft engines that facilitate aero-smoothness when integrated with the aircraft.

Before long, Cary shifted his recap of the propulsion system issues to a description of the aircraft manufacturer's managers that I would soon meet. He anticipated I would encounter French, German, and British employees of Airbus. "Each of them has inherent cultural traits and unique personalities," he reminded me. Of all the people Cary mentioned, the man that overshadowed all of them was a man called Jacques. "Being the Vice President of Industrial Programs, Jacques is an intense man in his early fifties, with an enormous responsibility and gripping influence. One feels his authority and presence when in a meeting with him. Jacques would stand out as the commander among a group of people," divulged Cary.

Cary talked about Jacques's vast knowledge of the aircraft industry, acute intuition, and last but not least, his attention-getting emotional outbursts.

"The man commands incredible respect," Cary emphasized. While listening to Cary, it dawned on me that Jacques could leverage his personality to intimidate the colleagues and suppliers not meeting his expectations. Closing the briefing, Cary highlighted his premonition, saying, "Many suppliers who encounter Jacques fear him."

His words seemed to validate the fore-warnings I had been given when leaving the States. Considering Cary's alert to the world I was stepping into and prior warnings from in-house colleagues, I wasn't looking forward to a meeting Jacques and becoming his next chopped steak.

While absorbing Cary's comments, I suddenly realized why some people at our Connecticut office had jokingly referred to me as "the Savior." Prior to this moment, their nonchalant quips were just noise. The Savior label had come more from nacelle supply managers, like Felix and Joe Fine, who undoubtedly had experienced the wrath of Jacques in prior meetings.

When I crossed paths with Gregoire, a watchful confidant of Jacques who had been planted in our company in the States, he displayed a simpering smile while referring to me as "the Savior."

Regardless, being on-site, closer to the concerns of the aircraft manufacturer, shed new light on the magnitude of the task. In fact, it added clarity to why I had been summoned to France. At this moment, the task of managing on-site upgrades, rectifying the delivery dilemma, and building trusting relationships with our on-site and the air-framer's people appeared daunting. Despite this seemingly impossible mission, I was determined to persevere and devote myself to eliminating our customers' concerns. After wrapping up his explanation, Cary drove me to the airport, where I could rent a car. Before leaving the office, I recalled hearing Chris express a reservation for a car on my behalf.

At the rental desk in the airport, what I thought would be a routine check-in became an exposé of French inflexibility. With a brusque *"Voila monsieur,"* the rental clerk, a clean-shaven guy in his thirties, handed me the keys and contract, stating the space where the car was parked. Upon finding the location he mentioned, I looked at the car in astonishment. No way, I thought, sizing up the vehicle. The car, a subcompact Peugeot, would be great for an accordion. After looking it over, an attempt to squeeze myself into the car confirmed my misgivings. The windshield was so close it could nearly touched my nose.

Returning to the rental desk, I asked, "Is it possible to get a larger car?"

Scanning the computer screen with a determined glint, the clerk who initially checked me in replied, *"Oui,* there are larger cars."

"May I change this to a bigger car?" I asked, showing him the contract.

Listening to me with his head skewed to the side, the clerk shrugged his shoulders. "This is not possible!" he answered with raised eyebrows.

Baffled, I continued my pursuit of a bigger car.

"You said there are larger cars outside. May I change cars?" I recited.

"Monsieur, your reservation asked for this class car," the clerk recanted.

After debating the change of cars for a few minutes, the clerk hastily typed and handed me a new contract. Going back to the car park, I readily found the car and discovered I had been given a vehicle large enough to haul a basketball team. A Peugeot as well, it was much more car than I expected. Thoughts of returning to the clerk crossed my mind, but they were quickly dispelled. I would hear the phrase "This is not possible" several times in the days to come, whenever I requested a last-minute change to a previously made arrangement or reservation.

OK. It's the culture. Give it a chance, I said to my perplexed self while getting into the car.

The drive from the airport to the hotel was my first driving experience outside of the United States and Canada. The circuitous route leaving the rental lot was a jarring ride over double-wide speed bumps. Driving among other motorists with unique driving habits in a country speaking an unfamiliar language gave me a feeling of uneasiness as I drove away from the airport. Upon entering the motorway close to the airport, a convoy of cars pushed me to the first *sortie,* where I exited. As I drove into the hotel's parking lot, Cary's earlier briefing, my decision to accept the assignment, and the obdurate car rental clerk swirled through my head.

Far from the exquisite cuisine I had envisioned when accepting the assignment, I had a sandwich delivered to my room. While eating it, I considered the enormous challenge facing me and the sky-high expectations of folks on both sides of the Atlantic. My head was reeling with memories of how far I had come in my twenty-six years of working with the company after starting as a two-year degree engineering aid.

It seemed I had always been attracted to a challenge. I'm not sure where the trait came from, but the seed was likely planted early in my life while working with my father. My dad was an imposing man, stout, strong-willed, and extremely independent. He had uncommonly light skin for an African American—so light that many white people thought he was white, and some Blacks envied his ability to pass for white. With his inflated belly and volatile temperament, family and friends jokingly likened him to the comedic actor, Jackie Gleason.

Dad came to Connecticut in 1947, driven by hope. When World War II ended, he and Mom migrated north from Portsmouth, Virginia, with their baby son—me. Prior to leaving the south, they both worked at the naval shipbuilding facility in Norfolk. My parents settled in South Norwalk, Connecticut, and eventually, my father got a job welding at a company that produced industrial boilers and storage tanks. He remained at that company for a decade while adding a girl and two boys to his brood.

During the recession of the latter 1950s, Dad left the vessel-fabricating company to start his own business. Before leaving, he rented an abandoned gas station in the center of a busy intersection in East Norwalk that became the site of his welding shop. He started his own business mending car parts, broken tools, and anything weldable that people brought in for repair. The shop was located at the apex of a small square, and its junk-yard appearance stood out among neighboring mom-and-pop businesses. Sharing the inner part of the square was a neighborhood grocery store owned by an elderly couple, Harvey and Rita. Landlords of Dad's shop, they visited him often to gab about life on the square. Across the street was George and Tony's Diner, a small, Greek-owned establishment that served breakfast and lunch to a regular clientele. Occasionally, patrons of the diner brought items to Dad to be fabricated and fixed.

Over the next five years, Dad's business grew from welding repairs to producing porch railings and fire escapes. While he struggled to establish the business and put food on our table, we lived in a public housing complex, where my two brothers, sister, and I bunked in a room just big enough to fit the beds. While we fussed daily in our close quarters, Mom worked as a housekeeper for a well-to-do family in New Canaan to supplement Dad's income and put clothes on our backs.

As the oldest of the four children, I was expected to help Dad after school and on weekends. I found his overbearing presence and menacing persistence unbearable when I began working with him. Often, he had to drag me out of bed to go with him. I couldn't have been much more than twelve at the time. Most days, Dad began work in a mellow mood, but he soon became an unyielding taskmaster. "Grab this, hold that, cut that pile of bar stock for the railings. Find the torch and welding rods, paint the railings, and sweep the floor again. When you're finished sweeping, re-stack the scrap steel in the shop and on the ground outside of the building," he'd endlessly bark.

Dad was merciless when it came to cleaning up, forever worried about complaints from Harvey and Rita about the appearance of the place. The shop was located at the crossroads of beach and business traffic, and he constantly reminded me about the shop's appearance and our visibility as the only Blacks on the square. Despite my endless sweeping and re-stacking of scrap metal around the building, passersby still grumbled. When hearing a complaint, particularly from Harvey or Rita, Dad's booming "Jun-Yah" would sound across the square. Regardless of the pace and Dad's blaring commands, I was inspired by watching a man with an eighth-grade education establish the business of his dreams as I grew into adolescence.

Many customers who came into the shop were confounded by my father's light skin and his connection with the colored boy working with him. One day, a pale, skeletal man, a regular customer of George and Tony's Diner, came into the shop, scanned Dad, and looked at me with a squinting stare. Appearing confused, he peered curiously at us with opaque blue eyes. Puzzled by the man's gawking, my father stopped what he was working on to ask, "Can I help you?"

"You mean you married a colored woman?" the man screeched.

Looking at the man with a sharp gaze, Dad took a deep breath and replied, "Excuse me, but I am a negro."

With his head lowered and gray hair dangling from his faded red cap, the man appeared to be drowning in guilt. "Sorry, I, I didn't know, he stuttered, "I thought you were white."

The customer walked outside, flabbergasted. Dad looked at me and shook his head. He didn't seem fazed by the customer's remark, but the astonishment written on the man's face and his difficulty accepting me as Dad's son was hard for me to swallow. It was an unforgettable moment! Eventually, the doubters became aware of our father-son relationship, but some remained perplexed by my presence. Despite the skeptics, Dad's business continued to thrive for another two decades.

Suddenly in 1980, Dad became ill—a victim of the occupation that put him behind a welding shield for over forty years. Following a protracted bout with throat cancer, he passed away. His departure deeply saddened me, but I greatly appreciated the seeds of perseverance he had sown in me. I attribute my interests, education, and career choice to Dad's tutelage at the shop. This caused me to pursue a career in the aerospace industry and to obtain a mechanical engineering degree from The University of Hartford, as well as a master's degree in operations management from Rensselaer Polytechnic Institute. While working as an engineering aid and quality auditor at Pratt and Whitney, I took classes for both degrees at night. The education I acquired under my dad contributed to the opportunity now given to me in France.

Feeling a bit uneasy, I went to bed, looking forward to plunging into the task. Unable to doze off right away, I lay there, convincing myself that I would succeed in getting the program on track and overcoming the demands that the future would bring.

Perhaps there were people on-site who didn't see why this savior was sent over to tell them how to jump on grapes, or propulsion systems, for that matter. Nevertheless, I was determined to achieve what Norm sent me to do—provide on-site direction, coordination, and ownership of propulsion system deliveries to Airbus. Prior to meeting anyone other than Cary and the people in his office, I could see that projecting a persona of piety could lead to an immediate rejection by those on-site—particularly those who had been here for years. I looked forward to meeting the on-site team, as

I was eager to observe, learn from them, and fit in quickly. I expected to be heavily scrutinized and held to a higher standard on both sides of the Atlantic. I believed that putting extra effort into being as helpful as possible to the people on-site was the most logical starting point for establishing good local relationships.

2

The Tour of Blagnac

As I turned the faucet handle above the bathtub the next morning, I looked skeptically at the glass screen stretching out my image. "This is a shower curtain?" I wondered, eyeing the skimpy glass partition. With the floor awash after my shower, I realized the plethora of towels stacked on the sink was a wise placement. While wiping the floor with the towels, I contemplated my day ahead with Cary and the onsite people I would soon meet.

Earlier, I awakened with uncertainty about how I would be received and accepted by on-site people when touring their facilities. Though a restful night had eased much of the angst from Cary's briefing, I remained uneasy yet hopeful about the day and task to come. Entering this new world of language, culture, and relationship building seemed colossal, but getting the local teams and their stateside counterparts to work together and support me appeared even more monumental. I felt an uncertainty I hadn't felt since starting with the company more than a quarter-century earlier.

Walking out of the hotel, I was comforted by the sun's warmth. Regardless of my misgivings about how I would be received, I looked forward to meeting the on-siters and exploring their contributions to our propulsion systems and customers. My desire to plunge into life in the south of France was just as pressing. Because I was the new kid on the block and expecting to be viewed that way , I didn't want to appear I came over to tell people how to do things they were already doing.

When arriving at the L-shaped brick building where Cary's office was located, I was surprised to see the parking lot empty, and I wondered if it was a national holiday. Considering the three-shift world I had left in Connecticut; I was amazed at how quiet the building seemed.

I stepped into the building through sliding glass doors, a blitz of lighting awakening the lobby. Nestled between two leafy plants in the center of the foyer was a desk with a vase of flowers on it. Opposite the receptionist's desk was a compact elevator that took me to the second (top) floor, where Cary and his offices were located. While walking out of the lift into a dimly lit hallway, the floor number "two" confused me. Had the elevator missed a floor? Cary's office should be on the third floor, I deduced.

"The lobby was the first floor, not zero?" I questioned. Apparently, the sign in the lobby displaying *Rez-de-Chaussee* (ground floor) was telling me something I didn't understand. As I counted the floors, I realized that the first floor was on the second level.

As I wandered the corridor, the lights went on. A few strides later, I arrived at the door to Cary's offices. Pacing back and forth to keep the hallway lights on, I waited for someone to arrive. Five minutes later, Cary appeared, with two men trailing him.

"I'm going to take you to places where you can meet the locals of our company and the key personnel of our on-site suppliers who handle our propulsion systems," Cary reminded me.

Cary and I entered the office, followed by Roland and Matthew. As we talked near the entrance, Chris strolled in, greeting us with a rhythmic *"Bonjour."* Removing her jacket, she sat at her desk facing the door with her head held high, laser-focused, waiting for the buzzer to announce the next visitor. She glanced at Cary and me momentarily before turning her attention back to the front door.

After talking briefly in his office, Cary and I began a tour of his group, starting back at the entrance. Greeting me with a more welcoming smile, Chris went about setting me up with supplies for my office. With a motherly tone, she lectured me about the phone system at a dizzying pace. Having a tin ear for French-English, I found Chris's instructions hard to follow.

After Chris's schooling about the France Telecom system, I followed Cary to an office next to his. Sitting at his desk, with eyes riveted to the window, was Roland. Appearing spellbound by a man washing the outside of his window, Roland hardly noticed Cary and I walk in.

Seemingly in his mid-fifties, Roland was the company's on-site technical expert. Short and thick with a bulging waistline, it appeared that Roland, like Cary, had no problem with the French cuisine. Moon faced with white, peach fuzz hair, he resembled a comic strip character.

"Besides Chris, he's been in this office position longer than anyone else in the group," Cary mentioned. "So long that there are people in the States who think Roland is French," he continued.

When he noticed us in his office, Roland greeted us softly. As we chatted, he sought confirmation from Cary. During the discussion, Roland injected subtle words of instigation and cynicism into his remarks. "Surely, it's his personality," I thought about his amped-up talk. I wondered if Roland was a prelude to others I would soon meet. While I assessed Roland, he blurted out a remark about my arrival in France.

"Oh, so this is why you're here," he said with goading sarcasm and eyes tilted toward the ceiling. As I pondered a response to the prickly comment, a man with curly blond hair eased into the office. Wearing a crisp white shirt and pin-striped suit, the elevated Matthew from the office next door extended a hand, reminding me to call him Matt. The on-site marketing manager, Matt appeared to be in his mid-forties. Matt's *"Bonjour,* welcome aboard" was Americanized and spoken at a volume the window washer, peering through the glass from outside, could likely hear.

Cary and I followed Matt to the conference room, where pictures of Airbus aircraft hung on the walls. While we discussed the market potential of the nuanced, twin-engine A330 aircraft, Matt spoke about the potential sales of our engines for A330 Airplanes.

"We're going to sell a lot of these babies," said an exuberant Matt. Nodding toward the door while Matt was on a roll, Cary signaled it was time to move on. Since Matt wasn't a player in the recovery strategy, it was time to go.

Located approximately three miles on the opposite side of the airport was the next stop on the tour. It was where engine and nacelle components were delivered after shipment from stateside and European suppliers. Contracted by our company, the Rohr Industries facility employed people who integrated engines with designated nacelle components (fan cowling, thrust reversers, and related units) that provide aero-smooth shrouding around jet engines installed on aircraft. Painting units in the colors specified by the airline customers and performing final inspections after marrying the components and confirming their proper fitting were the primary services provided by the facility. When a propulsion system was processed and verified as accepted, the facility sent the integrated units to the aircraft final assembly line for installation on an airplane.

"They're among the best in the world for what they do," said Cary as he pulled into the parking lot. Before getting out of the car, it was apparent that the supplier's success and esteem with the air-framer were dependent on receiving the propulsion system components from the producers within their required lead time.

"Accelerating processing to compensate for delinquent units had been the exception prior to this program, but late arrivals of current units are putting a burden on processing units in this facility," Cary mentioned. "Frustration, stemming from accommodating inconsistent deliveries from suppliers and the need to upgrade delivered components after arrival, has put the management in the building in the cross hairs of the Industrial Program

Management group in Airbus. These are the issues that contributed to the request for your presence," Cary continued.

Upon entering a brick block house opposite the main building, Cary and I were greeted by a lone guard dressed in a blue military-style uniform.

"Bonjour messieurs," he said with a bashful smile. Rushing to call the person Cary had arranged to meet, the guard received immediate authorization, tipped his cap, and waved us into the building.

The brilliance of the brick facade led me to believe that the building was new. As we entered the lobby, the citrus trees, wispy ferns, and cactus growing in white sand made the airy space seem like a botanical garden.

In the building were two men who worked for our company, Cary stated. As we walked to their office at the far end of the shop, my eyes were drawn to the high arched ceiling, where replicas of Airbus aircraft were suspended from the rafters.

"The airplanes are models of Airbus aircraft that receive propulsion systems processed in this building," Cary said. We approached a staircase to a mezzanine overlooking the shop floor, where we were greeted by a man running toward us.

"I noticed you coming while I was standing under an engine mounted on an A-frame," he said, breathing heavily. Freckle-faced and appearing in his mid-thirties, the buoyant guy introduced himself as Scott. Built like a reed with a hawk's beak nose, Scott had a friendly smile and a strange laugh. He said he was an American, which was obvious from his accent, and an engineer by profession. Scott stated that he had recently been assigned to the podding facility. Podding, as Scott called it, was a reference to the process the supplier's workforce performed in the building. It consisted of marrying jet engines with their designated nacelle components, which collectively resembled pods upon completion of the assembly process. While Scott talked about his inspection and oversight duties, his darting eyes and scoffing snickers projected the image of a prankster.

Standing on the mezzanine near the top of the stairway was a man leaning over the railing. As we ascended the metal staircase, Scott and Cary waved vigorously to him.

"Hi. I'm Ian," the man said with a squeaky British accent when we stepped onto the mezzanine. A workmate of Scott, they shared an office on this level. Ian was in his late thirties, I surmised, and broad in build, with amber locks of hair that shook when he spoke to us.

"I've been covering this process for more than five years," Ian said. Suddenly, he stopped talking for a moment, and I wondered if he was finished or had lost his train of thought. Regardless of Ian's manner of speaking, both men were in the building to oversee our propulsion systems while they were processed by the supplier.

Considering that Scott and Ian were located at the place where our propulsion system components arrived and were handled prior to delivery to aircraft, it seemed that they had the greatest visibility of the obstacles impeding our deliveries. Both men readily shared their experiences with the problems they'd encountered when receiving incoming units.

Returning to the shop floor, Cary and I searched for a manager in the podding organization. As we roamed a maze of workstations where mechanics worked on engines and nacelle components, Cary spotted Edith talking to workers at an A-framed structure. A compact woman appearing in her forties, Edith's flaming hair distinguished her from the people around her. During our introduction, Edith mentioned, "I manage the program activity for your propulsion systems processed in the facility. From my point of view, the program isn't going very well." She spoke good English and projected a gleamy eyed concern. Edith's sincerity gave me confidence in her commitment to our success. While Edith explained her duties and concerns with our program, Cary whispered more words of assurance.

"She never says no when our guys ask her to help accelerate work on delayed engines and nacelle components. At times, she goes beyond the limits of her management's good will to satisfy our needs," he continued. Cary's endorsement sealed my impression of Edith and the workers I observed as we talked. They appeared to be the supporting cast I had hoped for when leaving the States.

On the other side of the aisle were four men looking at a thrust reverser on a transport trolley. Other than the jet engine, the thrust reverser, which reduces the breaking speed of a landed aircraft, is perhaps the second most important component of a propulsion system. Among the men was a guy with salt-and-pepper hair broadcasting instructions to the other three men. Appearing unhappy about something he and the men were looking at, his voice resonated throughout the shop floor.

"It's my boss, Robert. He's in charge of the shop," said Edith, rolling her eyes. Edith introduced us when Robert walked over beaming at me affably . The men admonished by him seemed to welcome the relief of my presence. I estimated Robert to be in his fifties. His welcoming, "*Bonjour monsieur, Bienvenu*," had a gravelly tone. And despite his heavily, French-accented English, every word he spoke was amplified. Volume appeared his way of getting the attention of others. During our introduction, he surely got mine.

Blaring his assessment of the state of our propulsion program, which was similar to what Edith had said, Robert explained the key elements of the podding process.

"Well, the nacelle painting process is where the components are painted with the colors and patterns requested by the airline," said Robert, while showing us the paint booths on the other side of the building. We followed him to an A-frame (a triangular-shaped steel structure), where an engine was hanging.

"The A-frame is where engines and nacelle components come together," continued Robert with a brassy tone. Before he finished his description of the process, Cary made an appeal to have me located in the building close to Scott and Ian.

"Is there an office near the shop floor that he can use when he's here?" said Cary pointing to me. "Locating him closer to where incoming engines and nacelle components arrive would give him a better opportunity to respond to issues when they surface," Cary cited. As he listened to Cary's justification, Robert nodded in agreement and offered a small office on the mezzanine, close to where Scott and Ian were located. It was more space than I expected. The windowless nook was enough to cover my basic needs of a desk, computer, and the invaluable telephone.

Content with Robert's generosity, Cary and I followed him back to the shop, where he continued his explanation of the process. In the spacious, well-lit work environment, the workstations dispersed among the floor-to-ceiling pillars teemed with activity on jet engines and nacelle units for twin- and single-aisle aircraft. Inlet cowls, some more than eight feet in diameter, and thrust reverser half sections, nearly as large, were conspicuous. Occupying many of the workstations were the triangular, steel A-frame fixtures. After marrying them on the A-frames, the structures were used to fit, adjust, and inspect engines and assigned nacelles components. Upon simulating an installation of a propulsion system on a wing-mounted pylon of an aircraft, the integrated units were final—accepted by inspectors and representatives of the purchasing airlines.

With Cary's "We'll get on these problems right away," and Robert's "Good. It's about time someone does something," Cary and I departed the podding facility for our next destination. A repair-and-upgrade station was set up at a separate location to correct discrepant thrust reverser units. Driving there, Cary mentioned, "We're going to a place where the supplier of thrust reverser components and their contracted personnel coordinate and perform upgrades and repairs to specified units." The thrust reversers were the components of propulsion systems that, upon landing an aircraft, are deployed to reverse a portion of engine airflow forward, reducing the ground (braking) speed of an aircraft. In the building, repairs were performed by the workforce of a local company that specialized in modifications of airplane components and aircraft customization.

The work station was located closer to the podding facility than I imagined. In a dull gray building appearing a modified aircraft hangar, we were greeted by two of the thrust reverser manufacturer's on-site people. Americans, the two men stated they had been assigned there to oversee repairs developed by their engineers in the States. As they presented a brief overview of their duties, one indicated that they worked closely with contracted French mechanics to ensure the work met their company's technical requirements. Limiting our visit to the Sogerma facility (thrust reverser repair station) to an introduction to the thrust reverser manufacturer's on-site representatives, Cary and I departed to continue our tour of other pertinent facilities the next day. The time we spent with the podding folks had taken up much of the day.

"I'm sorry we cut the repair station visit short. What are you doing this evening?" Cary asked when dropping me off at the hotel.

"Nothing, I'll probably just hang out here," I replied.

Interested in seeing Toulouse, a city I had heard much about from visitors in the States, I drove in the darkness from tiny Blagnac into the center of France's fourth-largest metropolis. Nicknamed the *Ville Rose,* rose city known for its characteristic brick buildings some dating back to Roman times and *Basilica St-Sernin,* a striking landmark church.

Initially, I found the drive into the center of Toulouse wasn't so rosy. Driving in central Toulouse was an adventure, with its myriad streets created centuries before the automobile. While driving in the city, Cary's words of caution continued to resonate.

"Don't look in the rear-view mirror," he had mentioned several times as we rode to the podding facility. When I snuck a peek rearward on a large boulevard in Toulouse, it seemed that every car and motorcycle behind me was maneuvering to overtake my car. For reasons a Frenchman would know, they seemed to have a burning desire to improve their position by a car.

On street corners were two sets of traffic lights—a set located higher on a post and a second set placed at eye level. When the lights turned green, it was like a starter waving a flag to start a grand-prix race. Cars would sprint to a screeching halt at the next traffic lights. Driving over wide swaths of raised asphalt near intersections was reminiscent of rolling over a hump. They were different than the pencil-thin speed bumps I was accustomed to in the States, but I guessed one got used to them.

As I got a glimpse of an old-world city with its majestic brick buildings, innumerable cafés, and hordes of younger people walking the sidewalks, I noticed a vibrancy to the atmosphere and people. Although this was my first ride into the city, and I never got out of my car, I found the vigor of this city pulsating with life, infectious.

The next morning, a slim, well-groomed man was waiting for Cary and me in the lobby of the Sogerma facility. Upon introducing himself as the plant manager and hearing Cary tell him why I was sent over, Edouard shrugged a shoulder. At first, I was puzzled by Edouard's slack persona. Seemingly a man of few words, when Edouard spoke, I found his burdensome, French-accented English difficult to understand. It was clear that learning the language or acquiring an ear for listening to it was something I would need to do soon. During our first meeting, Edouard and his shop supervisor appeared slightly accepting of my presence.

"We hear you were coming and are happy you come to help," Edouard asserted before walking us through the building.

Edouard escorted Cary and me to a cordoned-off area in the shop that isolated the thrust reverser repair and upgrade work from their aircraft customization business. Like the podding facility, the shop was spacious, with a ceiling height capable of accommodating tail sections of larger aircraft. In fact, at that time, they were converting a large passenger model aircraft to a transport aircraft for ferrying fuselage sections and other large components from the manufacturers of the components to the on-site aircraft assembly line. The first of its kind, it seemed large enough to transport a small house.

The late morning sun, beaming through windows near a thrust reverser being repaired, added an invigorating luminescence to the area. As I watched a thrust reverser upgrade in progress, I became intrigued by the three mechanics working on it.

"These men are assigned only to this station," said Edouard, pointing a finger at them.

Noting the swagger displayed by the men working on the unit, I likened them to the characters I'd seen in the movie *The Three Musketeers.* Despite the absence of seventeenth-century garb, they appeared to be wrench-turning musketeers. At this time, little did I know that we were not far from the Gascony region of southern France, renowned for its *foie gras, Armagnac* (regional brandies similar to Cognac), and the homeland of the legendary D'Artagnan. The extended strides they took while working on a unit was reminiscent of the characters Athos, Porthos, and Aramis in the movie. After observing the noisy mechanics working at a leisurely pace, Cary and I departed to visit another group involved with propulsion systems.

Our next stop on the tour was located beyond a reasonable walk from the thrust reverser repair station. Cary drove through a labyrinth of aircraft hangers and equipment sheds to get to our flight-line destination. The epicenter of work associated with on-wing repairs, flight testing, and final preparation of propulsion systems on aircraft for airline acceptance, the group we were visiting played a vital role in the delivery of aircraft. Housed in a second-floor office in a small concrete building, our field representatives had a final view of propulsion systems before their delivery into revenue service. Positioned near the main runway of the Toulouse-Blagnac Airport, the office was an observatory for departing and arriving airplanes. The occupants of the office worked for our company and were a melange of nationalities, including Americans, French, an Englishman, a Kiwi, and a Tunisian, Cary stated before getting out of the car.

Gordon Triplett, an American referred to as Trip, managed the office. Burly and around fifty, I guessed, Trip's glossy gray hair, combed in a slick-back style, appeared to be from a bygone era. Upon our introduction, Trip rocked back in his chair with folded arms. He seemed irritated about something. Following a nonchalant handshake, Trip uttered an opening salvo that mirrored his demeanor.

"I see our Savior has arrived," he said raising his eyes upward. "I hope you're better than that last asshole who came over here to tell us how to do our jobs. He was clueless like others that come across."

"Happy to meet you, Trip," I replied.

In response to my salutation, Trip released a barrage of comments about the incompetence of my predecessor. Before long, his assertions shifted to the local culture and their lack of flexibility as he saw it. While discussing the status of our propulsion systems, it appeared that Trip was annoyed with my presence and the local culture, and that he had a disdain for people who couldn't speak English.

"They don't understand anything," said Trip, pleading his point. "You'll see what you're getting into," he continued.

To stem Trip's diatribe, Cary interrupted him saying,"Enough Trip."

Undeterred by the comment, Trip advanced his judgment. Undoubtedly, the two women in the office, both French, as well as others passing the doorway, could hear his critique. I was shocked by Trip's criticism of the locals. To others in the group within listening distance, the bombast could have been more of the same. Trip's opinions of others during our first meeting made a lasting impression. As his criticisms continued, thoughts of the Ugly American syndrome and the perceptions of locals weighed on me. "How are these remarks and biased notions of this American being interpreted by the local nationals?" I pondered as Trip spoke.

The other American assigned to the office was an angular man with deep-set eyes who couldn't be more than thirty, I guessed. Walking into Trip's office, he looked at me with an exaggerated, mocking grin.

"Hi, I'm Carl," he introduced himself.

Carl's hasty greeting projected a chilled haughtiness. Seemingly a less opinionated version of Trip, I found Carl's conveyance of a nice-guy persona unconvincing. His expressions told me that I shouldn't believe him, but at this stage in the assignment, I wasn't sure why. Carl's tightly folded arms, coupled with sarcastic remarks about other company people on-site, overshadowed his pretentious congeniality. Immediately, I became skeptical of Carl's inner self. During the discussion in Trip's office, Carl's repertoire of smirks, uncertain smiles, and raised eyebrows when facing Trip conveyed a disingenuous nature. Of all the people in the office, Carl seemed to be the most influenced by Trip. Trip and Carl clearly conveyed their initial feelings about my presence in Toulouse. When in the company of them, vigilance would prevail.

Geoffrey, an energetic Englishman, presented a more accommodating greeting when walking into Trip's office.

"Hi, I'm Geoff," he greeted me with cheerful laugh. Wearing pants with cuffs above his ankles, Geoff appeared to be deep into his fifties. He seemed genuine when we shook hands and regarded each other. After the receptions preceding him, Geoff gave me the feeling that malcontent about my presence wasn't lurking beneath his skin.

On future trips to the *piste* (flight line), I was encouraged by Geoff's optimism and eagerness to investigate problems. Though Geoff's submissions of remedies were offered in good faith, it appeared many of his recommendations were causing discontent among others in the group. Regardless of Geoff's enthusiasm, some office dwellers thought many of his suggestions were off-the-wall.

Geoff's contributions were dismissed with little justification, which appeared to affect his attitude toward others in the group. While presenting the results of a task that he had just completed, Geoff seemed uncertain while stating his findings. Speaking at an accelerated pace with a slight stutter, he explained to Trip what he had seen while observing an aircraft. I wasn't sure what Geoff was expecting as a response, but he received a nod of acknowledgment for his efforts. While taking on his next assignment, Geoff seemed overly reliant on receiving detailed directions and confirmation of his proposed methods of pursuit. Repeating instructions several times to Geoff set Trip's face ablaze.

"How many times do I have to tell you this?" said Trip, slapping a hand on the top of his desk.

As Trip and Cary shared a few words about a side issue, Geoff's frustration surfaced from a side of his mouth.

"I get this every day," he whispered. It didn't take long to see that Geoff craved direction rather than reactions to misguided instructions.

As I got to know Geoff better, he revealed a personal side of himself. The son of English missionaries, he mentioned he was born in Kenya.

"I lived there through the early years of my life," he told me. From my perspective, it seemed that growing up in a culture of vastly different people had cultivated Geoff's openness to me. I was comforted by his sensitivity to me, a person from a different culture.

Geoff's explanation of what missionaries endured in the 1930s and '40s to prepare for assignments in developing countries was fascinating. Being someone who dreaded visits to a dentist's office, I was agonized by his comments about the dental work (tooth extractions) his mom and dad endured to qualify for their missionary assignment. I could feel their pain sixty years after the agony and was overwhelmed by their commitment to their chosen task. "Succeed or fail, at least my teeth will be intact," I thought when Geoff finished his story. Despite the lack of ardor for his findings and suggested remedies, Geoff's purity and stories of his past captivated me.

The French nationals in the office were both women. Paulette, the office secretary, was a polite, attractive woman with a mane of chestnut hair. In the weeks to come, it seemed the hair became *la couleur du jour* (the color of the day). The other woman, Claire, was a technician who analyzed engine data collected from aircraft after test flights. Slinky with short blonde hair, Claire presented herself in a more austere manner than Paulette. Both women appeared to be in their early thirties.

Greeting me with a demure *"Bonjour,"* Paulette seemed genuine. Following a momentary salutation, Paulette continued scurrying about the office. Wearing little make-up, Claire greeted me with a terse smile and a firmer-than-expected handshake. Speaking to Trip with a disdainful tone, she asked for information about an aircraft.

"Trip, I need more information about this aircraft," she said, appearing peeved about his inability to provide the information she wanted.

While Cary and I chatted with the ladies, a man with disorderly light brown hair, wearing dark pants with a high waistline, came into the office, paused, and looked across the room. Paulette popped out of her chair, running to him with a message from the States.

Dylan Wallace, or "Dyl," as Paulette called him, was distinguished from others I had seen since arriving in France. He came over with extended strides and introduced himself.

"Hello, I'm Dylan Wallace," he said with an English-sounding accent. I'd been expecting a vise like grip from his sizable hand, but he surprised me with a pillow-soft clasp. A New Zealand-er, he mentioned, and overseer of the work assigned to a small group of flight-line mechanics, Dylan had a genial smile and accommodating gray-green eyes. Being a six-footer myself, standing next to him, it seemed I was looking up to speak with him.

Also reporting to the flight-line office were four mechanics. Vital fixtures on the *piste,* they spent their days installing retrofits and replacing parts on engines before and after installation on aircraft. Unfortunately, I didn't meet the mechanics on my first visit to the flight line, but before long, our paths crossed at the podding facility. Barring a need to go to the flight-line office to get a status or clarification about work they were performing, I saw little of the mechanics on future visits to the *piste*. Regardless, they seemed invaluable to the group and the program's recovery.

Leaving Trip's office, Cary and I crossed a wide expanse of tarmac to return to his car. While walking across the breezy, open space with a dozen or so aircraft awaiting delivery to airlines, I discovered many airlines I had never seen or heard of. Before this moment, I never imagined the multitude of Chinese airlines that existed. There were four different ones before us.

"What did you think about the group?" Cary asked as we entered his car.

"The flight-line people seem close-knit, but Geoff appears to be the outsider," I replied. "For Trip and Carl, the jury is still out," I continued. Cary responded by shaking his head.

Although Geoff was the most fascinating person in the flight-line office, observing the relationships among the trio of Trip, Carl, and Dylan had revealed that he was the odd man out. Pondering my impression of Trip's group, I concluded that the team's closeness had likely developed from their remoteness from others in our company.

As Cary drove me to the hotel, I considered the places I had visited. "What holds these distinct locations together?" I thought. At this time, it wasn't clear how the requirements from the States were communicated and coordinated among the locals on-site. "Who was responsible for disseminating, aligning, and executing the plans and requirements exported from the States?" I wondered. Still puzzled after seeing the local facilities, I realized why management of the aircraft manufacturer were perplexed about identifying an on-site owner of the recovery of the propulsion systems program. During the tour, no one had stepped forward as the owner of the situation on-site. It seemed that Jacques and his team were looking for that person. Deep in remembrance of the places we visited, it struck me that their expectations for improvements were riding on me. Failure wasn't an option because there were billions of dollars of aircraft to be delivered, and airlines were awaiting their acceptance and fly-away into revenue service. Our company's reputation as a dependable engine provider was at stake.

"Hope you learned something," said Cary as he pulled up to the hotel.

"I learned a lot both days. There are a lot of people involved with this program and numerous sites to oversee," I replied. "I'm looking forward to getting started."

"*Bonne soiree monsieur. Bon chance!*" (Have a good evening. Good luck!) "I'll see you later," said Cary upon going back to his office.

That evening, Cary returned to my hotel with Roland to take me to dinner. Riding into Toulouse as a passenger was delightful. Though I had driven many of the same streets the night before, the energy upon entering the city on the Boulevard de Strasbourg, a main artery of the city with brightly lit cafes and sidewalks crammed with people, appeared more lively than the night before.

"Many of these people are students. One of the largest universities in France is here," said Roland as Cary drove to the restaurant.

Parking under the *Place du Capitole* in the heart of Toulouse, we walked across the broad plaza to a backstreet close by. Virtually impassible by car, the street on which the restaurant was located likely dated back to medieval times. On a slender, sparsely lit bend in the street, we stopped at an establishment with a sign inscribed, *Cote de Boeuf* (side of beef) over the entrance to the restaurant.

Before going to the restaurant, neither Cary nor Roland mentioned what we would be eating. As we entered the open doorway of the *Cote de Boeuf* and its dim atmosphere, we were wrapped in a cozy embrace. The subdued dining area with its well-lit kitchen seemed to be from a bygone era. Greeting us with an exuberant *"Bonsoir messieurs,"* Helen escorted us to a table near the open kitchen. The most vocal person of the limited restaurant staff, Helen was a sturdy, mid-thirty-appearing woman. The epitome of multi-tasked, she was the maître-d ʼ, waitress, sommelier, and cashier, it seemed.

Helen waited with a ready pen in hand while Roland told her our orders. Helen and Roland exchanged words in French as they peered at me. Scribbling the orders on a pad, she dashed off to the kitchen. While awaiting Helen's return, our table was engulfed in a scent of garlic. A full-figured, sixty-looking woman walked from the kitchen toward us. Cary mentioned she was the proprietress and chef. Cruising the dining area with a quick smile, Rosey, as Roland called her, stopped at every table, greeting everyone with a, *"Bonsoir mes amis."* To emphasize her accommodating attitude, Rosey placed her hands on the back of my shoulders when she arrived at our table. The experience was reminiscent of Sunday dinner at Grandma's. *"Soyez le Bienvenu, monsieur,"* she said softly to me. It was a wonderful welcome to a first timer at her restaurant.

Broadcasting "Helen" from the kitchen, Rosey announced our meals were ready to be served. Hearing this, Cary glanced at me, then winked at Roland. Cary and I had deferred to Roland when Helen took our orders.

"Don't worry, we have you covered," Cary reassured me.

While peering at the oval-shaped meat on my plate considering what I was eating and tasting, watchful Cary and Roland looked at me with uncertainty in their eyes.

"Well. What do you think?" Roland asked.

"I like it," I replied.

"Do you know what you're eating?" Roland and Cary asked.

It was unlike any beef or lamb I had eaten.

"Magret. It's *magret de canard,"* (breast of duck) asserted Roland.

"I never imagined a grilled duck breast would have such a meaty texture," I responded to their gaping expressions.

Though the meat was a little on the rare side for my *bien cuit* (well done) preference, the *magret* and its wood grilling were delectable. The dinner, consisting of a medallion of *foie gras* on a crisp salad, roasted garlic potatoes, and the sinewy duck breast, was the beginning of my love of French cooking. Along with a bottle of red wine from a local vineyard, Rosie and Helen's accommodation, the evening, the place, and its wonderful food made a lasting impression.

After a week of getting acquainted with the Toulouse operation, I returned to the States. Upon my arrival in Connecticut, I briefed Norm about my view of the contracted suppliers processing our engines and nacelles, our on-site groups, and my assessment of the task ahead.

"There's a lack of cohesion among the stakeholders on both sides of the

Atlantic," I told Norm.

"In Toulouse, people complain about the speed and unreliability of information related to shipments of engines, nacelle components, and replacement parts. If people on both sides of the Atlantic aren't working together, the recovery will be prolonged and possibly fail. Our credibility with Airbus will be completely lost," I continued.

Listening with blank face, and raised shoulder,Norm replied, "OK, fix it. I'm sure you can do it."

While in the States, I met with the participants of the daily trans-Atlantic phone calls who were tasked with addressing urgent propulsion system issues and providing remedies to the folks in Toulouse. Hopeful of getting committed support from in-house people before returning to France, I pleaded for help from my stateside colleagues.

After checking in on Loretta and the girls, I was mentally charged and ready to dive deeper into the assignment.

Consumed by preconceptions of a first meeting with the airplane manufacturer's management, I returned to the hotel in Toulouse with thoughts of how they would receive me. My unveiling, planned for a meeting requested by Jacques, was intended to coincide with an explanation of our company's recommendations for improving propulsion system delivery problems. After investing heavily in the A330 and A340 aircraft programs, Airbus had lost patience with our delays.

During this era of producing longer-range, twin-engine airplanes, the competition between the major airplane manufacturers, Airbus, Boeing, and McDonnell Douglas, was fierce. Today, the battle continues between Airbus and Boeing, who took over Douglas in 1999. Any delays in the recovery of our program would set off alarms at the highest levels of the air-framer and in our company, I feared, meaning someone would likely be fired. Severe action, like removing a person in Norm's position, or those closely associated with him, would likely happen. Considering the struggle to improve delivery performance and satisfy the notorious Jacques, I was uneasy about the meeting.

Moments before the planned start of the meeting, Chris received a surprise voicemail from an unforeseen attendee. Jim Farmer, a senior manager of our company's scheduling department, called from his hotel room, stating, "I've just arrived in Toulouse." Confused about the location of the meeting room at the airframer's facility, Jim requested to be picked up at his hotel, further delaying our departure to the meeting.

Storming into the hotel lobby with his face on fire, Roland searched for Jim. Roland appeared ruffled when walking out of the hotel, and Jim blasted him. "It's about damn time," he said, wagging a disdainful finger at Roland. Instantly, a volley of unpleasantries erupted, further delaying our departure. Moments later, Roland drove us to the Airbus campus.

Troubled about the perception of our late arrival to the meeting, I walked to the Airbus office complex with Roland and Jim. Upon entering a radiant, metallic building on a site dominated by brick buildings, we wove our way through a maze of narrow hallways in search of the meeting. When we found the meeting room, my discomfort remained about how the Airbus management would view our late arrival. I worried they would see our lateness as a lack of interest.

As we stood in the hallway at the conference room entrance, we heard a voice boom from within.

"Well, *Meister De-a-mone,* how do you plan to fix this problem?" Said the voice in heavily accented French-English. Hearing the name, I assumed Rick Diamond, Norm's boss, was the person being scolded.

"*Eh bien!* What are *les elements* of your recovery plan?" the voice continued. After the query from whomever was speaking, the room fell silent.

Roland opened the door, peeked in, and the three of us entered the room. Sitting at a gleaming conference table opposite the source of the clamor was Rick Diamond, his chin buried in his chest. Cherry-faced and appearing stunned, Rick sat next to other managers from our Connecticut offices. The men appeared bewildered by the comments of the speaker. Undoubtedly, our management had come to the meeting anticipating a flogging, and boy did they get it. The sagging eyes of our attendees told us that the speaker's words had penetrated deeply. Unbeknownst to me, the three of them had come with Cary directly from the airport after arriving from the States.

They appeared tired and stunned by the assault of the person who had been speaking.

Seated at the conference table and around the perimeter of the room were ten or so stone-faced people peering at the speaker. As expected, Airbus was well represented and eager to hear the remedies for the problems delaying our propulsion systems. Entering the room, which seemed to only have standing room left, with the speaker in high verbal gear, put a spotlight on us latecomers. Showing up well past the start of the meeting, we drew the attention of everyone.

While we searched for a place to sit, a man sprang to his feet and approached us with a sunny smile. Extending a hand, he introduced himself.

"Bonjour, I am Didier," he whispered like a cinema usher. Didier's warmth flowed to his grasp. It was a relief to be warmly received by someone working for the air-framer. During my extreme uneasiness, Didier's accommodating demeanor made a great impression. He was the first manager of the airplane company that I had met. Apologizing profusely for the lack of chairs in the conference room, Didier dashed out of the room to get a chair for Roland and me.

While waiting for Didier's return, I watched the dreaded fury of the man called Jacques. His wavy, dark hair appeared recently coiffured. Jacques stood in front of a white screen in a combative stance, speaking with authority and gesticulations. Though he was no taller than others in the room—five-eight, I guessed—he was undoubtedly the vocal giant I had heard while standing in the hallway. Like Cary had stated, Jacques dominated meetings. Speaking with his arms and hands as much as his mouth, he was in constant motion. "So, mister who-ever-was-presenting, what do you do about this?" Jacques asked each presenter when they started speaking. Upon hearing a response, he didn't like, Jacques displayed a repulsive gaze and emitted a sound of breaking wind from his lips. What appeared to light Jacques's fuse was a mention of more engine and nacelle retrofits on-site.

"More retrofits? It's totally unacceptable," Jacques screamed with fire in his eyes. "We already see too many of your retrofits. Who's going to oversee all of these retrofits ?" he continued.

Highly insightful and intimately knowledgeable of airplane production, Jacques drove his message to our management. Throughout the forceful lashing, it became obvious that there was no pulling the wool over this man's eyes. Starting in the mid-morning and extending well into the afternoon, Jacques chastised our attendees relentlessly.

"You tell me no more than I hear this morning!" Said Jacques reprimanding our attendees seemingly in awe.

Steamrolling his way through an emotionally charged reprimanding of Rick and the responsible manager of the thrust reverser manufacturer, Jacques swept his arms and whirled his hands to emphasize his points.

"We hear it before. You have no credibility!" he repeated, leaving our people speechless. As I observed the expressions on our people's faces, I wasn't looking forward to being introduced at this time.

Continuing the verbal assault, Jacques paused and faced Rick.

"So, Rick, where is the industrial specialist I asked for two weeks ago? We need him now." Jacques asked with piercing rage. "I received a letter from Brady (Rick's boss) saying a man has been selected to provide overall direction and coordination for your propulsion systems. He will be the single point of contact for all activities related to engine and nacelle deliveries from Connecticut through podding and airline customer acceptance in Toulouse. He will also be responsible for managing the incorporation of the retrofits in Toulouse, the letter says," said Jacques, waving Brady's letter at Rick.

Pledging lofty expectations and great results from my involvement, Rick introduced me to Jacques and the air-framer's attendees. Blown away by Rick's enormous optimism and desire to appease Jacques, I stood up and faced him and the Airbus attendees.

"I will do my best to fix these problems as fast a possible," I uttered, cautious of over committing to Jacques and his colleagues.

Jacques leaned forward as I spoke, smiling and nodding affirmatively. After witnessing his intense fury, it seemed he expected immediate resolution of the issues and the program's recovery.

"*Soyez le Bienvenu monsieur,*" said Jacques, displaying lots of teeth.

Despite the emotion he had exhibited during most of the meeting, the calmer Jacques appeared pleased to see and welcome his requested industrial savior. Far less scornful than during most of the meeting, the demeanor of the current Jacques appeared to energize everyone. Suddenly, our attendees raised their heads. As Jacques shook my hand, I found him a likable, more humanized person. The transformation of Jacques, after my introduction, augmented my interest in correcting the issues delaying our propulsion system deliveries and my desire to live up to Brady's billing.

When the meeting ended, an audible sigh was heard. Attending management from our company and onlookers of the airplane manufacturer whispered to each other, "Thank God it's over." Other than my introduction, there was nothing said that appeared to raise Jacques's confidence in an instant recovery. Seated around the table, the air frame managers appeared skeptical of what our spokesmen had presented.

Upon leaving the building, the sunshine was blinding. As we walked, Rick stopped and clutched my arm.

"Wait," he said, "I'll know how well you're doing by how often I have to come back to Toulouse and face Jacques." Rick's gaze was sharp. His decree gave me an additional incentive to stay out of Jacques's doghouse.

While walking with Rick, I pictured the sight of our attendees sinking into their chairs during the meeting. The enormity of my task of directing and coordinating the activities associated with on-time deliveries of Pratt and Whitney propulsion systems now appeared more insurmountable. During the meeting, it became clear that Norm's predicted three-month assignment would take much longer than he had said. The multitude of sites to oversee and hundreds of retrofits to be accomplished within them appeared colossal. Surely, I wasn't the first person offered this assignment, and perhaps not even the second. Regardless of the number of people that were asked before me, in the eyes of Jacques and others in the meeting, I was "the Savior" who had been sent to resolve the concerns of the air-framer. They not-so-simply wanted unimpeded processing and deliveries of propulsion systems for their aircraft and customers.

Despite Jacques's impassioned chiding and skepticism about our improvements to the delivery situation, my debut at the air-framer ended on a positive note. With my introductions to the on-site players completed, I felt more relieved upon departing the airframer's facility than I had as the uncertain stranger who walked in. Meeting the on-site interfaces in their backyards gave me a glimpse of people who appeared to know the price of everything yet the worth of nothing. I would continue to be watchful of them during the assignment. I would focus on the issues that would satisfy Jacques by minimizing the impact on Airbus aircraft, I told myself while listening to Rick. "Experience is the hardest kind of teacher. It gives you the test first and the lesson afterward," wrote Oscar Wilde. With this in mind, it was up to me to dive into the task with my supporting cast, shed my worries about failure, and do the job I had been summoned to complete.

3

The Eighty Day Battle

"Can't we all get along?"

Declared Rodney King to violence erupting after the acquittal of police officers charged with brutally beating him.

Following introductions to local people involved with our propulsion systems, I looked forward to diving into the task. As the hub of propulsion systems integration, the podding facility was the logical place to begin my over sight of engines and nacelle components in process and their allocations to aircraft.

When I walked into the podding facility on the morning after Jacques's chiding, the day began with *beaucoup* handshakes. There was nothing unusual about Ian and Scott's handshakes, but the frenzy on the shop floor was decidedly different. It appeared that everyone in the building was greeting each other as they strolled about pillars and workstations. When hands weren't being clasped, cheeks were pressed against each other as men embraced women, women embraced women, and a man embraced a man.

If a hand was soiled or occupied, a pinkie, forearm or back of hand was extended to be touched.

Little did I realize that these daily workplace greetings were a ritual here and throughout the country. What happens on Mondays? I wondered. This must go on forever. Regardless of the time of day, I found it novel to watch the workforce embrace each other. While my impression of this work environment soared in the morning, I soon discovered the limits of these greetings.

I shook Robert's hand in the morning while crossing the shop floor and attempted a re-shake later in his office. Peering at my hand thrust before him, Robert responded with a cocked head and a wry smile. Casually, he flipped his hand as a reminder that our hands had touched earlier that day. Before a word was spoken, I realized Robert was flagging my *faux pas*. The rejection of my second attempt to shake Robert's hand lingered for a minute but made me realize how little I knew about the people around me.

Senior managers considered me the focal point for propulsion system processing and delivery. I found the tracking of engines and their nacelle components an enormous challenge. I was burdened with tracking thousands of repairs and retrofits, and there were times when I felt like the station master at a frantic train depot. Prioritizing, allocating, and directing units received after their need dates while monitoring those returned to their respective suppliers for upgrades required an acute focus. I had to be aware of the processing within the podding facility, as well as the upgrades being performed at the thrust reverser repair station and the flight line.

Things became more intense when units were sent back to their original producers. This was instantly visible to the airplane manufacturer's managers, and interruptions to the streams of deliveries to their aircraft caused consternation among them. When delays occurred, I would receive an instant complaint about what was needed and when it had to be there. Under such circumstances, the conversations weren't pleasant.

My honeymoon was over within a day of Jacques's sermon to our management. Dieter, a deputy of Jacques's, and his assistant Russell called, demanding propulsion systems for an aircraft on their final assembly line.

"I don't have any propulsion systems available now," I responded.

"But you will do it, yah?" said Dieter, with a profound German accent.

"Welcome to Toulouse," Russell blared in the background.

Following up on Dieter's request, I called our engine facility in the States.

"I have an urgent need for an engine to deliver to the Airbus final assembly line. They have lost patience with our delays. Their aircraft deliveries are being affected. When will I receive an engine?" I asked Bob, the engine assembly operations manager.

"Sorry pal, the closest engine available was rejected at test yesterday and has been sent back to the assembly floor to be fixed," Bob responded.

"OK Bob, when can I expect an engine? I need to tell my impatient Airbus colleagues something," I replied.

"I can't give you a date right now. The engine is being torn down. We'll have to investigate the problem," Bob answered.

"I'm waiting, Bob, and so are our customers," I mentioned in closing.

Managing the inconsistent deliveries of incoming units and being the watchdog for those sent back to their manufacturers was a colossal task in itself, but coordinating the information shared between the local facilities and their enablers in the States was far more demanding. Positioned at a critical juncture in propulsion systems processing, the podding facility was the likely place where problems would surface and impact the flow of units to the aircraft final assembly line. After routing units in need of repair and determining how best to cure them, my workdays continued with the folks at the thrust reverser repair facility.

In the building where thrust reverser repairs and upgrades were performed was a stream of units entering and exiting. Incoming thrust reversers were examined to confirm their pedigree, then upgraded by the musketeers to incorporate retrofits (design modifications) recommended by the manufacturer. After assessing units being processed and their allocations to aircraft, I'd often approach Edouard and Peter, the on-site leader of the thrust reverser producer, to request adjustments to their assigned work.

"Airbus has an urgent need for two thrust reversers," I'd tell Edouard to encourage him to speed up the work and get Dieter and Russell off my back.

"We're moving as fast as we can," he'd say in return.

From the beginning of the task, Airbus management was relentless when they wanted a unit. They had hundreds of millions of dollars of aircraft in process to be delivered to airlines around the world. With aircraft selling for tens of millions of dollars apiece, any delay was an attention-getter. The pressure to accommodate the airframer's expectations was immense. When a thrust reverser installed on an aircraft required a replacement unit, the demand was simply stated:

"We need it now, yah!"

Edouard's people repaired thrust reversers in an isolated section of the customization shop. With a backlog of units waiting induction for retrofits, and others exiting for installation on aircraft, the thrust reverser area was often frantic. Occasionally, units were recycled through the repair station for additional upgrades. Injecting such units into a constipated workstream made the task of prioritizing their processing and projecting their dates of completion more burdensome. Beyond the task of following units delivered to aircraft was the task of keeping track of those sent back to the manufacturer after removal from an airplane. Typically, thrust reversers were shipped back to the States to incorporate modifications beyond the on-site capability.

Undoubtedly, the stars of the repair area were the mechanics; wrench-turning musketeers, I imagined. Forever animated, the men repaired reversers with non-stop chatter and flair. Regardless of the work assigned to them, the musketeers relished their fellowship. They repaired a constant flow of components for several months, and there was always a unit outside the building awaiting their wrenches. Their merriment continued through May of that year, but in the next month, the mirth started to fade. Adjustments to the schedule, coupled with improvements to upstream units, resulted in a reduction of units needing upgrades or repairs on-site. Consequentially, the joyful musketeers became disdainful repairmen, their workload diminishing.

Three Americans were sent to France by the thrust reverser manufacturer to oversee restorations of units and provide technical support to the musketeers. When they arrived on-site, there appeared to be harmony between the newcomers and musketeers. Still, by mid-June, the quantity of repairs and retrofits had escalated beyond that of prior weeks. The shop load and increasing complexity of the repairs required greater product knowledge and hands-on skills beyond what was available on-site. Soon, the deficit was filled by the thrust reverser manufacturer, who sent people to address the workload. Seeing additional people arrive on-site appeared to effect the performance of the musketeers.

Countering the perceived threat to their job security, the mechanics appeared to reduce their pace of completing the repairs. The intensity I had previously observed was diminished, extending the time they were taking to complete repairs.

"The mechanics seem to be working slower than usual," I advised Edouard.

"They look like they're working hard to me," replied Edouard with a shrug.

Contrived or not, the change in the mechanics' pace of work made it more difficult for me to predict when a repair would be completed. Even harder to determine was communicating reliable delivery dates to my unyielding Airbus counterparts.

Despite my difficulty in aligning deliverable units with designated aircraft, Airbus continued to apply pressure. Ever persistent when requesting delivery dates and relentless in holding me to commitments, Dieter phoned me one day with a particularly strong request.

"A reliable bad date is better than a bad good date. I can't plan around an unreliable date," Dieter scolded me. "*Yah*, but you will give me a good date!" he repeated with an enduring German accent.

In seeking accountability from our side, Dieter and Russell were not only asking for projected delivery dates, but also my confidence in meeting them. They needed information they could trust for reliable aircraft planning. Although I dreaded receiving phone calls from Dieter and Russell, their pleas gave me an incentive to commit dates with certitude. As the month of June continued, the reliability of my commitments got better. Gradually, I saw the dependability of my dates building credibility and trust with Dieter, Russell, and others in their procurement unit. The phrase "A good, bad date is better than a bad, good date" was drummed into my mind so often that I would recite it in my sleep.

Dieter's pronouncement became so ingrained that I adopted the philosophy when pursuing our in-house producers and suppliers. It was my first thought when receiving delivery commitments from anyone. After providing dependable commitments to Dieter and Russell, they'd often ask impassively, "What about the contingency?" As a result, when seeking delivery dates for engines and nacelle components, I'd reflexively ask for backup units to ensure my given dates would be met. Faultless, totally success-oriented commitments became unacceptable to me.

To assist with the turn times of upgrades to our composite nacelle components, the thrust reverser manufacturer sent specialists to Toulouse. Carbon fiber materials, a lightweight and stronger alternative to aluminum, which had been used for decades, were becoming more widely used in the aircraft industry. Traditionally, aluminum unit repairs were conducted by means of metal smithery and mechanical fasteners (bolts and rivets). Mindful of the impact of the new helping hands on their job security, the musketeers were increasingly more sensitive to the newcomers.

The specialists, who came in on weekends to expedite repairs of units, became a paradox to reducing the backlog. We concluded that playing catch-up on weekends to finish the work that began during the week seemed a logical means of relieving the congested shop. Contrary to our best thinking, the sight of the additional outside support appeared to influence the output of the musketeers during weekdays. As usual, the chatter was there, but the pace of work became languid. Recognizing the drop-off in output, I once again turned to Edouard for help.

"There is nothing I can do," he would respond when hearing my concerns. Regardless of my complaints about the output, the musketeers became more open about their dismay.

Normally, the workweek of most French laborers and office personnel was five days, Monday through Friday—no different than the workweek for many Americans and others around the world. Having been in France for two months, I was beginning to see how regulated and binding the

French labor laws were—particularly when discussions were in the air about reducing the weekly hours from thirty-nine to thirty-five hours. Barring some exceptions, like those working in the airline industry, bakeries, and some neighborhood merchants, most businesses were closed on Sundays. Weekends were for family and relaxation, I observed. Weekend work was considered off-limits by regulators and most laborers. On the contrary, in the world I had come from, many American laborers were happy to come in on Saturdays, Sundays, or a holiday to fatten their wallets.

The specialists arriving from the States had a common understanding.

"We came across to assist in the recovery of thrust reverser repairs, upgrades, and propulsion system deliveries, regardless of the day of the week or time of day," most would say. Despite the added support at the thrust reverser repair station, Dieter and Russell saw the increase in the time it took to repair and upgrade units. My extended delivery commitments were transparent. When a commitment was broken, I would immediately hear from them. As the liaison who transmitted Dieter's need dates to the people at the repair station and gave the commitments to fill Dieter's needs, it was inevitable that I would be drawn into this untenable situation.

On a peaceful Friday in mid-June, the malcontent of the musketeers boiled over. Russell, Dieter's industrial assistant, called to warn me about a rumor he had heard.

"We hear someone has called the *inspector de travail* (French labor inspector) and told him that people are coming in on weekends to repair thrust reversers," he advised.

"We believe the inspector will investigate the repair facility this weekend."

"Who told the inspector about the weekend work?" I asked.

"I don't know," said a shrill Russell.

With a jittery tone, Russell mentioned, "Not the American specialists nor anyone else should come in this weekend to work."

Because this was my first exposure to a labor inspector in France and I was uncertain of the consequences of his findings, I called the thrust reverser repair station immediately. I told the team leaders at the repair station that we desperately needed weekend work to finish repairs in progress while warning them about not coming in this weekend. Despite the forewarning and the implications thereof, the repair station team stuck to their plan to work the weekend.

The next day, Saturday, the specialists worked without a visit from the inspector. It was my understanding that the musketeers (mechanics) did not come in. Upon visiting the following day, the inspector conducted his review. I heard that after quietly taking notes of his observations, the inspector closed his notebook and swiftly departed.

"After his no-show on Saturday, we didn't think he would be coming in on Sunday," said a thrust reverser manufacturer's on-site person. Obviously, the inspector chose his days well. A few days later, the findings, accompanied by a hefty fine (said to be tens of thousands of dollars), were submitted to the thrust reverser manufacturer. Stunned by the inspector's punishment, the leadership at the repair station became wary of working additional hours. Considering the severity of the penalty, the prospect of shrinking the backlog of repairs and upgrades seemed hopeless.

Upon observing the morale of the musketeers leading up to the inspector's review, it seemed their awareness of possible unlawful weekend work and the prospect of a violation of the statutory workweek may have been more than coincidental. I didn't know what had stimulated the inspector's interest, but it appeared that someone had tipped him off. Within a week, the buzz about the incident evaporated and wasn't mentioned again.

Carrying on with their repair work, the musketeers reverted to their spirited, playful, wrench-turning selves. The lengthy strides, reciprocal teasing, and raucous laughter returned to the repair station. Mindful of the impact of their presence in the building, the specialists adjusted their schedules to weekdays only. Before long, they began to help the musketeers. Although the working relationship between the musketeers and visitors from the States was better, their engagement made me more judicious about stating delivery dates to Dieter and Russell.

During the early days of settling into the task, the six-hour time difference between western Europe and the eastern time zone of the United States greatly influenced my workdays. Generally, mornings were devoted to the podding and repair facilities, while afternoons were consumed with telephone calls, during which I'd correspond with my supporters in the States. In these discussions, the primary focus was on resolving the *issue du jour*—tracking the hundreds of parts needed to upgrade propulsion systems in Toulouse. Issues were causing upstream delays of units that were desperately needed on-site. Lost parts, shipping problems, and upcoming upgrades dominated our daily conversations. Of greater interest, particularly among the more senior-level managers, was the billion-dollar question: "When will we recover and be back on schedule?" A question easy to ask but much harder to answer.

Attendees of these daily teleconferences were primarily the same people. Chairing the meetings from my office in the podding facility, I was usually accompanied by Scott and Ian. Dylan also joined us, often breathless when he arrived. It seemed he always sprinted from wherever he had been. Pending the problem of the day, a representative of the repair and podding facilities sat in with us as well.

Participants in Connecticut, located at sites twenty-five miles apart, added complexity to the coordination on their side of the Atlantic. During the first few calls, it appeared that the stateside attendees were alien to one another.

"Who's asking for this?" I'd hear from a party in our Middletown facility, speaking defiantly to someone on the line in East Hartford. Prior introductions notwithstanding, these statements were said all too often. Gaining agreement and cooperation from representatives of organizations traditionally at odds with one another seemed impossible from my vantage point. Integrated Product Development (I.P.D.), a concept created a few years earlier, sought to meld diverse requirements and promote dialogue between previously polarized departments like product design and development, part producers and engine assembly, and Engineering and Manufacturing.

The concurrent introduction of new commercial and military engine models exposed inter-departmental fault lines. Chasms between departments like Engineering, Manufacturing, and Quality Assurance were evident by an apparent lack of shared interest in the issues of the other departments.

"That's not our responsibility," was frequently stated by some participants of our calls. Granted, inter-departmental teaming was maturing and, in many instances, working well, but some of our discussions revealed the deeper divisions that remained between some organizations, notably Engineering and Production, and the vocal personalities within them.

"You guys in Middletown are always complaining," said an engineer in East Hartford to Quality and Production methods engineers in Middletown. It seemed hopeless to overcome this, I lamented when initiating the calls. At times, getting agreement on a way forward was like obtaining a bipartisan compromise in the Congress of the United States in recent years. As a result, meetings lasting two and three hours were hindered by finger-pointing and mistrust. In some meetings, promises said with conviction were forgotten.

"The parts and paperwork you need for the retrofits will be shipped out today," committed Frank, a program manager in East Hartford, upon responding to my plea in Toulouse. It didn't happen. Disappointed by unfulfilled commitments, the people on the Toulouse end of the phone were losing confidence in the people on the other end. When calls began, the eye-rolling and innuendos of those around me appeared to be reflexive responses to the same old, same old. A faint "This is bullshit" was occasionally belched to an unbelievable commitment stated over the phone.

The organizational clashes that arose during some of the calls seemed to result from the cultures of the organizations. Cultural struggles between organizations on different continents are understandable, but the in-house departments in the company appeared to be in separate worlds. Commitments stated solely to appease people on the other end of the calls were being repeated by the same voices, I noticed. Fed up with the failure of follow-through, the guys on the Toulouse end of the calls became less trusting of what they heard. Clearly, the biggest obstacle to the recovery of the program was the mistrust among the participants assigned to support the effort. When the calls commenced, I envisioned mediating disagreements when they surfaced. However, my Toulouse location was putting me in a position of being viewed as "one of them" by some participants on the other end of calls.

Shortly, it became apparent that the more viable means of reducing the propulsion systems' processing times were changing the routing of the major components. At this time, engine and nacelle components were subjected to two fit-ups. An initial marriage conducted by our engine assembly department in the States was followed by a final integration of engines and nacelle components in the podding facility in Toulouse. The sequence was designed to identify marriage problems early before shipping the units to France. In today's manufacturing world, steeped in process efficiency and streamlining, redundant processing would be considered taboo.

Since an in-house business unit of roughly seven people had been established to conduct the initial marriage of propulsion systems, I concluded that a recommendation to eliminate the function would be considered treasonous. In the midst of debating the removal of the in-house step, the appeal to continue the preliminary processing was rejected. Finally, when a set of components failed to fit in Toulouse, the decision became a *fait accomplis.* Following the fitting incident, the finger-pointing began. As I discussed the event with Rick and colleagues in the supply chain after Norm's stunning departure from the company, it was decided to eliminate the prior fit-up step.

Regardless of speeding up the recovery, folks in the States balked at relocating the fit-up processing equipment (A-frame apparatus) to Europe. Terminating the step in the States resulted in reassigning the workers in the defunct business unit to other places in the organization. However, the annulment of the sequence resulted in hard feelings among some people of the unit and those in nacelle supply management pushing for the move. The animosity lingered for years. After the demise of the nacelle processing unit, I found the task of obtaining delivery commitments for engines and nacelle component deliveries difficult.

At the podding facility, the day-to-day drama continued. One day during a conference call with the States, I heard two men arguing in an adjacent office. I wasn't sure who they were or what had provoked the altercation, but the commotion was loud enough to hear through my closed door. The intensity of the voices speaking French made the scuffle more confusing.

Opening the door to my office, I noticed a fist-sized hole in the closed door across the aisle. Peeking into the office through the hole in the door, I saw papers strewn on the floor. Quivering with anger, the occupant of the office was leaning over his desk, with his untucked shirttail hanging over his pants. Glancing at me as I opened the door was a heavy-breathing Henri.

"Are you OK?" I asked, puzzled about what had happened. Henri remained silent. At our plant in the States, I had heard about incidents of fights among workers but never thought I'd be this close to a workplace scuffle. Such a thing was rare in our company, as generally, a fight resulted in termination.

Walking through the lobby of the podding facility the next morning, I noticed a wiry, youthful-looking guy sitting on a chair with a bluish halo around one eye. I didn't know his name but recalled seeing him walking through the shop. With his eye swollen and a bandage wrapped around his hand, he gazed outward. Later in the day, it was revealed that he had been in an argument with Henri. No one mentioned what had caused the disagreement, but their outburst of emotions was startling.

Weeks later, when I passed Henri in a local supermarket, he spewed a litany of expletives when mentioning Claude's name, continuing to pummel me with verbiage as I walked away. I didn't understand a word he was saying, but I could see that the incident hadn't left him. For reasons unbeknownst to me, one day, Henri disappeared and was never seen at work again.

For an airplane manufacturer, the most dreaded news from a supplier would likely include a request to remove propulsion systems installed on aircraft. Known as a recall in most industries, it's a setback that adds considerable complexity to the processing of aircraft and recovery of a propulsion program. Pending the nature of the problem and the quantity of units affected, it's devastating to those involved in planning for replacement units and creating the workarounds required to reduce the impact to the end item users (the Airbus and airline customers).

In the midst of planning my day at the podding facility one June morning, I was surprised when the phone rang at 9:00. It was too early for a caller from the States, I deduced. As I picked up the receiver and heard Dieter's voice on speaker phone, I sensed that the purpose of the call was more than the usual request for a delivery status.

"Jacques wants a meeting with your vice president in two days," Dieter asserted. Before I could ask why, Dieter restated the demand and added his usual supplement. "But you will do it, yah!" he commanded.

"OK, I'll call the States when they wake up. It's 3:00 a.m. over there," I replied, seeking some understanding.

"But you will do it!" said Dieter in return.

I felt bad about calling so early, I agreed to call the States now.

"So why does Jacques want a meeting in two days?" I asked.

"Because he read Joe Fine's letter recommending removal of suspect nonconforming thrust reverser units installed on aircraft," Russell shouted in the background.

At the time, I hadn't seen the letter or heard anything about Joe's proposal. Before hanging up, Dieter made another request.

"Jacques wants you to come to his office immediately, yah," he said.

Before leaving the podding facility, I called Cary to inform him about Jacques's urgent meeting. "I'll have Roland join you at the meeting," Cary offered before hanging up.

When I arrived at Jacques's office, Roland was pacing in the hallway.

"Are you sure you want to go in there?" Roland asked with a smirk.

"No, not really," I answered.

Stepping out of Jacques's office, Dieter invited Roland and me in.

"*Bonjour messieurs*," Jacques greeted us with a tight-lipped smile.

Before explaining why, he had summoned us, Jacques asked his secretary to bring some refreshments. When she returned with sodas and snacks (mini Madeleine biscuits), Jacques took a bottle of Orangina from the tray and began reading Joe Fine's letter aloud. Upon reciting a statement recommending the removal of thrust reversers from several aircraft, Jacques paused to remove the cap from the bottle.

Blaring, "Joe Fine," with his face ablaze, Jacques twisted the cap of the bottle repeatedly. Seeing him choke the neck of the bottle with one hand while contorting the cap with the other, I wondered what he would have done to the bottle had Joe been present. From Jacques's reaction, it appeared Joe, a technical manager at our home office, had faxed the alert a day before. Observing Jacques's reaction to the advisory, Roland and I listened in awe as Jacques finished reading.

"I want a meeting with Brady (Rick's boss) in two days," Jacques demanded.

"I'll see he gets the message," I replied, relieved that the meeting was over.

Upon leaving Jacques's office, I couldn't get back to the podding facility fast enough. Before going to Jacques's office, I had called Brady to give him a heads-up about the proposed meeting. Brady sounded fully awake when I called him the second time. He mentioned that he hadn't seen the letter but would discuss it with Joe. Digesting Jacques's appeal as we talked, Brady proposed the meeting be held in three days. I called Dieter immediately.

" Jacques won't be happy, but I'll tell him," said Dieter with a dim tone.

Three days later, Brady came to Toulouse with Joe Fine and other managers (one from the thrust reverser manufacturer). Waving the letter like a flag, Jacques opened the meeting with a blazing summary of the proposed recall, beginning with, "The removals of the thrust reversers will put me in the *merde* (poop) and create *beaucoup* problems at our final assembly line."

Emphasizing the impact of removing the thrust reversers from the wing, Jacques spewed discontent, with an extravagant wind-breaking sound sputtering from his lips.

Sitting next to a somber Brady, Joe Fine presented a summary of the problem affecting the units. During his explanation, Joe mentioned that the carbon fiber material used to produce the skins of the units was delaminating and required reinforcement to fix them. Stronger and lighter weight than aluminum, the composite material had gradually become the material of choice in the industry. After stating his summary of the non-conformance and justification for the recall, Joe proposed a plan for fixing the units.

"An on-wing repair would save time, but the reliability of such a critical fix would be risky to perform on wing," said Joe, with earnest surety.

Listening intently to Joe, Jacques took a deep sniff, scribbled a note on a piece of paper, and slid it to Brady. Standing defiantly erect, Jacques raised a shoulder, cocked his head, and emitted a more sonorous blurt.

Reminiscent of the multiple wind breaking I recalled him emitting during my introductory meeting, the louder verbal flatus at this meeting mirrored Jacques's agonized emotions. Reading the note, Brady faced the attendees with a strained smile.

"You have no credibility!" Jacques said, repeating the written message.

"We're sorry this has happened with these thrust reversers. I apologize for the inconvenience," said a solemn Brady.

Watching Brady's confession with piercing eyes, Jacques cleared his throat. Moving his hands in a rolling motion, he said, *"Nourrira,"* several times. Neither Brady nor any non-French speaking attendee knew what *"Nourrira"* meant, but Jacques's rotating hands were sending a message. In fact, Jacques was saying that he wanted us to feed him with upgraded replacement thrust reversers as the suspect units were taken off the wing. More precisely, he wanted us to feed them with upgraded units before suspect units were removed from aircraft.

With his hands planted on his hips, Jacques raised a question that underscored the purpose of the meeting.

"What is your plan for replacing thirteen units, and when will we see them?" he asked Brady with a steely gaze.

Seeking to rescue Brady from Jacques's question, Joe Fine jumped in. "We have some replacements available now," he offered.

Nodding his head, Jacques acknowledged Joe's overture with a nonchalant glint. Clearly, he wasn't happy with what was available at that time.

"When will we have them and more?" Jacques pressed.

"We are putting a replacement plan together and will be ready to share it with you in a day or two," Brady replied.

"OK, we wait for your plan," Jacques responded with a shrug. With a peevish smile, he closed the meeting.

Throughout the meeting, Brady had exhibited a sterile smile. Undoubtedly, he was embarrassed. Regardless of the anguish he was feeling, I was impressed with the emotional intelligence displayed by him during Jacques's outward disapproval. Brady's composure made a lasting impression on me and how I would want to comport myself under similar circumstances.

The *Nourrira*, Jacques's plan for feeding replacement units to aircraft, provided an opportunity for supporters of the recovery to collaborate on a nearer-term solution. As the participants worked together to return units to the thrust reverser manufacturer, who would quickly upgrade them and return them to Toulouse, the reliability of their promises improved. Within a week or two, the chasm between enablers in the States and the on-site repair station people began to shrink. A sense of common cause, I reckoned.

Among the people participating on the daily calls, there remained little or no trust, particularly those in the States versus those in Toulouse. Feeding the suspicions of the people in Toulouse was the feeling that the committers, who weren't feeling the pain, weren't fulfilling their commitments.

"It will be sent out today," became a statement heard during many calls.

"Why should we believe it?" Someone on my end of the phone, would ask.

Despite promises that, in some instances, were aspirational assumptions resulting in insufficient follow-through, the daily communication gradually sensitized the distant attendees to the urgency of the air-framer and the expectations of our airline customers. The daily calls also served as reminders that Jacques's confidence in the operation was at stake. Reliable commitments and flawless execution were essential to keeping him calm. The folks on the stateside end of calls didn't feel the heat, but on my end, we were charred by the dismay of the air-framer. The conference calls continued for several weeks before participants saw progress in Toulouse.

Fault lines between the contributing organizations in the States, component suppliers, and the processing units in Toulouse played a role in the polarized environment. Each group seemed to live and operate within its own silo. Their day-to-day activities and operational objectives weren't intertwined or even connected in some instances. Although the meetings were conducted in English, at times, the discussions were foreign. A sense of organization and nationalism heavily influenced working relationships among certain groups, particularly the folks in Toulouse. Nativism among the on-site people made them more focused on the needs of the air-framer and the local suppliers.

The geographic separation of the trans-Atlantic teams resulted in some participants being less responsive to requests made by those from afar. At times, it seemed as though protectionism was impeding cooperation. Because they were located thousands of miles from Toulouse and far from the adversity at the airplane manufacturer, the accountability of some stateside folks appeared diminished. Weighing the overall impact on the people in Toulouse and the dissatisfaction at the air-framer, it was incumbent upon Dylan, Scott, Ian, and me, who were closer to the firing line, to inspire the stateside people during these daily calls. I was often frustrated with the lack of support from the other end of these calls. They became an exercise in futility, making it harder for me to give Dieter and Russell reliable delivery commitments. Adding to my trouble were events coming out of the blue (bird strikes, lost parts, and unforeseen labor disputes).

A week after Jacques's urgent meeting, I walked into the podding facility and noticed a mass of people standing at the coffee machine on the shop floor. Not concerned about it, I continued across the shop to my office. As I reviewed a commitment I had made to Russell about deliveries of propulsion systems, I looked over from the mezzanine to see how the work was progressing. Scanning the shop floor, I saw no one at their workstation or working on anything. A look at the other side of the floor revealed dozens of people talking at the coffee machine. Nervous about breaking my commitment to Airbus, I searched for Robert or a recognizable supervisor to help me understand what was happening. Upon approaching the congregation at the coffee machine, I noticed Edith, our program manager, among the people.

"What's going on, Edith?" I asked. "Nobody is working."

"You don't understand. It's normal," said Edith.

"OK, I get it. It's a strike," I replied. "But, for how long?"

"*Oui*, it's a strike. Normally, they are over in a day," she replied.

Dejected by losing a day of progress on delivering urgently needed propulsion systems, I continued to look for a higher-level manager. Shortly, I came across Robert and Jean-Luc, the shop foreman, talking to a striker.

"Robert, Jean-Luc, is there something you can do to get these people back to work?" I asked in bewilderment.

"He doesn't understand," said Jean-Luc, flashing a smile of chaotic teeth.

"Can't help you, *mon ami*," said Robert with a shrug.

With my commitment at stake, I went to the second-floor office of Jean, the head of the podding facility. I was not willing to give up.

"Jean, is there something you can do to get my propulsion systems worked on? I have deliveries committed for tomorrow," I pleaded.

"No. There is nothing I can do. It's a way of life here," said Jean.

Expecting no sympathy from my colleagues at Airbus, I called Dieter and Russell to share the bad news.

"Yah, we wait for your delivery," asserted Dieter.

"I'll deliver them when possible. No one's working here," I informed.

"Welcome to Toulouse!" Dieter and Russell laughed, ending the call.

Outside of the workplace, I was becoming more accustomed to the local life. After living for a week in the hotel near Cary's office, I moved into an apartment in another hotel. Located on a busy route farther from Toulouse, the hotel and its amenities were a dream. Upon arriving at the hotel, I met the assistant manager, a shapely, mid-thirties-looking woman who greeted me with an austere expression. She escorted me to a unit on the second floor at the far end of the hotel. Perhaps this is the normal demeanor of French women in this position, I pondered while she explained the terms and conditions of the agreement.

By contrast, the staff at the front desk beamed with affection. Smiling incessantly, the bright-eyed men and women behind the counter appeared to relish the hospitality they extended. From my first day, they made me feel at home and accepted. Returning to the hotel after arduous, frustrating workdays, I found their gleeful receptions of "*Bonsoir monsieur*, did you have a good day?" soothing.

The unit Sylvie showed me was ideal for an avid golfer, as it overlooked a golf course. Prior to accepting the assignment, France conjured thoughts of food and wine, but golf? Unthinkable! I took a deep breath while leaning out of the bedroom window. I was in heaven. The fragrance of fresh-cut grass was as welcoming as the buoyant "*Bonjours*" from the front-desk staff.

In the weeks following my entry into the hotel, I established a work routine where my days began at Cary's office. After gathering mail, faxes, and phone messages from the States, I'd depart for the podding facility and repair station to assess the progress of the *Nourria.* From there, it was decided which units needed pushing. The bulk of my time at the repair station was consumed with overseeing thrust reverser repairs and upgrades. Typically, I spent the afternoons presiding over our trans-Atlantic conference calls.

One sunny morning during the second month of the assignment, I walked pass a room where the musketeers changed clothes and ate their lunch. Gazing through the window, I noticed two women busily cleaning the tiny space. One of the women, appearing to be in her mid-twenties, was emptying waste baskets, while the other, taller woman swept the floor. Both women beamed warm smiles as I walked by the open window.

Beyond a facile *"Bonjour,"* I couldn't converse with them at all. Later, I discovered the two women were related to each other, a mother and daughter team, someone mentioned.

As I continued to the shop floor to review units recently received in the facility, my mind drifted to my inability to speak French. The language barrier at this facility and in most places I went to was a wake-up call that had stimulated my interest in learning the language. While circulating among the worksites, I could communicate in English, but my inability to speak with others was obvious outside of the workplace.

Using the cassette tapes provided via a home study course, I pursued my interest in learning the French language. At the hotel, I filled my evenings with listening to tapes and studying the text accompanying them. As I became more comfortable with the language, I ventured into speaking it in the repair station. After mustering the nerve to attempt to speak French, I struggled to say the right words, though there was no shortage of corrective help. Edouard, the musketeers, folks at the podding facility, and the staff at the hotel instantly corrected me. To my chagrin, the corrections came far too often for my confidence in speaking to others.

"It's said this way, not that!" I'd constantly hear.

"What were you saying?" some would ask.

At first, I found the interruptions of my attempts annoying and embarrassing. The frequency of the corrections told me how dismal my French was. Soon, I avoided speaking anything more than the basic words I knew before coming to France. Nonetheless, as time went on, I learned to accept the corrections as an expression of the cor-rector's pride in the language and how it was intended to be spoken. This would be considered rude by the American culture and was far from anything I had previously encountered when speaking, but I found the help invaluable in learning the proper pronunciations and usage of words.

I found the French language pleasing to the ear. Conversing with the French in their language was much harder than I had anticipated when coming to France. The unspoken language the French exhibited was more helpful to my understanding of the words being said. Facial expressions and body language like flailing arms, fluttering hands, wagging fingers, arched eyebrows, pouting lips, and the ubiquitous shrug added meaning to words and their intentions. With hands fanned outward, palms facing up, and shrugged shoulders, the locals responded to my efforts to speak the language. The French love their language. They value it highly and use it with great care. To their credit, no one gave me a pass on misspoken words.

Eager to road test what I was learning, I ventured beyond the workplace, supermarket, and *boulangerie* (bakery) near the hotel to a broader population in Toulouse. For starters, I began the testing in the center of Toulouse, selecting restaurants on a whim. The Pizzeria Vecchio restaurant had caught my eye on my first ride into the city. Housed in one of several brick buildings lining the lively Boulevard Allee Jean-Jaures, the restaurant, with its brightly lit Romanesque façade and people lined up waiting to get in, was teeming with life. "What hunger is to food, zest is to life," says Bertrand Russell. The piquancy of the place and its patrons, consisting of university students and repeat customers, was irresistible.

When in Toulouse, I always found the time to visit the Pizzeria Vecchio. Though the cuisine was Italian rather than French, I found the vibrant atmosphere and accommodating staff magnetic. Catching a glimpse of me walking into the restaurant seemed to ignite the servers, Nadia and Jean-Pierre, their boss, Marc, and his brother, Hassan. I was treated like a dignitary when I showed up, and it didn't take long for the pizzeria to feel like home.

Both Marc and Hassan commonly greeted me with hearty handshakes and visible joy. They were men of Moroccan descent, I was told, and neither Marc nor his brother could speak or understand much English. Despite my inability to converse with them in French, our hands and facial expressions became our means of communicating. Intuitively, we were able to understand each other. Before long, a rapport of mutual acceptance and trust developed from my perception of their intended words and their perceptions of me.

When speaking with the brothers and others on the staff, there was a feeling of open expression. There were none of the innuendos or false pretensions I had been experiencing at work. At the restaurant, I had no concerns about someone's intentions when hearing words, I couldn't understand. On busy nights with customers lined up at the entrance, Marc and his brother would go out of their way to greet me.

"Who is he?" I'd often hear reverberating through waiting customers on the sidewalk. Waving me into the restaurant ahead of the line would create a buzz among them.

"Who are you? Where are you from?" people seated at neighboring tables would ask me.

They knew I wasn't French, but the fervor produced by my presence led many diners to wonder if I was more than I actually was.

Within a week or two of my first visit to the restaurant, I had formed a closer friendship with staff members Nadia and Jean-Pierre. Besides her natural beauty and charming personality, Nadia spoke English better than anyone on the staff. She came to my aid on countless evenings. Generally, Marc and I were able to understand each other, but other times, we would have to rely on Nadia to interpret for us. Absorbed by the accommodating nature of the Vecchio family, I continually went back to the place. The gratifying reception and overall treatment I received at Vecchio propelled me through many challenging workweeks.

Although the A330 aircraft and its propulsion systems had been certified by the aviation authorities, the flight-test program was ongoing. When I arrived on-site in April, testing had been in progress for more than a year. Subjected to stringent safety and airworthiness requirements by the regulatory authorities (the F.A.A., French-D.G.A.C., and European-J.A.A., or E.A.S.A. today), several test aircraft were being used to validate the performance of the aircraft and their power-plants. Most days, there was a test flight of one aircraft to confirm its conformity to technical and regulatory mandates.

In general, the flight test personnel and I lived in separate worlds. Located in a hangar adjacent to the flight line, the charter of the flight test team was to prepare the aircraft and its propulsion systems for the test program of the day and maintain and service the airplanes before and after flights. My duties were more focused on feeding aircraft on the final assembly line with new and replacement propulsion systems, in addition to clearing the issues that were impeding, or could impede, delivery of aircraft. Occasionally, our paths crossed when a replacement propulsion system, or spare part, was urgently needed for a test aircraft.

Walking out of the thrust reverser repair facility on the afternoon of June 30, my eyes were drawn to the sky. Its mid-day brilliance had suddenly darkened. As I got into my car to return to the podding facility, I noticed a cloud of black smoke billowing from beyond the buildings in front of me. I asked a woman getting into her car what had happened and heard her reply: "A crash." The woman's comment was confirmed by a man pacing back and forth in the parking lot. "There has been an airplane crash," he said with a mournful tone while puffing on a cigarette. I gasped, wondering if there were survivors.

As I drove to the podding facility, I heard the incident confirmed over the radio. The report described the affected airplane as a large, twin-engine aircraft matching the approximate passenger capacity (250) of an A330 aircraft. The broadcast closed with news that there were no survivors. Further details revealed that all people on board, including a crew of three (pilot, co-pilot, and flight engineer), and four non-revenue passengers (representatives of a prospective airline customer), had perished in the crash.

Hearing the announcer's description of the airplane, I aborted my visit to the podding facility and rushed to Cary's office. While driving there, I thought about the engines installed on the aircraft and their manufacturer. As I entered Cary's office, the despondence of everyone was telling.

"Yes, our propulsion systems were on the aircraft," said a doleful Cary.

Considering the intense interest a new model aircraft creates, it wasn't surprising how quickly the shock waves of the tragedy spread through the aircraft manufacturer, aviation authorities, our company, and the airlines. Following the incident, I received numerous daily inquiries about the role of the propulsion systems in the disaster. Needless to say, the event overshadowed the *Nourrira*, which was well underway. Back filling the propulsion systems lost in the crash made it even more difficult to obtain replacement units to back fill removals from aircraft, subject to the *Nourrira*. It was a struggle to keep up with the current requirements.

In the aftermath of the incident, the aviation authorities and the airplane maker conducted an extensive investigation. Before long, we learned that the A330 flight test aircraft (MSN42) had been undergoing a performance test in a particular mode of take-off and approach configurations, the objective being to test how the aircraft behaved with the center of gravity of the airplane near its aft limit—meaning that tons of water, carried in bladder-like containers, was placed in specific locations in the rear of the aircraft. A part of the test was a simulation of an engine failure, which was performed by shutting down an engine and switching off a hydraulic circuit. During the test flight, the autopilot system was set to fly the aircraft to an altitude of 2,000 feet (610 meters).

Having just successfully completed a landing, the aircraft was in the process of performing a take-off. While the aircraft was being flown by the co-pilot, the actions of shutting an engine down, turning off the hydraulic circuit, and engaging the autopilot were being done by the captain. Following a successful take-off and the shutdown of one engine and a hydraulic system, there appeared to be a problem with the autopilot system—it took three attempts to engage it. When the autopilot finally engaged, the aircraft began to ascend to 2,000 feet. Rising sharply, the aircraft started to lose speed, decreasing below the minimum speed of the 118 knots required to control the aircraft. During the investigation conducted by the aviation authorities and the airplane manufacturer, an extreme focus was put on the actions taken by the cockpit crew and the performance of the autopilot system. *

Within days of the incident, the investigation exonerated the propulsion systems from contributing to the event. This was relieving to those in the propulsion system business, but hearing that there were no survivors was chilling. For weeks, the sorrow lingered among my colleagues on both sides of the Atlantic. In the days following the incident, I drove past the crash site on my way to the podding facility. Occasionally, I pulled to the side of the road, looked toward the runway, and sank into a momentary malaise.

As the investigation proceeded through the summer, I strived to keep the people in the podding facility, the repair station, and my colleagues in the States focused on the expectations (committed delivery dates) of Airbus. During my visits to the flight-line office, the cynics and skeptics of the group were increasingly visible. Trip and Carl projected malevolence that created an atmosphere of relational uncertainty. In this environment, the best two hours of the workday were lunchtime, which became a welcome respite from blazing issues of the hour and the discordant supporters on the perimeter. Lunches with on-site colleagues like Dylan, Scott, Ian, and the occasional visitor from the States were a midday relief from the madness of the workplace.

Among the many restaurants in the region serving *déjeuner* (lunch) to their devoted patrons was Les Marroniers, favored by workmates and visitors from the States. Situated in the center of the sleepy village of St. Martin du Touche, close to work and the Toulouse city limits, the restaurant exemplified the unhurried dining culture of the region. Far from chic, the eatery was a quintessential mom-and-pop establishment, serving regional fare in a convivial setting. With paneled walls adorned with photos of local points of interest and tables covered with ruby-colored table clothes, the modest furnishings complemented the café.

Though the restaurant attracted customers with its food, ambiance, and outrageously low prices, the real charm of the place was its owners, Gilbert, and his wife Janine. Generally greeting our lunchtime party with glowing smiles and a joke or two, the couple's passion for customer satisfaction was demonstrated in the meals they served, and Les Marroniers was often filled with diners. *Sans reservations*, it was virtually impossible to get a table in the restaurant at lunchtime. Not long after starting the assignment, the restaurant gained my acceptance of the food and hospitality, and the feeling became mutual with the owners.

Gilbert had a compact build and a touch of gray around the temples, but his most distinguishing feature was his nose. Slightly flattened and skewed to a side, it appeared it had collided with someone's fist. Exceedingly chatty, Gilbert enjoyed circulating among his customers, creating laughter. Whether he spoke French or French-English, the interplay seemed to fuel his energy. Despite the self-amusing tomfoolery, I heard he had good culinary credentials, and I never left his restaurant hungry or feeling like I had a bad meal. Although regional dishes like *cassoulet* (a slow-cooked, white bean stew), *confits de canard* (duck legs preserved in duck fat), and *foie gras* were popular menu items, Gilbert's mussels in garlic cream sauce with a side of crispy *pomme frites* were sensational. They were food for the soul, brother!

On weekends, I spent much of my time assessing the upcoming week's activities at the podding and repair facilities. By anticipating the flow of incoming and outgoing units at both places, I could determine where my oversight was most needed in the coming weeks. I gradually began moving about comfortably on my own and feeling more connected with the local citizenry and people of vastly different cultures.

Not long after moving into my hotel apartment, I developed a friendship with Kumail, an on-site technical representative of Malaysia Airlines. A short, deeply tanned man with an incessant smile, Kumail lived in the apartment directly below mine. Kumail was a beginner at golf who had a strong desire to learn the sport.

"I see you have a set of clubs, Kumail, can I help you?" I asked, looking at his beginner set of clubs.

"Oh yes, I'd like that. I'm just learning," he replied with a wide smile.

Soon, playing a few holes of golf became a nightly ritual when returning to the hotel. After a second round of golf, Kumail invited me to his apartment for Malaysian snacks, as he put it.

We discussed our families—he had two children—and engines for his upcoming aircraft while Kumail and I ate something he put together in the spur of the moment. Green, slightly sweet, and resembling julienne-sliced green peppers, Kumail's crunchy snacks had an exotic flavor unlike anything I had ever eaten.

"This is great. I like the snap and spicy flavor," I praised Kumail.

"I'm glad you like it. It's just a simple snack," said Kumail. "Tomorrow, we can have more, if you like," he continued. Which we did, again and again.

Regardless of the severity of workday issues, time passed faster than I imagined it would. With the July 14th Bastille (Independence) Day holiday a little more than a week away, I anticipated Rick informing me that my three-month assignment would be ending. I was saddened when thinking about departing the assignment. Contemplating leaving Toulouse before propulsion systems powering an A330 aircraft were delivered to an airline made me determined to stay and see the job through. Since the investigation of the crash had not been closed, there was a lot of skepticism about when the initial delivery would occur.

Some managers in our company had misgivings about selecting a person of my ethnicity for this highly visible task, I imagined. Behind the scenes, there had to be people who viewed Norm's selection of me as risky. Sensing I was a pioneer for this assignment, I knew I would be closely scrutinized and would likely be held to a higher standard. This in itself motivated me to complete what I had been sent to accomplish. Thoughts of returning to Connecticut, feeling like a refugee in a department restructured beyond my recognition, provided additional incentive to stay in France. Besides, in my absence, Norm had been replaced by a person from outside of the company.

Thoughts of going back to a new-old world weighed on me for weeks. Nonetheless, the cultural exposure, international experience, and my desire to succeed in the task were decisive reasons to stay. A few days later, I received that call from Rick, who told me, "Your tour of duty in Toulouse has been extended." To me, the extension indicated that I hadn't failed, or screwed up enough to anger Jacques.

After digesting the best news I'd heard in weeks, I looked back at the prior eighty days of the assignment. When starting this task, I had naively expected that my cast of supporters would be unified and mutually focused on the day-to-day needs of the recovery. When mediating inter-departmental squabbles during the trans-Atlantic calls, Rodney King's plea of two years prior, "Can't we all get along?" resonated with me.

But by July, only three months after the start of the assignment, I realized that my expectations of unity had been delusional. Cultivating a sense of common purpose was really needed to move the recovery forward. A renewed focus on improving delivery performance was awakened in me during these eighty days. Adapting to the locals and receiving their acceptance elevated my interest in embracing the language and culture. For the road ahead, success would likely be measured by the timing of the deliveries of the first aircraft and clearing the obstacles impeding them. In addition, confidence in our ability to consistently deliver on our commitments would be determined by our ability to make doing so a way of life.

* Learmount, David. "A330 Crash Caused by Series of Small Errors." Flight International, August 10-16, 1994.

4

Connecting in the Vineyard

"England and America are two countries divided by a common
language."

George Bernard Shaw.

Granted, separation by an ocean was a factor, but there was more
contributing to our discord than the Atlantic. Speaking distinctly
uncommon languages and located more than 3,000 miles apart,
it's little wonder that the cultures of the United States and France are so
different. Americans speak, while the French *parlent.* Yanks converse with
an Anglo order of wording while Francs use comparable words inversely.
Regardless of the words and our respective interpretations of them, we
were missing the mark and appeared separated by ideological barriers. The
primary concern of our Franco-German counterparts was the deliveries of
our engines, and nacelles weren't meeting their expected dates.

"Just deliver on the dates you agreed to," they'd remind me.

As I approached the end of a third month on this assignment, I found oversight of a propulsion system program considered impossible to control from the States was as onerous to manage in France. My time here was destined to exceed Norm's ninety-day prediction. After weeks in the line of fire of the airplane manufacturer, it was painfully clear that they weren't asking for the world when blaring, "Do what you said you were going to do." Instead, they were telling us, "A commitment is a commitment." Being closer to the fervor of Jacques, Dieter, and those working under them certainly opened my ears, but it also permitted me to a perspective I couldn't see from the other side of the Atlantic. In the mind of the air-framer, the precipitous on-site upgrading of engines and nacelle components justified the need for an accessible owner of the issues and activities on-site. Consequently, they summoned me to mitigate their misgivings.

Since arriving in April, I had found myself a convenient target of emotionally charged frustration and posturing by my air frame colleagues. Despite their sharp words, it was incumbent upon me to remain focused on my pursuit of the recovery. The skepticism and mistrust I observed when coming to France continued into July. With Bastille Day less than a week away, I looked forward to some hours of relief.

When departing the repair station on the Saturday before the holiday, I wasn't certain where I was going. An oppressively hot day, by noon time, anyone who came into work had left. Driving south from Toulouse, I entered the A-61 motorway (a major highway) heading toward the Mediterranean Sea. With the city of Toulouse fading in the rear, Cary's driving tip became more vivid as I drove.

"Never look in the rear-view mirror while driving here," he said jokingly and repeatedly.

"Why?" I asked.

"Because it will scare the hell out of you," he quipped.

Following an uneasy drive from the airport on my first day in France, I had gradually become accustomed to the aggressive driving habits of motorists here. A peek in the rear-view mirror revealed a convoy of cars glued to my bumper. The bluster I felt from cars passing me made the 130 km (80 mph) speed limit seem nonexistent. I was amazed to see bug-eyed

Renaults, rattling Citroens, and wheezing Peugeot 205s years past their prime exceeding the speed limit. Regardless of where I was in the region, these venerable vehicles were driven hard by their owners.

Surrounding the highway was countryside of farmland and vineyards. Before long, the landscape was awash with fields of *tournesol* (sunflowers) basking in the brilliant sun. In front of them were clusters of poppies extending to the roadway. The rolling terrain showed signs of habitation, with distant villages and centuries-old churches visible from the roadway.

Appearing on the right side of the highway was the Canal du Midi. Started in the year 1666 and completed years later, the inland waterway linking the Atlantic coast of France with the Mediterranean Sea was still in use. Overcome by curiosity, I exited the highway to get a closer look at the waterway. Shimmering in a soft breeze, the listless flow of water was shaded by a parade of trees on both banks. Beyond the trees, I could hear a faint "put-put," confirming that the canal was in use.

When I returned to the motorway, the appearance of medieval Carcassonne, with a tapestry of vineyards before it, came out of nowhere. Pulling over at a rest stop opposite the walled city, I took a moment to view the kidney-shaped fortification and a vision of military architecture of the Middle Ages. The 1500-year-old fortress, dating back to Roman times, displayed the evolution of the materials and construction techniques applied over the centuries. Built on a foundation of massive blocks, later development of the battlement consisted of smaller cubes of stone alternating with progressions of bricks laid in a herringbone pattern. The ramparts included yellowish buildings and towers with slits in them for bowmen, it seemed.

Gazing at the fortress, I mused about the warfare of that time and the centuries-old battles the structure had endured. Breathing a fusion of wildflowers and pine-scented air while viewing the fortification, I peered in amazement at one of the most scenic views I had ever seen. Before long, I reentered the highway, continuing toward the Mediterranean. Moments later, Narbonne, a moderate-sized city with a history dating back to Roman times, came into view. Catching my attention on the left side of the motorway was

St. Just, a medieval Gothic Cathedral. Resisting a strong urge to stop and take a closer look, I continued towards the Mediterranean.

A short while later, my one-hour drive revealed a view of the sea. Unveiled at the crest of a steep grade was a gleaming view of the Mediterranean. Appearing far away a few miles later, a sign showing *Narbonne Plage* caught my interest. Leaving the motorway, I followed signs through a labyrinth of roundabouts to a placard marking the road leading to the beach. The surroundings were desert-like, with scorched foliage and thirsty grape vines.

The road to the beach was a narrow strip through parched prairie, desolate vineyards, and smoky rock formations. It was a bland contrast to the highway, which displayed scenic villages, stunning edifices, and rolling countryside. As I drove at a leisurely speed on the narrow strip of pavement, I was leery of vehicles coming from the opposite direction. As I continued towards the beach, the terrain changed. Alone among ashen cliffs and dehydrated brush, with no sight of the sea, I began to experience an eerie feeling. Fighting the temptation to return to the motorway, I pulled over to consider going on.

"You've come this far, so keep going," I reasoned. Continuing my pursuit of the beach, I came upon a sizable vineyard with a roadside stand. Surrounding the small stone building was distressed vegetation, seemingly suffering from the heat. Soon, I found myself among craggy rocks. The air carried a scent of the sea. Breathing salty air made me hopeful of water ahead. Moments later, the roadway came to a glistening expanse of carillon water, where hundreds of umbrellas were pitched in the sand. Gazing at the fan-shaped basin while descending to the beach, I was amazed at the multitude of bathers strewn across the shore.

After finding a place to park far from the sand, I removed my shoes and socks and rolled up my pants up to just above knee level. I surveyed the glazed humanity as I walked toward the sea, my strides accelerated by searing pavement. Oiled to the hilt, the crackle of roasting skin was almost audible.

Among the countless people, the more vivid folks were women sunning *au naturelle* from the waist up. *Madame, mademoiselles,* and *mamans* (moms) with children were soaking up the sun. For a guy coming from reserved

New England, I found the liberation pleasantly different. Taking a winding route through villages of parasols, I strolled gleefully to the sea.

My first step in the gentle ebb of the water released tension I had stored over the past three months. While wading in the ankle-high water, I peered beyond the crowd of people into a flotilla of catamarans sailing offshore, then to the horizon. My God, I thought, North Africa must be out there somewhere! After gazing at a rocky jetty, a hundred feet away, I turned back to the multitude of people in the water. As I stood in the ankle-high water, my observations of people at the water's edge was more focused. Occasionally, my beach-combing was interrupted by waders charging a swell. Returning an errant ball to a couple playing paddle ball prompted a jubilant *"Merci monsieur"* from them.

As I hiked along the beachfront for nearly an hour, it became apparent that my perception of French beaches, buoyed by films and magazines, had been contrary to what I was seeing. There appeared to be a collective shrug among the nonchalant folks under their umbrellas. The sight of me wearing rolled-up pants, aimlessly walking the shoreline, must have appeared odd to those watching me. The farther I strayed from the entrance to the beach, the more liberated the people appeared.

The bodies of the bathers in and out of the water varied from deeply tanned, sinewy figurines to plump, greasy roasters. Reclining on her elbows in the gentle surf was one of many middle-aged women in the water. She gazed skyward through colossal sunglasses, posing like a goddess. Standing behind her was a burly, gray-haired man wearing a skimpy swimsuit. With arms folded over his robust belly and his face browned to a crisp, he surveyed the beachfront like a watchdog.

"Bonjour monsieur," Madame said, clutching her wind-blown hat.

"Bonjour, madame," I replied, side-stepping her.

Seeing her basking in the hot sunshine partially clothed made me feel more self-conscious about my absurd attire. To avoid continued feelings of guilt, I moved on quickly. When the whimsical *"ooh-la-la"* subsided, I gained a deeper appreciation of *madame's* enjoyment of her freedom and the culture's acceptance of it. Rather than being promiscuous, as some may imagine, her exposure was an assertion of liberation. The joy of uninhibited exposure seemed to permeate the people along the shore. Educated by the throng at the beach, I returned to the parking lot.

I thought about what I had learned as I got into the car. The reality of the excursion opened my eyes to the misconceptions I had had about the culture. The experience had also been beneficial in relieving the uneasiness that had festered in me for weeks. As I left the parking lot, the voices from the beach faded into the terrain. A five-minute drive brought me back to the vineyard and roadside stand I had passed on the way to the beach. Behind the stone building were vines with slouching clusters of dark fruit. Curious about the structure, I pulled to the side of the road.

Inside the building was an ample woman looking outward from behind a wooden counter. The woman was brown with leathery skin. Her life appeared etched in the furrows of her brow and her disheveled white hair.

"*Bonjour monsieur, voulez vous gouter?*" (Do you want to taste?) she asked with a raspy tone. Knowing nothing about the wines on the counter and puzzled by so many to choose from, I hesitated to respond. To my unfamiliar eyes, they all looked the same. Blocking the brilliant sun with a hand, the woman waited patiently while I considered my selection. Displaying a grimaced smile during my deliberation, the woman grabbed a bottle and poured a sample of it into a glass.

"*Voila monsieur,*" she uttered, sliding the glass to me.

My first sip of the ruby liquid drew a pause. "It's no different than any wine I've tried in the region," I thought. At this time, it was just me and the server. She spoke no English, and my French was American-English. Our communication was confined to short statements and marked by idle gazes. As I assessed her offering, the proprietress peered impassively at me.

While savoring the wine in quietude, a car pulled up with a dusty halt. Emerging from the pint-sized vehicle were two women. One woman was rusty blond, trim, and freckle-faced, with her hair tied in a ponytail. Sturdy and far shorter than her travel mate, the other woman was deeply tanned, with dark hair reminiscent of an aroused porcupine. Rushing into the building, both women bellowed "Hello" with British-sounding accents.

Having exhausted my limited French on the first sample, I was relieved to hear the women speaking English. Considering the exposure, I had encountered at the beach, the sight of them wearing jeans and shirts with rolled-up sleeves was strange. But the sight of my silly garb at the beach had surely appeared strange as well. Regardless of where these early thirty-looking women were from, they appeared touristy.

"Bonjour mademoiselles. Voulez vous gouter?" asked the proprietress. Freezing for a moment as I had, the taller lady pointed to a bottle. Standing at the far end of the four-to-five-meter counter, they giddily sipped their sample. While turning up their glasses, they occasionally looked toward my end of the counter, then quickly turned away.

"Where are they from?" I wondered, observing their banter.

"How do you like the wine?" I asked while trying another wine.

"It's OK," the taller lady replied.

Swallowing with a gulp, her companion raised her glass and nodded.

"Where are you from?" the taller woman asked, tossing her hair backwards.

"From America. Can't you tell?" I replied.

"Where are you from?" I asked.

"I'm from New Zealand, and my friend is from Australia," the taller woman said. Stating my name, I walked to their end of the counter to extend my hand to both ladies.

"My name is Margaret, and she is Debbie," the taller one said.

Margaret's height and hair color resembled a guy in our flight-line office.

"Do you have relatives in France?" I asked, thinking she might know him.

"Ah no, definitely none," Margaret affirmed.

Perhaps it was the hair or her leanness that swayed my thoughts of a connection, but what the hell, they were both New Zealanders, I concluded while finishing my sample.

During my exchange with Margaret, her companion remained silent. Suddenly, Debbie burst into talking about how they had happened to stop at the stand. Appearing eager to participate in the conversation, she mentioned that they had been touring the south of France and unintentionally wandered onto the beach road. Expecting a shorter drive to the sea, as I had, they settled for the vineyard instead. While she continued to speak about their misadventures, cars streamed by.

A snazzy green convertible spewed dirt as it came to a screeching stop. Two men got out and rambled to the counter. Their skin appeared opaque in the afternoon sun as they entered the stand. Wearing dark pants and plaid shirts, they seemed more alien than Margaret and Debbie.

"Good afternoon, *madame*," one greeted the seasoned server with a pronounced British accent. Waiting to be served, he brushed back strands of wind-blown hair from his reddened face. The other man, plump with bushy white hair, held the brim of his cap in the gusting wind.

"*Bonjour messieurs. Voulez vous essayer?*" the proprietress asked, inviting them to try.

"*Oui madame.* We'll try that one," the red-faced respondent commanded.

Judging from his swift response, the man had a better grasp of the wines and language than the ladies and myself. After receiving their selection, the men huddled at the opposite end of the building. While they sipped the wine, the volume of their voices increased.

"We'll try another," one of the men demanded, stroking his inflamed cheek.

As the recent arrivals nursed their wine, the ladies and I tried another wine and continued to talk about our travels. The voyagers from down under alluded to being in their second week of sightseeing in Europe. Their tour stopped in the city of Montpellier, France, about 70 kilometers away, and they had decided to spend the day exploring on their own.

The detached conversations between the ladies and me, and the recent arrive-rs, continued for a good twenty minutes while cars continued to flow by. As I observed the boisterous guy at the other end of the counter happily enjoying his selection, I leaned closer to see the bottle.

"How do you like that one?" I asked the red-faced guy.

"It's nice," he nodded.

During our chat about their selection, another car stopped at the stand. Engulfed in a cloud of dust was a tiny car with a license plate from the U. K. Two men, appearing ten years older than the seemingly mid-fifty-year-olds at the counter, approached the building at an unhurried pace.

"Bonjour, madame," both said with British-sounding accents.

"Good afternoon, folks," one said softly while scanning the counter.

With his hat turned up on one side, I got the impression that he was an Australian. Both men appeared overdressed, wearing long-sleeved shirts with rolled-up sleeves. Flexing blue suspenders over a maternal bulge, the hat-less man responded to the proprietress's offer. After being served the wine, they stepped away from the counter to converse alone. Though our three groups at the counter began tasting in isolation, it wasn't long before the conversations merged.

"You must try this one," the sunburned guy proposed.

Sampling his suggestion, we smiled approvingly. "You're right. It's a good one!" we responded. Harold's knowledge of wines became apparent when he spouted jargon unknown to most of us, or so it seemed.

"The color, body, fruitiness, tannins, and structure of this wine make it a good one," he said about his recommendation. Continuing to lecture us about wine making from fermentation to bottling, I wondered if he was appraising the wine or trying to shower us with his knowledge of oenology.

Watching our discreet chatter blossom into open dialogue appeared to have an effect on the stone-faced proprietress. As our sociability ramped up, her nonchalant, expressionless demeanor softened to a grin. Unable to speak to us in English or understand much of what we were saying, she bridged the language gap by offering a bottle of wine.

"It's her best," proclaimed David, one of the last arrive-rs, after tasting it.

We all gave it a try, and the consensus was, "It's great." The effects of the samples made me hungry for something to munch on.

"Maybe the *maison* has some *fromage* and a baguette to snack on?" I asked the proprietress jokingly.

"Non monsieur," the server replied with a chuckle.

The boisterous wine aficionado, with his face appearing more ripened, bought a bottle of wine. Gleefully, he poured a sample of his purchase into each person's glass. Putting the half-emptied bottle on the counter, he cupped his glass in his hands and gave it a few swirls. Raising the glass to eye level, Harold examined the ruby color of the wine, plunged his nose in the glass, and took an abrupt sniff. With his routine in high gear, I sensed the moment of truth to come. Raising his eyes, Harold put his lips to the glass and took a sip. After rolling the wine around in his mouth, he spit it into a barrel at the end of the counter.

Following Harold's demonstration, David bought a bottle to share with the group. Before finishing David's selection, I ended the pattern of red wine tasting by choosing a white wine on a shelf behind the counter, knowing nothing about what I was buying. The nutty taste of the amber-colored wine brought on an even greater desire to snack. Before long, the generosity flowed to Debbie, who bought the next bottle. The buying frenzy continued until each person had bought a bottle.

As the time and tastings passed, our lips became looser. Each bottle uncorked greater camaraderie. By now, it was apparent that our dialects were distinctly different. Undoubtedly, the woman serving us knew we were English speakers from different places. While listening to our chatter about our names and countries of origin, the proprietress's eyes brightened.

I was the only American and the first of the seven to stop at the stand. Considering I was an African-American man roaming the south of France alone, my story drew curious glances from the others.

"I've been in France about three months, overseeing the recovery of a troubled aerospace program," I explained, feeding their inquiring eyes.

Following my explanation, Margaret and Debbie shared their stories. Apparently, they were employees of an Australian company. They were touring the region with a group and had strayed from fellow tourists.

"The wine is good and we like it, but we drink beer, when it's hot and cold," Margaret said.

Arriving after them was Tom, a Scotsman, and Harold, a flush-faced Irishman. During our introductions, Harold stated that they had been in France three days and had come to the town of Beziers, for a music festival.

"Somehow, we wandered off course," Tom mentioned, appearing frustrated about the diversion. Harold, who dominated much of the conversation, stated that he was a history professor at a university in Ireland and planned to retire in a year or two.

Tom, a bus driver from Glasgow, was muted by the more garrulous Harold. Despite his reticence during our tastings, Tom perked up when golf and whiskey entered the conversation. With my ears still calibrating to French-accented English, I found Tom's brogue burdensome to follow. I felt embarrassed, continually interrupting him by saying, "Would you mind repeating that, Tom?" Gradually, as the dialect penetrated my conception of English, I found his tales of sheep-friendly golf courses and geese-guarded scotch distilleries fascinating.

Lecturing us like Harold had, Tom explained how Scotch whisky-producing recipes had been guarded for centuries by the honking alarmists.

David, a pot-bellied Englishman, and Walter, a Canadian, were the last to join us. Dave, at times, was as voluble as Harold. He seemed to be knowledgeable of everything we discussed. While we drank, he bellowed his know-how about viticulture and continually injected opinions that were contrary to Harold's remarks about the wines we were tasting. The depth of his opinions of the wines and his jargon-laden critiques of Harold's thoughts were far beyond my wine know-how. Shortly after we began openly assessing the wines, David and Harold engaged in a verbal pissing contest about their impressions of a wine that neither of them liked. When Harold mentioned, "This wine tastes like dusty raspberry," David countered with, "No, mate, it tastes like raspberry shit!" The rest of us listened quietly to their banter after each uncorking.

As Harold and David sparred about their opinions of the wines we were drinking, truth be told, I had no idea what either of them was talking about. My judgments of the wines were far less complicated. "Were they smooth tasting or harsh going down?" I'd consider while drinking. Despite the vigorous cross-talk between David and Harold, I found their knowledge of wine educational. From *terroir* to tasting, there wasn't much either of them didn't know about wine making, it seemed. Seeing them differ in a heated exchange led me to conclude that neither of them would have conceded a lack of knowledge to the other.

Walter, David's traveling companion, presented little vocal competition. Seemingly content with every wine we tasted, he nodded often, leaving his judgments of the wines to David. Both men revealed that they had been retired for several years. Coming from Toronto, Canada, Walter mentioned that he had worked for an automobile manufacturer for thirty-five years before retiring. David said he was a dentist from Birmingham, England. Both Walter and David stated that their wives had gone shopping, leaving them to go off on their own.

Located south of Narbonne, near the Mediterranean Sea, the La Clape wine appellation is an esoteric land of mostly red wine vintners. The La Clape AC (*Appellation Controlee*) requires red wines be produced of at least two-thirds *Carignan* (a lesser planted grape outside of the region) and the remainder *Grenache, Cinsault, and Terret Noir* grapes. The combination of these grapes produce rather intense, dark-red wines. Produced to a far lesser extent than the red wines (that account for ninety percent of the local production) are dry and sweet white wines. These wines are produced primarily from the *Clairette* grape, a white grape grown in the Midi and Cotes du Rhone regions of France. The wines are soft and aromatic. During the spirited repartee between Harold and David, I learned that the richer, golden-colored white wine I had bought was produced from a grape known locally as the *Malvoisie*. "A wine with finesse," as David described it.

Although the wine tasting was curtailed as we shared our separate backgrounds, the awakening of our diversely spoken language provided an excuse to share another bottle.

"We have to try another bottle," blared Harold, toasting our language.

"Here, here," David confirmed.

The conversation continued to flow about the oddity of our coming together in this off-beat vineyard. Though there were many wines on the shelves awaiting our selection, the pace of the tasting began to fade with the sun. The yawning proprietress hovered over the counter with her arms folded. During our moments of connecting, the woman was incredibly patient. Barring the lack of anything to munch on, which I still craved, Susanne, who identified herself earlier, was hospitable. She appeared amused by our bonding and disclosures of where we had come from, but her eyes were telling us, "It's time to go." Reading Susanne's desire to close the vineyard stand, we bid her a goodbye and made our way to the cars as the sun was sinking.

Originating from oceans apart, it was incredible that the seven of us, speaking the same language with distinctly different dialects, had come together and connected in this vineyard. Before getting into our cars, we closed the gathering with a round of handshakes. Each clasp conveyed an expression of the camaraderie we established earlier. For me, the connections were an antidote to my tension-packed assignment, fraught with confrontations, personality conflicts, and us-versus-them mindsets.

Shrouded in darkness, we drove off to the motorway. Upon leaving, it was obvious that we would never see each other again.

As I reentered the A-61 motorway, the memories of my recent adventures remained alive. The carefree crowd at the beach, compared to the conservative folks I met in the vineyard, revealed a stark cultural contrast. Liberated by searing sun and the sea, the people at the beach embraced their culture. Connected by the wines of a secluded Languedoc Vineyard and a recognition of our lingual commonality, the assemblage at the vineyard had lapsed into ardent discussion and social harmony. Merging our different dialects of the same language had elevated our interest in the encounter.

The sky ahead was brightened by flashes of lightning. When reaching the spot where I had first seen the Mediterranean, the bolts became more vivid. From a distance, the flickering appeared artistic, but a few miles down the road, images of trees and stone structures were etched in the darkness. Accompanying the tangled abstractions were bursts of thunder crashing through the clouds. Suddenly, rain began pelting the roof of the car like a zealous drummer. Overworked by the deluge, the sluggish windshield wipers permitted a murky vision of the vehicles in front of me. But as swiftly as the storm arrived, it faded to distant flickers. Lowering a window, the scent of roasted earth filled the air. With stars appearing through parted clouds, I could see a glimmer of Toulouse on the horizon.

For a spontaneous get-away, I found the connections I had made with the people at the beach and those at the vineyard educational. In a few un-stressful hours, I had gained insight into a misunderstood French beach culture and greater appreciation of the extent of the English language. I was now geared up to return to my appointed task with a clearer mind. As I approached Toulouse, I wondered about the issues beyond the horizon and the adventures to come. It's said that "travel expands one's horizon." For me, the time I spent exploring the beach scene and mingling with the strangers in the vineyard were culturally invaluable. Long afterward, I considered our connection in the vineyard and why the event resonated so much with me.

Looking back on the day and lonely times preceding it, I thought about why we, in the vineyard, had bonded quickly, and the keys to our fusion.

First and foremost, studies have shown that chatting with casual acquaintances can contribute to one's well-being, particularly for one who is alone and has doubts about the trustworthiness of some in their daily environment. Simply stated, the wine had a definite influence on our bonding. It served as an ice breaker for developing conversation and relationships. The tastings provided the common ground for promoting mutual interest prior to acknowledging our diverse speaking of the same language. Casual discussion of the wines became the lubricant for opening up to each other. Before long, two people in the group began to compete for the attention of the others. Driven by human nature, personalities, and the speakers' quests for dominance, the ensuing banter became more entertaining than problematic.

Expanding our discussion beyond the wines we tasted served to extend the conversation to the lesser wine-savvy folks. Tom, the Scottish gent, for example, came out of his shell when golf and whisky were mentioned. Bringing Tom into the discussion gave me an opportunity to learn about things I hadn't experienced (for example, playing golf in Scotland and the unique means of protecting recipes for making Scotch whiskies). Tom morphed into another person when sharing his knowledge.

If nothing else, the day revealed that there could be a greater sense of belonging with strangers than with some of the folks we deal with every day. Asking pertinent questions that convey genuine interest in the person before us as opposed to veiled, peevish quips serves as a bonding agent. The acculturation we experienced during our conversation appeared to be shared by all at the vineyard. A sense of trust had been established, which I found refreshingly different than many workdays.

What struck me the most about the connection in the vineyard was the ennoblement I had felt while in the presence of this diverse group. Regardless of our differing accents, the sensation of the experience and memories of it continued well beyond the day. With Bastille Day coming up within a week, I looked forward to more unusual experiences and challenges after the Independence Day holiday.

5

A Moniker is Born

"Titles are but nicknames and every nickname is a title,"
says Thomas Paine's Rights of Man.

Invigorated from the enlightenment at the shore, I was back at work Monday, bounding between the podding facility and thrust reverser repair station. Although it was another workweek with hundreds of retrofits to incorporate, many on-site people chose to take the Bastille Holiday week off. Nonetheless, the reduced coverage, including at the airframer, allowed me additional time to assess our progress and focus on the thrust reversers subject to the *Nourrira*. "It will make Jacques happy and keep him off my back," I thought.

At noon the next day, I went to the Les Marroniers restaurant to see who would show up to join me for lunch. I saw Ian before leaving work, who mentioned he was going home for lunch.

"Ah, you're alone," said a cheerful Gilbert when I walked into the restaurant.

"So far, I'm alone. I don't know who else is coming," I replied.

"OK, sit here," said Gilbert, seating me at a table near the bar.

Soon, Carl showed up at the restaurant.

"Ian told me you were coming here," said Carl with a wily smirk.

"I wasn't sure who was coming, but I came expecting someone to show up. It's good you came," I replied.

"Did you hear Trip might be leaving?" Carl promptly asked with cocked head and subtle smile before erupting.

"We don't need you here," he blurted loudly.

"OK," I smiled, looking him in the eyes.

Carl's remark and confirmation of my intuition cast a larger shadow on our scant relationship and openly revealed where my presence and acceptance of it stood with him. Shortly thereafter, we finished lunch and quietly left the restaurant. His caustic, heart-felt statement made me more determined to succeed in this task.

Still energized from memories of the shore and in an adventurous mood, I drove to the center of Toulouse two nights later. Located near a busy intersection reminiscent of Hollywood and Vine, I thought the Pizzeria Vecchio would be a great place to join locals partaking in their favorite pastimes of good eating and people-watching. Arriving at the restaurant on the eve of Bastille Day, I looked forward to seeing my friends, Jean-Pierre and Nadia. After frequenting the establishment half a dozen times, I had gotten to know them better.

Spotting me among the crowd on the sidewalk in front of Vecchio's entrance, the head waiter Jean-Pierre approached me with an extended hand. Built like a stump, I thought he showed a likeness to the actor Danny DeVito. Gazing at me with cordial eyes while whirling his arms in a comedic fashion, Jean-Pierre confirmed my pronouncement of "Danny," his nickname. Visibly stunned by my assertion, Jean-Pierre peered curiously at me. Moments later, when the moniker sunk in, he gushed an exuberant, *"Oh, merci monsieur,"* followed by a vigorous two hand shake of my hand.

When seeing me, Nadia, an attractive waitress of Moroccan descent, presented a less animated *"Bonsoir."* Appearing about thirty in age, the sparkle in Nadia's soft brown eyes, silky sienna hair, and *café au lait* complexion highlighted her Mediterranean heritage. Forever smiling and radiating her accommodating nature, Nadia was a magnet for repeat customers, I noticed. After a second visit to the restaurant, I had been captured by her welcoming charm. As much as Nadia relished her job, the more I looked at her, the more it seemed she had missed her calling. "She's worthy of a higher position," I thought while watching her engage with customers. "Ambassador de Vecchio? Why not?" I imagined, observing her applying her captivating charm on patrons seated near the entrance.

By now, Jean-Pierre and Nadia had become my extended family. Despite coming from continents far apart and having varying origins, we were bound by common sensitivities and understandings of the stigmas about us in our current societies. By sharing personal experiences, we were able to establish a camaraderie that bridged our cultural differences. We showed genuine interest in each other while talking openly about social encounters, promoting harmony and trust between us. On my prior stop-ins, we discussed their perspective of attitudes toward people of their ethnicity and the historical plight of Blacks in America. During our chats, I felt at ease to unlock myself.

At a sidewalk table at arguably the best pizzeria in town, I gorged on a pizza laden with *jambon* and *champignons* (ham and mushrooms). While eating the abundant disk and washing it down with a local wine, I watched hundreds of people pass the restaurant. Exhibiting distinct strides and styles of affection, couples navigated tables on the sidewalk with finesse. Young and old alike, they strolled by gawking diners while holding hands, hugging waists, and with arms wrapped around shoulders. Some passersby appeared to be auditioning for roles beyond themselves. The more sedate couples clasped pinkies. Regardless of age or the size of the person, there was a cornucopia of hair colors and styles. Blue-black pageboys, Rapunzel-length hairdos in shades of reds, pinks, greens, and yellows, and clean-shaven domes were there for the viewing. For the customers participating in both national pastimes, the parade of strollers was a delight to watch.

After exchanging parting words with Jean- Pierre and Nadia as they served customers, I dashed off to another familiar place, a reasonable walk away down spindling side streets. The "Thirty-Nine-Forty-Five Club" was another beacon of hospitality. Deriving its name from the World War II years in Europe, the staff of the speakeasy-like bar-restaurant wore regalia of military officers of the Second World War. From my very first visit to the club, the jovial proprietors, Claude and Sarah, made me feel like family. Before long, their staff, particularly three brothers who worked at the front door and in the kitchen, adopted me.

Patrick, seemingly in his mid-thirties, was the club's chef and the youngest of the brothers. Slightly built with hair little more than peach fuzz, Patrick's smile and affable manner projected brotherly kinship when we talked.

"How are you, my brother?" he often greeted me.

Shortly after meeting him, Patrick told me he was born in West Africa. The ease of sharing his background and the comfort he showed while speaking to me indicated that he'd spent his prior years mingling with people of color. A child of French expatriates like Claude, Patrick mentioned, "I lived in the Republic of Cameroon, a former trust territory under French rule that gained its independence in the 1960s." When he was young, his family migrated to Toulouse, the center of European aviation, to seek work in the burgeoning aircraft industry.

Speaking fluent English while talking about his background, Patrick shared interesting stories about the contrasting worlds he grew up in. He was a jazz enthusiast like myself, and we quickly discovered the common interest that promoted our relationship. When discussing music, I learned he knew more about jazz artists and the civil rights movement in America than I expected. I found our chats about the roots of jazz music provided an exit ramp for Patrick's disclosures of the friction that existed between the nation in which he grew-up and country in which he now lived.

Beyond his good nature d, laid-back demeanor, Patrick was an extraordinary chef. The self-effacing type, Patrick off-handedly mentioned that his primary job was teaching culinary arts at a local school. Considered an accomplished chef by diners in the restaurant, Patrick could not only cook great French meals but could also create excellent Chinese, Moroccan, and African dishes. During my visits to the restaurant, Patrick would ask me to try and critique his specialty *du jour*. Regardless of how busy he was, Patrick would approach me with his creation of the evening. They were always flavorful yet exotic. I looked forward to eating any of his offerings.

After sampling Patrick's saffron-and-cumin laden meat and vegetable creation and speaking with the staff for an hour, I departed to my next destination. With the exotic taste clinging to my palate, I walked to a karaoke bar a few blocks away. Arriving at the dimly lit, hole-in-the-wall establishment with a sign flashing "Karaoke" over the doorway, I opened a creaky door and approached the smoke-filled bar area. Girard, the proprietor, Patrick, the disk jockey, and Megan, the barmaid, bade me a rousing good evening. Leaning on the bar with a thousand-watt smile, the neck-less Girard extended a meaty hand to shake and a book of songs for me to select from.

I chose a Frank Sinatra song, "My Way," and was surprised when Patrick called my name to come to the stage before I'd received the beer I had ordered. Being a neophyte to karaoke, the thought of singing before an unknown crowd without lubricating my throat was a test of fortitude. Nonetheless, as I stood on the scant stage in front of a shadowy audience, I began to sing. Similar to my prior visit to this inconspicuous haunt, my singing garnered thunderous cheers and a standing ovation. "Are they being polite or applauding my talent?" I pondered while absorbing their clamor. Bowing to the generosity of the audience, I left the stage glowing like an ember. Walking back to the bar area, I was struck by the thought that maybe the listeners sensed a connection between me and the song's lyrics. With my tell-tale American accent, they knew I wasn't one of them.

As I resumed the conversation I had started with Girard, a youthful woman interrupted us, speaking French, switching to Spanish, and adding a few words in English. My first thought was that she must be testing her language skills. After having been in the region for three months, I was accustomed to locals testing their French-English on me. Speaking English intermittently in Spanish, she introduced herself as "Isabelle."

"I come from Barcelona to Toulouse a year ago," said Isabelle, fondling a tawny braid dangling over her shoulder. "I am still getting established and recently found a new job," she continued.

After exchanging a few words with each other, Isabelle asked me to sing a song with her. I countered with a request: that she select the song. She chose the Marvin Gaye song "Ain't No Mountain High Enough," and we made our way to the stage and sang it like we had rehearsed it. While singing along with us, many in the audience stood up, showing their approval. I was astonished by the sonorous cheering, and Isabelle blushed with glee. We took our bows and departed the stage.

As we returned to our seats at the bar, the crowd prepared for the next singers. While listening to a sextet of women giggle their way through a song, Isabelle leaned closer to tell me she was leaving.

"I have to pick up my baby," she said, tossing the braid to her back.

"No problem, I understand. *Bonne nuit*," I replied, bidding a good night.

At the entrance, Isabelle paused. "Would you walk with me to the babysitters?" she asked with a childlike tone. Considering the sincerity of her request, I agreed.

The streets outside the bar were much darker than when I arrived. Lights in the buildings around the bar were dimmed by shutters. Headlights of a passing car revealed a parade of parked cars straddling the sidewalks. We talked as we strolled, our voices bouncing off the buildings lining the street.

Before long, we approached a cluster of buildings at a fork in the road where cars were prohibited from entering. After pounding a maze of sidewalks for nearly an hour, I was wondering, "Am I being led astray?" Around us were faded brick buildings with fancy grill work adorning the windowsills. Concealed from the street, most of the windows were covered by shutters in need of paint. Finally, we stopped at a three-story brick structure similar to others around it. Isabelle asked me to wait, saying, "I will be right back." Pacing back and forth, I surveyed the lifeless street. Other than a faint bark of a dog in the building Isabelle had entered, the only sound I could hear was my shoes smacking the sidewalk.

Minutes later, Isabelle returned with a man appearing to be in his sixties. Lean, listless, and seemingly perturbed, the man scanned me.

"Bonsoir monsieur," he greeted me, sucking his teeth.

Shaking my outstretched hand, the man flashed a drowsy smile. With ruffled white hair and deeply wrinkled pants, it appeared the man had been sleeping in his clothes. Standing in front of the building, Isabelle and the man resumed a feud it seemed they had started in the building. As I listened to them speak to each other in French beyond my vocabulary, I wondered what had provoked this bickering. "Where's the baby?" I thought. I picked up on three words the man was saying with disdain: *"chien, merde,* and *l'argent."* (Dog, poop, and the money.)

In an argument going nowhere, Isabelle snatched the leash the man was holding. Tugging vigorously on the other end of the red strap was a scruffy, brownish-gray dog with a patch of white on its chest. Resembling something akin to a terrier, the dog walked with a profound limp, with a rear leg not touching the sidewalk. Alas, it dawned on me that this was Isabelle's baby. With the dog sitting on her feet, Isabelle concluded the dispute abruptly with a lively about-face.

"Bonne nuit, monsieur," she said, throwing a hand skyward.

Uttering verbal flatulence while wagging a finger, the man stormed back into the building. Considering Isabelle's relationship with the man and her anticipation of the quarrel, my intended role was as a guardian. It was a set-up! I concluded. Stepping away from the building, Isabelle asked me to escort her and the dog to her home.

"It's not fair," she said in anger.

"OK, why not!" I agreed, scanning the abandoned street.

Strolling to Isabelle's place, I wondered about her argument with the man.

"What was that all about?" I asked.

"I borrowed money from him and hadn't paid him back," she replied.

"How much do you owe?" I inquired, confused about her needing the loan.

"Not much," she whimpered. "He watched my dog several times while I was working and wanted to be paid for that," she continued. Mystified about her financial dilemma, I became suspicious about her source of income. When I asked her a second time, she replied, *"Je ne comprends pas l'anglais,"* erasing her understanding of English.

With the dog limping along, we talked sparingly as we proceeded to Isabelle's place. As we crossed a wider boulevard, the dog struggled to get over the curb. Seeing the dog's hobbling effort to keep up, I was tempted to pick him up. Sharing my sympathy, Isabelle picked up the dog and cradled him in her arms. Two blocks later, on a deserted side street, she stopped unexpectedly.

"We're here," she said, putting the dog on the sidewalk.

Several streets from the dog sitter's home, I found that the wilted rose-colored building in which Isabelle said she lived was similar to many dwellings in the city. I was saddened by her frail façade and the scraggly dog by her side. Tossing a braid over her shoulder while entering the building, Isabelle uttered a meek *"Merci monsieur."*

Isabelle walked the dog through the drab lobby and ascended a narrow staircase. Following them to the first step, I waited for a moment to hear a door open and close. Satisfied they had gone into her apartment, I left the building in search of my car.

Relying on directional instincts to find my car, I wandered the gloomy streets I vaguely remembered from earlier. After walking for half an hour trying to remember where I had parked the car, the appearance of the Canal du Midi jogged my memory. Guided by the gentle flow of the canal, I crossed a street I recognized. Seeing the central train station of Toulouse a few blocks beyond the canal made me confident that I was heading in the right direction. Crossing the broad boulevard where Vecchio's Pizzeria was located made me feel even better. Finding the car parked with the right-side wheels on the sidewalk, I slid into the driver's seat and drove to my out-of-town apartment.

The sun, streaming through the bedroom window the next day, opened my eyes to the Bastille Day holiday. I arose at noon to voices of golfers below my window. A Thursday holiday, Bastille Day began quietly, like a usual Sunday. With nothing planned, I returned to the center of Toulouse.

Contrary to the prior evening, the streets of the city were festive. On side streets, streams of people weaved their way around the cars parked on the sidewalks. In a city where parking is a premium, navigating cars parked on sidewalks was normal.

Driving past the karaoke bar, I zigzagged my way through streets I vaguely remembered from the night before. When the streets narrowed to alleys, with buildings appearing less rosy, I parked and continued on foot. Walking a short while, I spotted Isabelle and the dog at a busy intersection. Wearing pink and yellow pants, Isabelle could have been seen from anywhere in the city. Strolling idly with a gimpy dog of dubious roots made her stand out among the people on the sidewalk. Isabelle spotted me approaching from across the street and waited for me to cross.

"*Bonjour, monsieur.* How are you?" she greeted me with wide eyes.

"A little tired," I yawned.

"Would you like to come to the fireworks with me and Andi?" she asked.

I was excited about an opportunity to experience a French Independence Day celebration and accepted the offer. It was late afternoon, brutally hot, and the sun had fallen to the tops of the buildings. We rambled through backstreets as we had the night before, Andi hobbling with us. Walking with two steps and a hop, the dog struggled to keep up. Before long, I became sympathetic to the dog's struggle and found myself growing fonder of him.

While roaming the side streets of Toulouse, we spoke English and French (my American version) with Isabelle's injections of Spanish. Caught up in our conversation, we unexpectedly made our way back to the karaoke bar. Seated at a table on the sidewalk was Girard, smoking a cigarette. With a sociable grin, Girard invited us to sit down and join him, offering us a plate of sliced *saucissons* (dried sausage), olives, and a baguette. We gladly accepted Girard's offer.

"Where do you come from?" Girard asked, raising an eyebrow.

"Just walking. We go to fireworks," Isabelle replied.

Regardless of being a backstreet establishment, the karaoke bar provided great people-watching. It was a *flaneur's* (lounger's) delight. Why else would Girard be sitting outside on such a warm evening? Chatting quietly amongst each other while eating Girard's snack, we gazed at a procession of passersby. Everyone was fair game for our prying eyes. One by one, we pointed out a person we were eyeing and shared our thoughts and impressions of their oddities—their hair colors, hairstyles, the clothes they were wearing.

Seeing more people coming onto the street, we ended our visit with Girard. Andi, who had been lying quietly under the table, sprang to his feet and took a mega stretch. Walking toward the center of the city, we entered a throng of people heading towards the Garonne River, where the fireworks were to be launched. We were quickly swallowed by the crowd. Worried about Andi getting trampled, Isabelle picked him up and carried him. At the river, where viewers had gathered, we looked forever for a place to sit.

Not long after the sun vanished below the buildings on the other side of the river, the sky was ablaze. Fountains of red, yellow, and orange fireworks rose from the riverbank. Contrasting the colorful spectacle were white fusillades, appearing to be geysers rising from the river. Launched higher in the sky, red, green, and yellow rockets spewed glittering tentacles. For a moment, night returned to day. With a backdrop of centuries-old buildings and the landmark bridge, Pont Neuf, before them, the erupting fireworks above the river were stunning. Even higher in the sky, fireworks blossomed into astrological figures. One after another, images of a winged horse, presumably Pegasus, the Gemini twins, Castor and Pollux, Taurus, the bull, and the figure of Orion (a hunter with belt and sword) filled the night sky. It was a celestial exhibition unlike any I had ever seen, and the displays of mythical characters continued for several minutes. Each launch drew louder "oohs" and "ahs" from the viewers.

I glanced at Isabelle. Images of the astrological characters splashed across her eyes. Peering skyward with an open mouth, she appeared childlike. We couldn't have asked for a better place to enjoy the spectacle. After about an hour, the luminous launches became more frequent and amplified, building to a finale of mid-day brightness.

When the blast ceased, the crowd made their way back to the city streets. Wading through a sea of people, we walked several blocks to where I had parked the car. Coaxed by Isabelle, a wide-eyed Andi stepped into the car, surveying everything. Isabelle was intent on showing me her workplace and introducing me to a friend, and I agreed to take her there. Driving to the place, I remained curious about Isabelle's source of income. Unlike the heavily congregated streets where the fireworks were held, Isabelle directed me to a tree-lined boulevard in a quieter section of the city. Stone structures, rather than brick, were more prevalent in this part of town. At Isabelle's behest, I parked the car on a narrow street near a grand roundabout.

At the entrance of Isabelle's employer, a genial warmth radiated from the sidewalk. Still bedazzled by the fireworks over the river, I peered at a brass plate on the door inscribed with an incomprehensible phrase. As she tapped on the stately wooden door, Isabelle raised a rhythmic *"Bonsoir"* from within. Immediately, the door opened, revealing a wisp of a man with a cigarette dangling from his lower lip. *"Bonsoir Isabelle et monsieur. Bienvenu,"* he welcomed us, extending a sinewy hand. Exposing tarnished teeth behind an amiable smile, he waved us in.

Following a shake of his chilled hand, the man escorted Isabelle and me to stairs leading to a cavernous room below. In the dimly lit room, a fusion of earth and stale cigarette smoke filled the air. On the opposite side of the room was a bar and a section of polished planks for dancing, I presumed. We were surrounded by red velvet curtains and empty bistro tables, and I looked around for others in the place. Besides Isabelle, Andi, and the man I had just met, there was no one in the club. "Where is everyone?" I thought while looking around. Instantly, Isabelle excused herself, disappearing with Andi behind a curtain near the bar. Puzzled by the sudden exit, I waited, wondering where she had gone and who else was here.

Shortly thereafter, Isabelle returned with a brawny guy dressed in jeans and a black dinner jacket. "Must be the bouncer," I imagined, gazing at his frame. Approaching me with a hearty *"Bonsoir monsieur"* and extended hand , he presented himself.

"I am Philippe, manager of the club," he said, speaking good English.

I stated my name. Philippe knew I wasn't remotely French, but the perplexity on his face appeared to rule me out as being English.

"Where do you come from?" blared Philippe with a curious glance.

"From America," I replied.

"Bien sur," (surely) Philippe quipped with a no-shit eye roll.

Sensing Philippe's hunger for more details, I mentioned the state I had come from. Taking a deep breath, Philippe lit a cigarette and took a long drag on it. With eyes frozen on me, he appeared statuesque in the smoke-filled light. As he snuffed the cigarette vigorously in an ashtray, his austere gaze softened to a grin. "What's up?" I thought, bewildered by his new demeanor. Immediately, Philippe stepped closer to share what he had been thinking.

"So, you are *Le Yankee Noir,*" he said, broadcasting his proclamation to the city. Alas, I realized, in his trance, Philippe was connecting my complexion and the state of Connecticut.

"The Yankee Noir. Guess you're right," I chuckled.

Letting the assertion sink in for a moment, I grabbed Philippe's hand and shook it again. While we stood toe-to-toe measuring each other up, Isabelle, holding Andi, came closer. Forming a trio of arms around waists, we recited *"Le Yankee Noir"* several times. When the amusement subsided, Philippe continued his inquiry.

"So why are you in France?" he asked, peering at me with deep interest.

Upon listening to my explanation of what had brought me to the region and the challenges I saw before me at work, Philippe grinned.

"Bonne chance monsieur," (good luck) he said with a shrug.

"Merci beaucoup," I responded.

After continuing our discussion of my adventures in France for another half hour, I departed the subterranean club, leaving Isabelle and Philippe.

The next day, a Friday, I was back at work bouncing between the podding facility and the thrust reverser repair station. A multitude of retrofits were still awaiting incorporation into engines and nacelle components. However, being the end of the festive holiday week, many people chose to extend their holiday into the weekend.

On my next visit to the Club Rouge roughly two weeks later, I looked forward to seeing Philippe and hearing his deep-throated *"Bonsoir, Yankee Noir."* Soon, others in the club seized onto the moniker, and the proclamation stuck. I enjoyed the acceptance and goodwill that Philippe projected when saying *"Le Yankee Noir."* The sensation was penetrating.

As time went on, Philippe and Isabelle continued to be acquaintances, but we never became closer than that. Our body clocks were in different places, and there were times when I was skeptical of bridging our societal differences. They were people of a later-night society, unlike me. My charter and associated activities consumed daytime hours, a period when they were likely sleeping. Nonetheless, when we were together, we were respectful of each other and accepted the other for what they were. By conveying civil decency toward one another, we were able to bridge our societal divide.

Upon awakening the next day, I reflected that the finale of the French Independence Day celebration had come from Philippe. I couldn't have imagined a greater ending to a holiday. Philippe's declaration of *Le Yankee Noir* and the acceptance I had felt from those words touched me at an intense time and likely will cling to me forever. The relationships I established and fortified during this two-day period, and the feeling of acceptance I enjoyed from them, propelled me into the next weeks of the assignment and through years of involvement in the region.

In the days after the holiday, an A330 aircraft powered by our propulsion systems had yet to be delivered into revenue service. Regardless of the mishaps, naysayers, and obstacles in the path of the deliveries, it was comforting to feel the acceptance of locals in the region.

6

The First Aircraft Deliveries

"The way to secure success is to be more anxious about obtaining than deserving it."
William Hazlet's, "Qualifications to succeed in life," 1826.

Adapting to the local culture was exciting during non-working hours, but at the forefront of my thoughts was getting our first propulsion systems powering an A330 aircraft delivered into service before the end of the year. From September through November 1994, deliveries of engines and nacelle components to Toulouse were more scrutinized than in prior months. Hunting down nacelle components produced by suppliers in Europe and in the States devolved into a battle with time.

Returning engines and nacelle components to their original producers to install required upgrades had been ongoing since the beginning of my assignment. As a result, committing delivery dates to Dieter and Russell continued to be difficult. Regardless of my explanations of the problems causing the delays, I was shown no mercy.

"But you will do it, yah," Dieter would bellow when ending a delivery discussion. I heard these dictum so often that I anticipated hearing those words before they were spoken.

Little had changed since my initial arrival in Toulouse. I continued to vault between Cary's office, the podding facility, and the nacelle repair station to ensure their delivery commitments were meeting my commitments to Airbus. It was easier said than done. Getting off-site enablers and local suppliers to comply with the air-framer's expectations of continual on-time delivery performance was an uphill battle. Working in an environment where some in-house supporters and on-site personnel appeared more focused on cynicism than the task at hand made work life more challenging. Tension mounted as I encountered these people daily. Seeking engine and nacelle components to accommodate the needs of the air-framer, sending recalled units back to suppliers for major retrofits, fixing components on-site, and obtaining replacement units from off-site locations became a logistic nightmare. A charting freak by nature, Dylan was in ecstasy when tracking units coming in and those being returned to their producers. Luckily for our Toulouse team, he relished this arduous score keeping.

I came to realize that expecting unity among all of the designated contributors was a delusion. Missing from many of the enablers far away from Toulouse was a sense of urgency to get an aircraft in service before the new year. Being closer to the heat of Jacques's breath sharpened my focus on maintaining our delivery commitments and increasing confidence in our ability to do what we had committed to do.

The affection shown by locals like Jean-Pierre and Nadia, the staff at the hotel, and others in the region fueled my interest in adapting to the culture. Moreover, their acceptance propelled me through demanding workweeks. At this time, all on-site eyes were focused on the delivery of the first aircraft. As a result, the removal of obstacles impeding deliveries became a priority.

While long-time residents like Dylan and Roland were sensitized to the needs of Airbus, there were contemptuous souls who weren't as committed to supporting me, in my opinion. Generally, the groups at the flight line and nacelle repair station exhibited a tribal allegiance. Their extreme devotion to the group's mode of operation and thinking appeared to result from them being situated at the end of the delivery stream. Although these groups had a stake in the delivery of propulsion systems and the parts thereof, disputes arose daily, often associated with an urgent need versus the ability to accommodate it. Typically, a dispute would go something like this. The following is an example of a call from someone in the flight-line office to someone at the repair station or podding facility:

"Hi Jon, we need a thrust reverser today to replace a unit damaged on an aircraft," someone in the flight-line office might ask.

"We don't have anything available now and won't for a few days," Jon or Peter may respond.

Reacting to the response from the overseers of the repair station, Trip, or someone else would launch a rebuke.

"You clowns can't get your act together."

Such responses made my job and the jobs of others at the podding facility and repair station more difficult.

It wasn't long before I would look forward to the leisurely atmosphere at the Les Marroniers Restaurant and the lighter conversations during lunch. Barring a rare exception, I found the time at the restaurant served to assuage the tension-filled workdays. After eating at the restaurant for several months, Gilbert and I developed a liking for each other—so much so that he began referring to me as the "chef," or boss, and the "chocolate man" when serving me coffee. To me, Gilbert and Janine were "Pop and Mommy," as I'd call them. My understanding of the "chocolate man" comments came from Gilbert's astute observation of my affinity for the seventy-two percent dark chocolate squares he provided with his strong coffee.

During one lunch, a person at our table looked at me curiously when Gilbert, saying, "chocolate man," placed chocolate squares in front of me. I looked at the person and shrugged it off. What mattered most to me in this situation was the relationship I felt with Gilbert and my perception of his intentions when making the comment. It wasn't the last time I heard the remark from Gilbert or observed his backhanded placement of the chocolate before me. There were much bigger things to be concerned about, like getting the first aircraft delivered before the end of 1994, rather than worrying about a lunch-mate's construed perception of an unintended slur. I considered that the person viewing "chocolate man" as a racial slur was telling me more about them than about Gilbert. Was he instigating or revealing his view of me?

For months, the air-framer, French Air Regulatory Authorities (D.G.A.C.), and the European Joint Aviation Authorities (J.A.A.) were absorbed in the investigation of the autopilot system of the A330 aircraft. After several months of inquiry into the system, it was confirmed that the autopilot system was operating properly on the day of the crash incident. Rather than dwell on needless changes to the autopilot system, the focus of the investigation turned to the cockpit operating procedures that were being carefully scrutinized by the investigators. **

As the procedural studies continued into autumn, concerns mounted about when an aircraft powered by our propulsion systems was going to be delivered into service. At this time, delivery of the first aircraft was a moving target. Some people on-site and in house silently wondered whether it was ever going to happen.

While concerns about the deliveries remained, the holiday-heavy month of November rolled in at a time when every minute was precious. All Saints Day was on the first day of November, and a week and a half later was Armistice Day, marking the end of World War I. A week after that, on the third Thursday of November, was the Nouveau, celebrating the first tastings of wine produced in that year. An event occurring on a workday rather than a declared national holiday, the Nouveau still creates an air of anticipation among the locals. Toward the end of the month (the fourth Thursday) was Thanksgiving in the States. Other than the month of May, with national holidays on May 1 (Labor Day) May 8 (World War II, V Day) May 12 (Ascension, a post-Easter holiday) and May 23 (Whit Monday, the day after Pentecost Sunday), there wasn't a more labor-friendly month on the French calendar.

Commemoration of the Nouveau provided an opportunity for on-site people of our company to come together and dine as one. Occupants of Cary's office, folks from Trip's flight-line office, and Scotty and Ian from the podding facility converged at the Les Marroniers restaurant. A totally new experience for me, the evening of the Nouveau offered a wonderfully welcomed break from the fervent pace at work.

For the Nouveau, Gilbert was the entertainer for the evening. Any day in the restaurant, Gilbert could be seen shuffling about the place, wearing gleaming white clogs and greeting patrons at each table. With a toothy smile and laugh, Gilbert spoke to patrons like they were best friends. It took a few visits for me to accept that Gilbert, who seemingly had a greater penchant for comedy, could be a serious chef.

Janine, an ample woman who appeared to be in her late forties, was the authoritarian of the place. She was often seen puffing a cigarette planted in the corner of her mouth that would rise and fall as she spoke. As I listened to Janine bark commands to Gilbert and others on the staff, it didn't take long to understand why the guys called the restaurant "The Generals." When Janine tended the cash register, there was no doubt who was in charge.

In the center of the dining room, our party of ten or so was engulfed by other tables. I found it interesting that in an open dining room, where every seat was occupied, the conversations were muted beyond the confines of each table. It was a conversational etiquette similar to what I had seen in other restaurants in the region. Other than the clinks of knives and forks striking plates, the mood at each table was low-key.

With the majority of the people at our table originating from English-speaking countries, it's a wonder that the patrons at adjacent tables weren't distracted by our chatter. Most of us had come directly from our offices to the restaurant and wore neckties and sports jackets. By contrast, the people at neighboring tables were far more casually dressed in jeans, casual shirts, and sweaters. After showing a Nouveau menu scribbled on a blackboard, Gilbert took our orders. He returned minutes later with our selected starter, and our chatter was reduced to whispers.

Gilbert unveiled a salad of colorful veggies covered with an array of animal organs, served family-style on a pewter platter. A signature salad of the restaurant, the medley of greens, tomatoes, and artery-clogging delights—*foie gras* (goose liver), *gesiers* (gizzards), and duck hearts scattered over the greens—was a platter of artistry. Though the *salade gourmande* was pleasing to the eye, I wondered about its journey through my body as I waited for the tongs. Hoping what I heard about the French paradox was true, I was counting on the Nouveau wine to cover me this evening. "It's an insurance policy for a *bon vivant*," I thought. Judging the joyful faces at the other tables, they were not worried about the cardio effect of their meals.

When the main course was brought to the table, Gilbert's cooking skills were on full display. The *gambas* (large shrimp) bathed in a creamy whiskey sauce and *coquille St. Jacques* (scallops) sautéed in an herbal garlic-butter sauce were magnificent. His cooking skills were confirmed. Prior to bringing our orders to the table, bottles of the Nouveau, some labeled *primeur* (first) from the Gaillac region were uncorked. They were lighter-bodied and fruitier than any red wines I had tasted, their youth was even apparent to a newbie like me.

While we ate, Dylan lectured us about the Nouveau phenomenon.

"The first release of Beaujolais wine is celebrated every third Thursday of November," he reported to eye rolls at the table. "The wine is between seven and nine weeks old," Dylan rambled, rolling his eyes after a sip. Described by some as a marketing monstrosity, the Nouveau is revered in places like Japan and China.

"Locally, the French have a love-hate feeling about the wine," Dylan continued. "Most people love to celebrate the event and any happening, but many are not particularly keen about the wine."

After burning the midnight oil at The Generals, we returned to work the next day to resume our quest to deliver the first propulsion systems powering an A330 aircraft. Since the deliveries to Thai Airways and Malaysia Airlines (MAS) had been postponed to resolve issues with the aircraft and their propulsion systems, the pressure to close open items became more intense through late fall.

Although I had been back to the States four times, I'd been on the assignment for almost eight months, and I missed my family—particularly my daughters, who were both in college. The younger daughter was living at home with her mother, going to a school within driving distance. Within a week of the Nouveau, I was back in Connecticut for the Thanksgiving holiday. As my family gathered at my home for dinner, the phone rang. Gobbling like a comedic turkey, Dylan called from Trip's office seeking urgently needed parts for an aircraft. Laughing, Dylan made a plea for some replacement engine parts.

"We need a fan inlet case and some fan blades right away to replace parts on an engine that were damaged by a bird strike," he said. The bird strike, which happened during a test flight of an aircraft in the delivery stream, wasn't an unusual event, but other than calling on Christmas, Dylan couldn't have picked a worse day to seek anything. I called our Middletown assembly building to find there was no one there.

Dylan's voice on the phone was drowned out by someone in the background blaring, "Happy Thanksgiving" repetitively with a derisive tone. The sneering sentiment of Carl notwithstanding, to me, the importance of the call was not who was spewing mockery but to convey the urgency of getting the replacement parts delivered to the first aircraft. The next day, Black Friday in the States, I went to our engine assembly plant, thirty-five miles from my home, to find a parts handler to fill Dylan's request. Though it was a seemingly impossible task with limited resources, eventually, I was able to find someone to gather the necessary parts. Two days later, I returned to Toulouse, finding that I'd arrived a day before the replacement parts. Soon the calendar turned to December, making people in our company and at the air-framer more nervous about the first aircraft delivery.

"Will it happen before or after Christmas?" some questioned.

During the four months prior, I had heard remarks from both sides of the Atlantic that "I was being unreasonable" when requesting engine parts and replacement thrust reversers. Felix, the nacelle procurement manager, told me that "Your demands for thrust reversers are unrealistic."

"If my requests seem outlandish, they were stated to get propulsion systems delivered to A330 aircraft sooner rather than later," I told him. Perhaps my greatest motivators were Dieter and Russell, who called daily with merciless demands for backup engines and nacelle components to cover aircraft in progress. They weren't sympathetic to excuses about delayed units. They couldn't be dissuaded from using their greatest weapon, Jacques, when things weren't going well and they weren't getting what they wanted. From a front-line perspective, it seemed Jacques was the ultimate lever for getting anything that the air-framer wanted.

We were delivering aircraft to Thai Airways and Malaysia Airlines, and proceeding was a go one day and no go the next. Then, on December 9, 1994, after weeks of this operating dilemma, the first A330 aircraft (MSN060) powered by our propulsion systems was delivered into revenue service to Thai Airways. Among the folks who had contributed to its delivery, there was an enormous sigh of relief. A month earlier I thought that a delivery may never happen, so I was elated to see the first Thai aircraft gone. Less than a week later, Thai received a second aircraft. Considering the countless issues requiring resolution before the planes were accepted, the aircraft were delivered unceremoniously. The pomp and pageantry of the delivery of the first aircraft was so muted, I asked Cary if it had been delivered at all. If Cary had not confirmed the departures, I would have deduced that they had departed by not seeing them on the flight line or hearing an authoritative complaint from Dieter.

Though aircraft were being prepared for delivery to Malaysia Airlines, the next airline scheduled to receive our propulsion systems was L.T.U. International, a German airline operating scheduled and charter services on medium- and long-haul routes. After the second aircraft was delivered to Thai Airways, a swap-out of the thrust reversers installed on the L.T.U. airplane was planned before delivery. Considering the destination of the delivery and the work required for airline acceptance, it was decided that the work would be performed in Germany, at the Airbus facility near Hamburg. Shortly after the decision was made, the plane was flown to Germany. Considering the acute focus on the success of the swap-out, I was strongly urged by Dieter, Russell, and the management of our company to "Get my butt to Hamburg."

I couldn't get to Germany fast enough. Planning a strategy to perform the work, the thrust reverser repair station assigned three mechanics to the task—the musketeers, as I thought of them. Performing repairs and upgrades daily at the thrust reverser repair station in Toulouse, the musketeers were the most experienced repairmen available to get the swap-out done. The greater challenge for them would be conducting the exchange of units on-wing rather than working on an individual unit in their accustomed shop environment. That added risk to the task.

Arriving at Finkenwerder airfield near the air-framer's plant in Germany, I checked into a hotel in the nearby village of Buxtehude. Accompanied by Jonathan, an engineer representing the thrust reverser manufacturer, the mechanics had already checked into the hotel and were awaiting our arrival.

"When do we start?" they asked when seeing us walk into the hotel lobby.

"Tomorrow morning," I replied, confident of the outcome.

That evening, Jon and I strolled the meandering streets of the village of Buxtehude. Having vast knowledge about the thrust reverser's design, Jon spoke confidently about the task facing us as we walked about town. Engrossed in a discussion about the details of the work, we found ourselves in the midst of a Christmas market—a reminder that Christmas was less than two weeks away. In the chilled night air of northern Germany, countless villagers walked among the lighted booths. Brassy music filled the air, adding a festive mood to the evening.

As we scanned the arts and crafts exhibits while perusing the canvas booths, I noticed a strong scent of cinnamon-spiced wine. Upon closer inspection, I noticed many of the people among us carrying mugs filled with a warm beverage. Before long, we came upon a booth selling *Glühwein,* a German word that literally translates to "glow wine." In the booth, stirring a vat of the concoction, was a stout, rosy-cheeked man. Upon asking him what he was stirring, he paused.

"Uh, I mix red wine, some brandy, cinnamon stick, and citrus fruit," he joyfully told us with a husky Germanic accent.

Smiling profusely as he ladled the brew, the merchant handed a cup of the warm cheer to Jon and me. After one sip, I discovered the belly-heating effect of the cherry-cinnamon-citrus blend. Despite the enticing scent of sausages grilling in the next booth and the *glühwein* mixture engulfing the market, I longed for a breath of distilled air. Soon, we departed to the hotel while we could still walk to it.

Upon arriving the next morning at the entrance to the air-framer's facility, I found a man waiting for me. A clean-cut guy in his late twenties, I surmised, the man greeted me with a vigorous handshake. I had no idea what position he held, but the fancy car he arrived in had me intrigued about his status. He prefaced our handshake with a "You must be?" statement, leading me to believe there was a connection between him and the air-framer's people in Toulouse. Assisting with my guard post clearance, the man, named Horace, escorted me to the building where the swap-out was to be performed.

Before reaching the hanger where the work was to be done, I could see the L.T.U. aircraft had arrived. Judging by the size of the building and the height of its entry doors, it appeared the structure had been built for aircraft smaller than the A330. By contrast, a smaller, 150-passenger A320 aircraft was parked outside of the hangar. Having a higher tail section, the L.T.U. A330 was partially towed inside the building, leaving the orange-painted tail section outside of the doorway.

Inside of the hangar, Jon and the musketeers were busily unpacking the installation tooling. Fixtures had been sent with the aircraft to disconnect, remove, and install the replacement thrust reversers on the pylon of each wing. As they prepared the first unit for removal from the wing, a thick-set man drove into the area on a mobile crane. Displaying an expansive grin while maneuvering the vehicle closer to a wing, the driver lifted a thrust reverser half that the mechanics had disconnected from the pylon. Swinging the boom of the crane away from the wing, he lowered the component to the floor. Although the driver performed the task with casual ease, I found his handling of the unit near the wing and fuselage of this multi-million-dollar aircraft nerve-racking to watch. Most likely, the confidence exhibited by the driver had come from years of installing and removing engines and nacelle components on smaller aircraft, but the intensity of observing the disengaged unit swinging near the wing roused Jon and me. Both halves of the first thrust reverser were taken off the pylon and placed on pallets without a problem, thank God. After removing the second set of reverser halves from the other wing, the operator got off the crane and removed his cap, revealing a glistening brow. Smiling from ear to ear, he walked over to us and shook everyone's hand.

Later in the day, when upgraded units were towed into the hanger, the crane operator got back on the vehicle, lifted the first half-unit above the wing, and stopped. With the unit hanging from the boom, he climbed down from the vehicle and walked away. Puzzled by his sudden halt, I pursued the operator to understand his reason for stopping.

"Why are you leaving?" I asked in bewilderment.

Appearing stunned by my query, he pointed to his watch. The workday had ended, his gesture was telling me. Seeing him turn and continue to walk away, I stopped him and asked, "Would you please get on the crane and lower the unit to the floor?" Seemingly perplexed by my request, he peered at me with a blank stare and pointed to his watch. Gazing through the doorway, I pointed at the unit dangling near the wing. After an interchange of me pointing at the hanging unit and the crane man pointing at his watch, he got on the crane, started it up, swung the unit away from the wing, and lowered it to the floor. Dismounting the crane, the operator walked away, seemingly fuming and mumbling to himself.

With no one in the facility to operate the crane, we departed for the day. While leaving the building, it dawned on me that it was my birthday. Overhearing me talking to myself, Jon and the mechanics piped in with a suggestion for the evening.

"We must celebrate in Hamburg," they said jokingly.

Riding in separate cars, Jon and I followed the mechanics into the city. Located in northern Germany along the Elbe River, the city of Hamburg is an affluent metropolis. Second to Berlin in size and population, Hamburg is the home of one of the largest harbors in Europe. Being the principal port of Germany, Hamburg may be the most cosmopolitan city in the country. As the shipping and trading capital of Germany, Hamburg became a melting pot of many cultures.

Leading the way, the mechanics guided Jon and me from the hotel, through the port tunnel, and into the city. It appeared the mechanics had done this before. They navigated the streets like Hamburgers. Centered on two long boulevards, central Hamburg was throbbing with life. Despite heavy destruction during World War II, the stately buildings of the city were beautiful. On this chilly weekday evening, there were loads of people out and about the city.

Unknown to Jon and me, the mechanics had decided where we were going for dinner. They chose a restaurant in the St. Pauli district, near the Reeperbahn Boulevard. Jon and I deferred to their choice. Home of countless entertainment venues, ranging from pubs to bars featuring adult entertainment to musical theaters, the area was reminiscent of New York's 42nd Street. The eatery, located at the confluence of five lively streets, was bustling—bright, festive and teeming with people. Before long, the tributaries of the Reeperbahn were choked with festive strollers.

As we ate, the mechanics commented about the wines we were drinking .

"You call this wine?" said one mechanic with a sneering French accent. Soon, another mechanic jumped in with a similar critique of the wine. I found it interesting that there were no comments about our unanimous selection for dinner. Despite a boastful remark from one mechanic about the magnificence of French cuisine, everyone appeared to like the medley of grilled fish we had ordered.

Though it was a Tuesday in mid-December, the Hamburg streets were awash with people. Undoubtedly, it was the holiday effect. While dining, we were entertained by strollers passing our window. Some people stopped to gaze at us eating, while others displayed playful grins and ogling glances. A reverse people-watching, I supposed. The musketeers seemed to get a kick out of the onlookers, mocking gawkers as we ate. Their mimicking continued through dinner and after we finished our meal.

Before leaving the restaurant, I received a birthday toast from the guys, who crooned *"Appy Birthday"* before shaking my hand. Their enthusiasm garnered the attention of other customers. Though my birthday had been far from my mind when leaving the airplane hangar, it felt great to share it and the beginning of the forty-ninth year of my life with these people.

"To our success," I responded, tipping a wine glass to them and on-lookers seated at tables near ours.

Leaving the restaurant, we were swept into the hordes of people on the sidewalk. Meandering among them for a good twenty minutes, we settled on a small pub broadcasting pop music to the parade of passersby. Inside the establishment, the black walls were adorned with posters advertising local concerts and sporting events. As I looked around the pub, it didn't take long for me to realize that the five of us were the only ones there.

As a rotund man wearing red shorts and a tie-dyed tee shirt took our orders for beer, a woman walked onto the stage. Dressed in a black evening dress and displaying a cheerful smile, she began to dance. Soon, another robust woman joined her on the stage. While they moved about performing leg splits and rhythmic contortions, I departed through a curtain of beads concealing the bathrooms.

Returning to our table, I was surprised to see a mechanic dancing on the stage with the ladies. The amplified music and screaming from the trio on stage drew people into the place. The mechanic connected so quickly with the ladies' dance routine that some may have assumed he was a part of the act. During the trio's performance, the other two mechanics shouted words of encouragement. Hoping the mechanics would take our cue, Jon and I departed to the hotel.

The next morning, I was shocked to hear Jon say that he had received a phone call during the night about the mechanics. It appeared that sometime after leaving the pub, the mechanics were stopped by the police for exceeding the speed limit. It seemed strange that someone could be pulled over for speeding in a country known for its high-speed autobahns. After receiving the call, Jon found his way to the police station to attest to the mechanics' mission in the region. They were immediately released. After listening to Jon's drowsy adventures of the mechanics, I drove to the Airbus for the second day of the swap-out.

Walking into the hanger where the L.T.U. aircraft was parked, I was greeted by the plant manager. Seeing a grave expression on his face, I sensed something was wrong. Standing next to the plant manager was a man peering at me with a serious gaze. With lips turned downward, the man declared, "I am the labor inspector. You violated a German labor regulation."

Noting my perplexity, the inspector gave me a deep-throated summation of my oblivious *faux pas*.

"Yesterday, you ask the crane operator to work later than his normal hours," said inspector with a stern tone.

"Seeing the crane operator get off the vehicle with the thrust reverser dangling from the boom made me nervous. I was worried about damage to the unit, the aircraft, and the safety of someone near the aircraft," I replied.

Hearing the crane operator's concern from the inspector about working beyond normal working hours, I continued to plead my case to him.

"Had the hydraulic system of the crane failed, the thrust reverser and plane could have been damaged. A person could have been hurt," I told him, pointing to the crane.

Looking upward, the inspector considered my justification. After weighing my testimony for a few minutes, he closed his manual hastily and took a long sniff.

"So, I've decided to dismiss the grievance," he said with a tenuous smile.

Feeling enormous relief from the inspector's decision, I clutched his hand. Instantly, he and the plant manager walked over to the crane operator to explain the judgment. Observing our conversation from a distance, the crane operator scoffed at the conclusion, stomping the floor. Tugging on the brim of his cap while the inspector was speaking, the crane operator appeared agitated by what he had heard.

Visibly unhappy about the inspector's judgment, the operator climbed on the crane and drove to a pallet where a thrust reverser half had been placed. Seeing the operator move the unit to the aircraft, I approached him and extended a hand. Displaying a half-hearted smile, the operator shook my hand. Peering at each other with our hands joined, the operator seemed uneasy, but I felt relieved that a load had been taken off my back.

Joining Jon and the mechanics who had just arrived at the aircraft, the crane operator lifted the first reverser segment into place below the wing. Less energetic than the day before, the mechanics went about securing the unit to the pylon. While the second half of the unit was being installed, the labor inspector and plant manager walked out of the building with smiles on their faces. I felt solace from their departure. Displaying a slight grin, the operator seemed more accepting of the outcome of his complaint.

During the installation of the remaining thrust reverser segments to the aircraft, barring a momentary lapse of a dropped wrench and kit of attaching hardware, the mechanics were their old selves. The effects of the night before had me concerned, but the continual chatter and usual swagger were on full display. Though I had feared the worst when they arrived in the hanger, I was comforted by what I was now seeing from the mechanics .

Later that afternoon, I felt even better when a quality specialist in the facility and *L.B.A.* (German Civil Aviation Authorities) accepted the work. After obtaining the acceptance of the *L.B.A.*, we all breathed a sigh of relief. An enormous hurdle had been cleared for the delivery of the L.T.U. aircraft and follow-on aircraft being processed in Toulouse.

Six years prior to this thrust reverser replacement, I was sent to Munich to collaborate on introducing another propulsion program. In Munich, a team of German, English, and American manufacturing specialists came together to coordinate the manufacturing integration of engine components produced by partner companies of the International Aero Engines (IAE) consortium for the Airbus A320 aircraft program. Though we spent a few days in the German MTU facility working on a mutually agreed production plan, this experience in Hamburg provided a much closer view of the culture in a German manufacturing facility. The departure of the crane operator in Hamburg at the precise end of his workday revealed how closely a worker monitors his time. It was much more exacting than I had thought.

The thrust reverser segment hanging from the boom may not have been at risk of falling, but the sight of it dangling near the wing had bothered me. Undoubtedly, the tension surrounding the delivery of this aircraft had contributed to my fear. The crane operator's focus on his agreed working hours was probably no different than most shop workers in the world, but from my vantage point, the accomplishments of all involved with swapping out the L.T.U. thrust reversers was a stirring experience.

When departing the next morning on my return flight to Toulouse, I thought about the proceedings of the prior two days. I waved to the mechanics through the window of the plane as it moved away from the Finkenwerder terminal. They were packing the tooling in crates for shipment to Toulouse, and I wasn't sure they could see Jon or myself, but the three of them waved vigorously at the plane when it taxied by the hanger. Unquestionably, they were thrilled that their work had been successfully accomplished. "The musketeers came through again," I reminisced as the plane sped down the runway. Although frightening to watch, during the installation of the units, I commended the crane operator for his skillful positioning of the thrust reversers on the pylons projecting forward from the wings of the aircraft.

In retrospect, the key to our success was the collective recognition of the importance of the task and our common acknowledgment of the consequences of failure. There were thousands of people around the world whose lives were counting on us. It's the nature of work in our industry, I've found after three decades. When engaged in a critical task, apprehension, combined with competence, tends to elevate one's focus on their work.

No one's entitled to succeed. I believe that success must be earned by those involved with the task.

After the intense three days of the thrust reverser swap-out, I looked forward to going home to Connecticut for Christmas and having a quiet holiday season with my family. At this time, we were still far from a predictable on-time delivery of engines and nacelles to the podding facility and having a confident air-framer. Though reduced, retrofit activity was still necessary at the podding facility, repair station, and flight line, as evidenced by the recent swap-out of thrust reversers on the first L.T.U. aircraft. There was much to do on both sides of the Atlantic to get propulsion systems delivered repeatedly on schedule.

During the first six months of 1995, surprising changes were brewing. It was terrific that the first aircraft had been delivered and the door had been opened for deliveries of aircraft to airlines beyond Thai, Malaysia, and L.T.U., but a greater measure of success was ending the on-site retrofit and repair work on thrust reversers and engines and getting them delivered from the States in accordance with the podding facility lead times. Squeezing the lead times to accommodate late arriving engines and nacelle components continued to put a burden on delivering propulsion systems, putting them in jeopardy of being late.

By the end of March 1995, the flood of engine and nacelle retrofits and repair activity was significantly reduced, particularly at the thrust reverser repair station. The work there had dried up so much that the thrust reverser manufacturer terminated their contract with Sogerma and returned all their on-site people to the States. The musketeers remained at the facility doing aircraft customization, I presumed. I never saw much of them after the operation shut down. By mid-April, engines were being delivered to Toulouse at a more reliable rate. Before long, propulsion systems were being delivered on contract dates.

"Yah, you do it!" said Dieter on the phone, expressing his acknowledgment.

"We did it, yah," I jokingly replied to him and Russell on the speaker phone.

"OK, we need you to keep it up," said Russell in the background.

"I'll try. You can count on it," I committed.

Propulsion systems continued to be delivered on the dates mutually agreed with the air-framer. One day in May, I received the ultimate indicator of our newfound success. As I passed Jacques on the Airbus campus on my way to a meeting, we stopped to say hello to each other.

"*Ca va, mon ami?*" Jacques greeted me with a wide smile.

"I'm doing great, thanks. How are you?" I returned.

"It's OK. You're still here?" said Jacques, appearing surprised to see me.

"Yea, I'm still here, Jacques," I uttered as we parted ways.

Jacques's query was telling me I could go home. I took it.

As I approached fourteen months of eating in the wonderful eateries in the region, a reality hit me. The foods I had eschewed when growing up—like liver, gizzards, and hearts—were now tasting delectable. Yogurt and even oysters that my mother, with her southern coastal roots, urged me to eat were going down much easier now. The grilled meats I ordered in French restaurants gradually became pinker than my habitually overcooked requests. Red wines, which I had rarely consumed in the prior years, were now my preferred wines. "What happened?" I wondered. Had I adapted to the French culture?

Becoming more consumed in the region and feeling accepted by a growing number of locals served to elevate my interest in adjusting to the culture. My engagement with the people of the region resulted in my shedding a few pounds, reducing a notch in belt size. Immersed deeply in the assignment, I overlooked eating different types of foods in more reasonable portions. My eating habits changed, with lunch being my main meal. In restaurants, the table was mine for the day or night. I never felt rushed to give up a table to accommodate waiting customers. I never heard wait staff annoyingly bellow, "Is everything OK?" It seemed the inquiring words were grilled and baked into the meals and conveyed in the accommodating nature of the establishments I had eaten.

As we entered the month of June, changes in the workplace were accelerating. Early in the month, Trip was informed he would be reassigned to another customer support position outside of Europe. Not long thereafter, rumors flew about Cary, Roland, and Matt being replaced. By the middle of June, the inevitable also happened to me. On a quiet June morning, I received a call from Rick with astounding news.

"Hi," said Rick with an upbeat tone. "I just wanted you to know that new positions have been created in the company and our organization for propulsion system manufacturing program managers covering Operations activity at commercial air-framers (Airbus, Boeing, and McDonnell Douglas) and our military customers. Considering the great job you've done over there, I would like you to be our manager of propulsion systems manufacturing management for Airbus aircraft programs," Rick mentioned. "You will work out of an office in Middletown, Connecticut." (Middletown was the location of the engine assembly facility where my journey to Toulouse had begun.)

"Rick, I don't have to think about it. I gladly accept your offer and will be back before the end of June." By accepting this new position, I absorbed Scott and Ian in the podding facility and Trip's flight-line personnel in

Toulouse. I was also given some manufacturing program people in the States to interface with the engine program organization and to assist me in my duties of providing propulsion systems that met the needs and expectations of our air frame and airline customers. Getting to this point of consistent on-time deliveries had taken fourteen toilsome months, but in the years to come, I would find it harder to sustain this level of success.

Returning to Connecticut after more than a year stint in France, I felt like an alien in a new world. Re-entering an organization restructured beyond recognition, the uncertainty of having a new boss, and seeing the removal of many people I had worked with for twenty years weighed on me several weeks after coming back. However, through this period of transition, there was a silver lining. I was back on the same soil as my family. Surely it was great to be home, but with the issues surfacing in the days ahead, there were times when it seemed that I was commuting to the United States.

** Learmount, David. "Airbus Wary Over A330 Changes." Flight International, August 17-23, 1994.

7

The Transfer

Considered less glamorous—perhaps undesirable from an occupational perspective—by some in the aviation industry, the producers of aircraft nacelle components receive little applause, I've found. Enclosures covering wing and aft-mounted aircraft engines and the aero-structures (cowling) shrouding aircraft engines appear to be just along for the ride, which contributes to these feelings. It's understandable why passengers likely don't notice the nacelles when they look at the plane they are boarding. Yet the perception is dispelled when the flight lands and the engines are accelerated. Revved up to increase the velocity of air passing through the engines, the thrust reversers block fan air and reroute it forward to reduce the aircraft's braking speed. Visible to passengers looking at the wings during a flight, the nacelles play a vital role in integrating engines and aircraft, providing an aero-smooth transition from the propulsion systems to the pylons on which they are mounted.

Stationary during flight operations, the fan cowling positioned forward of the thrust reversers just ride with the aircraft. In addition to being painted in the colors of the airline, they're often adorned with distinct logos of the airline or the propulsion system manufacturer. Considering the size of these components (some exceeding 120 inches in diameter) and their importance to the aircraft, rumors of a transfer of suppliers would raise eyebrows at an aircraft manufacturer.

Prior to the announcement of the transfer of fan cowl production from the current Italian supplier to another in-country producer, there were times when the attaching holes in fan cowls didn't align upon installing them on engines. The misalignment issues created a domino effect, causing significant delays in processing propulsion systems at the podding facility, delaying deliveries to the aircraft manufacturer, and detaining deliveries of aircraft to airlines—potentially creating a financial nightmare. Believe me, I received an agonizing number of "Yah, but you will do it," calls from Dieter, or my partner, as he now called me.

A notable misalignment incident occurred in the fall of 1994 when an engine and its mating forward fan cowls revealed an installation problem.

"We need the propulsion systems, yah," Dieter reminded me daily. Attempts between our podding facility team and the supplier to resolve the conundrum over the phone proved ineffective. Subsequent remedies proposed by the supplier were fruitless, adding to the dismay at the podding facility and among my air frame colleagues. Before long, everyone was frustrated, including the supplier of the fan cowls. When the issue continued to impact the deliveries to the air-framer, the reaction was predictable—a phone call from Dieter, during which he stated those familiar words:

"Yah, you will do it now."

Dieter was constantly pressuring me to deliver units I couldn't provide and had added Jacques's name to his pleas to ensure my diligence. With an acute focus on the matter, I was able to convince the supplier to send repairmen to Toulouse to fix the cowls. Showing up on a Friday morning at the podding facility after their nine-and-a-half-hour drive from Turin, the repairmen were immediately taken to a propulsion system installed on an A-frame. Notified of their arrival, I joined Scott and Ian, who were observing the repairmen looking at suspect units. Greeting me with wary eyes and genial smiles, the supplier's repairmen appeared ready to begin their inspection of the available units.

"Did you bring the alignment fixture?" I asked, seeing only their hand tools next to them.

"It's in the car," a repairman replied, scratching his head.

Sending a man to get the tool, the lead repairman and helper began a visual review of cowls on transport trolleys. Returning minutes later with a fixture, the men began using it to check holes in an engine fan case and holes in its mating fan cowl. Appearing distraught after starting the inspection, a repairman made a startling revelation.

"We bring the wrong tool!" he said, raising arms and shoulders.

"How can this be?" I reacted.

Stunned by the shocking discovery, I invited the lead repairman to my office in the podding facility, where we called the supplier and conferenced in our procurement department in the States. Speaking Italian, the lead repairman explained the predicament to his supervisor.

"How soon can you get the correct tool here?" I interrupted.

"The tool will be sent out today," said a voice on the other end of the line.

Additional probing on my part resulted in a commitment to have the tool hand-carried to Toulouse. While on the phone, another surprise arose. The repairman told his supervisor that they only had enough money to cover a day or two in Toulouse.

"It will take a few days to complete the work," he continued.

Sensing my consternation, the repairman's supervisor committed to reserving rooms at a hotel and sending money with the correct tool.

"If they run out of money, can you help them?" asked the supervisor.

"OK, but your men need money, now!" I responded.

Getting final instructions from his boss, the repairman hung up the phone, saying a few words in Italian. Peering at me with blank gazes, the men shrugged and bade me a "good weekend."

Strolling in the center of Toulouse two days later, I noticed hands waving vigorously as I passed a sidewalk café. Seated at an eatery on a broad, tree-lined boulevard, it appeared the men were trying to get my attention. As I walked over to the table where the wavers were sitting, I saw four jovial men with empty beer bottles in front of them. Jubilant about their good fortune, the repairmen invited me to join them.

"We have lots of money," said a joyful repairman, pointing to the courier that had brought the money and the correct tool.

For my sake, I was relieved to see the supplier had honored its commitment. Eyeing a parade of people passing the café, I chatted with the repairmen about the work to come and their estimate of the time required to complete it. Anticipating an early call from Dieter the next day, I wanted to provide an immediate response when asked. The vitalized repairmen made me as buoyant as them and more confident of the outcome. They bade me a "*buona sera*" when our discussion of the work had ended.

Within a day and a half, the men corrected all of the fan cowls in the podding facility. Immediately after they finished, I called Dieter to share the news of their completed task. Telling Dieter and Russell that the cowls had been corrected and deliveries of the associated propulsion systems would soon follow compelled both Dieter and Russell to say, "Great job."

Though I felt comfort from the praise of Dieter and Russell, I remained worried about a return of the problem. I shared my skepticism with Cary. Within a week, we traveled to Turin in northern Italy to meet with the management of the repairmen and confirm that the supplier had taken the necessary steps to prevent another cowl problem.

During our introductory discussion with the management of the cowl supplier, Cary and I expressed concern about the impact of the problem to the airplane manufacturer. We emphasized the sudden surfacing of the problem and why we felt compelled to come to their facility. Listening quietly, a man wearing a shop coat and another dressed in a sports jacket appeared disheartened by our presence. After presenting an extensive summary of their analysis of the root cause and corrective action taken, they told us that the tools and gauges that contributed to the problem had been removed from the workstation in the shop.

Soon, we were escorted to the workstation where the questionable holes were bored in the cowls. Arriving in the department during shift change, we were greeted by a machine operator who had just clocked in. Eager to demonstrate his skills on the machine, the man installed a cowl into a holding fixture. Recalling the explanation earlier in the conference room, I walked to a workbench not far from the machine and picked up a tool, which appeared to match the description of the tool allegedly removed from the workstation. I turned to our escorts.

"Is this the old or new gauge?" I asked, handing it to the perplexed shop superintendent. Seemingly embarrassed, the superintendent looked at the machine operator, shaking his head.

"I don't understand how this happened!" he shrieked.

Confounded by the revelation, I peered in amazement at them.

"We'll remove it right away and make sure it won't come back to this operation," the men assured us.

Restating the pain that the problem had caused at the podding facility and the air-framer, Cary and I departed the cowl supplier and returned to Toulouse. From this incident, I took away one lasting lesson: "Intuitively, when something doesn't feel right, and there is uncertainty of closure, go with your gut." Our impromptu visit to the cowl supplier proved to be worthwhile and reassuring in the end.

Although the cowl alignment problem had been resolved, concerns about other issues, from part fitting problems to re-sourcing, lingered. Working out of the States in my new position of propulsion systems manufacturing program manager for Airbus aircraft programs didn't dim my focus on what was happening in Toulouse. In fact, being the principal industrial liaison between our company and Airbus, pushing engines and parts out of Connecticut and suppliers, plus having people in the podding facility and on the flight line in Toulouse put a greater burden on me.

Seven months after assuming my new position, when I was feeling comfortable about the resolution of fan cowl problems, another issue surfaced. With rumors abuzz about a transfer of fan cowl production to another supplier, there was a tsunami of concerns throughout the supply chain and at the air-framer. When a management team from our company and management of the current and future fan cowl producers converged in Toulouse to announce the transfer, the intensity in the conference room was electrifying. Stating, "The proposed transfer of the cowl production was influenced by the Italian government's desire to consolidate key industries into centers of excellence," they announced their proposed transfer of cowl production. They did not present a detailed plan for the move from the current supplier to their facility but shared a rough timetable for relocating the work with Jacques and others in the room.

Jacques peered at the presenter of the proposal with a stony face. One could imagine what was going through his mind while listening to the announcement. Absorbing the information calmly as the supplier's representatives presented the basics of the move, Jacques scribbled notes on a pad. Appearing to be developing his own plan, as he often did, Jacques looked over his glasses from time to time while surveying the room and asking questions about the timetable for the move. Somehow through his questioning and rapid responses from the supplier's senior manager, there appeared to be mutual respect and a relational bonding developing between both men. Upon closing the meeting, it was agreed to allow a few months to fully develop the transfer plan and reconvene again in 1996.

The next meeting was held at our engine assembly facility in the States, six months following the announcement of the transfer. Representing the air-framer's management was Jacques, Dieter, and Maurice, a colleague of Jacques's who led their Quality Assurance Department. I hadn't met him before. Attending the meeting for the current supplier was Ezio, who bore the responsibility of coordinating the transfer with his counterparts at the new supplier. During Ezio's presentation of the proposed transfer plan, Jacques appeared restless, shaking his head often while listening. I wasn't sure what Ezio said that set Jacques on fire, but suddenly, Jacques erupted with a deafening assault on him.

"*OK, je ne comprends pas votre plan,*" Jacques said with a blast of verbal flatulence, blaring his lack of understanding of the plan Ezio was presenting. Appearing to be in a state of shock from the barrage, Ezio displayed a forced grin. Stepping out of the conference room for a moment, I was bombarded with questions.

"What's going on in there?"asked a person sitting at a desk near the room .

"Is everything OK in there?" another guy muttered.

"Everything's fine," I replied, hoping to end the queries.

Not long after returning to the conference room, the meeting adjourned. I felt bad for Ezio, who was still smarting from Jacques's lashing. The next meeting was set to be held at the new supplier's plant in Venegono, Italy to assess their capability of absorbing the cowl production work.

I remember the next meeting as much for my issues with getting to the new supplier's facility as for its outcome. It was mid-February, 1997, with a New England chill in the air, when I embarked on a trip to Milan, Italy. I expected a routine transfer in Paris and was shocked when hearing my transfer flight had been canceled. Inquiring about the cancellation, a ground staffer told me, "There is an air traffic controllers' strike in Italy." Starting at nine in the morning, airline personnel proposed alternate flights to get me from Paris to Italy. Discouraged by my inability to get to Milan, I waited through the morning and much of the afternoon to be rerouted. Finally, after being inundated with flight options for much of the day, I accepted a flight to Lugano. Perusing a map of Italy with an airline employee, I presumed Lugano, with its Italian-sounding name, was a drivable distance to Varese, Italy, where my hotel was located. Ending a day in the Charles de Gaulle Airport, I boarded a regional jet going to Italy. Or so I thought.

Making a quick stop in Bern, the capital of Switzerland, the plane descended like a corkscrew. As I peered through the airplane window, I noticed that the small terminal appeared sunken in snowy mountains. Following a spiraling ascent after take-off, we climbed above the peaks, where the snow seemed close enough to touch. Before long, we began our descent to Lugano. Gazing outside, I marveled at the scenery of honey-blue lakes and the crimson snowy crests of the surrounding mountains. As the plane descended, the landscape appeared lifeless below.

Upon landing in Lugano, I had a feeling of being on another planet. In twilight, the place appeared desolate. As I walked to the baggage claim area not far from the arrival gate, I noticed that the airport terminal had a remoteness about it. A woman awaited her luggage at the baggage pickup area. We were the only people there, and we looked at each other, wondering if our bags had made the flight. Saying "Hello" to one another revealed we were both Americans. Not long thereafter, the luggage wobbled in.

With my suitcase in hand, I went to the area where car rental companies were located. Telling the agent that I was going to Varese, Italy and wanted to return the rental at the Milan, Linate Airport raised two stunning concerns.

"We only rent sub-compact cars for one-way drop-offs in Milan," said the agent, peering over his glasses.

"Nothing bigger?" I replied, anticipating what was coming.

Having no other option to get to Varese, my only choice was to take the vehicle. While putting the contract on the counter, the agent hit me with an even more astonishing revealing. Speaking heavily accented English, he quoted the rental price in francs.

"Francs, why not Lira?" I asked, assuming I had landed in Italy.

"No, that's not possible," the grinning agent retorted.

"Then where am I?" I wondered.

"*Monsieur*, you're in Switzerland," the agent answered with a wry smile.

Baffled by the disclosure, I asked for directions to Varese. Instantly, he put a map on the counter, penciled in the route to take, and summarized what he had drawn. Arriving at the space where my rental was parked, I was surprised by the size of the green Fiat Punta awaiting me. Placing my suitcase on the tiny back seat, I set off in near darkness to the city of Varese.

The route prescribed by the rental agent was steep and winding. With the exception of an occasional car coming from the opposite direction, I had the route to myself. Driving a good distance in dark solitude, I was surprised by how quickly the roadway became ablaze with motorists. I hadn't seen a sign showing I had crossed the border into Italy, but the driving habits were telling me something. Arriving from nowhere, the headlights of the cars to my rear were glued to the bumper of my car. Drivers of these cars seemed determined to push me to Varese. A blast of a horn served as a reminder that I was well off their pace. When navigating sharp bends on the glazed descending roadway, a quick "toot" of a horn signaled that I was being passed. Although I was dead tired, there was no way I could have dozed off with the alarmist behind me.

As I entered Varese (just south of the northern lake region of Italy), without a map of the city or directions to the hotel, I was confused. Spotting a brightly lit mom-and-pop grocery store on a busy boulevard, I pulled over to get help. I sought directions from a man behind the counter, and his quick smile and shrug provided an immediate response to my predicament. He had no idea what I was saying. Departing the store, I continued further on the well-lit avenue until a service station appeared. It was a larger establishment than my prior stop, and I was encouraged to stop there.

Inside the convenience section of the gas station was a man behind a glass enclosure wearing a New York Yankees baseball cap. Seeing the Yankees cap made me hopeful of being understood by the clerk.

"I'm looking for the Palace Hotel," I mentioned, praying the attendant would understand me. Saying a few words in Italian, the clerk opened his hands with palms facing upward and shrugged. Dejected by my inability to be understood, I showed the clerk my itinerary, noting the street where the hotel was located.

"Ah, OK," he replied with a friendly smile while drawing a map on a napkin. We used our fingers, facial expressions, and smiles to establish a mutual understanding of where I needed to go, confirming our acceptance with an OK. I shook the attendant's hand as he laughed and mentioned the words, "New Jersey." Hearing this statement stunned me. As we continued to talk to each other with our hands and facial expressions, it appeared that the attendant had a relative living in the state of New Jersey. Thus, the connection with the baseball cap, I took it. Departing the gas station, I was uplifted by our speechless discussion. Shortly thereafter, I ascended a steep hill where the castle-like hotel was perched.

As I entered the opulent lobby of the hotel, my impression was, "Wow, it's definitely the Palace." Palatial red velvet and rich wood consumed the reception area. After being checked in by a receptionist wearing a dark velvet jacket, I entered my room and crashed on the bed. It was the first sleep I had had in nearly two days without the sound of jet engines singing in the background. Not long after nodding off, the phone rang. It was a company colleague checking to see if I had made it.

"Would you have any interest in going out for dinner?" the voice asked.

Having a greater appetite for sleep than dining, I reluctantly agreed to meet him in the lobby. I was drained from the trip to Varese, and the meal couldn't end fast enough.

Over the next two days, we devoted our time to listening to the production plan of the receiving fan cowl supplier and assessing their capability to absorb the work in their shop. Representing the air-framer at these meetings were Russell, who I was very familiar with, and Pascal, from the airframer's Quality Department. Although I hadn't met the management of the new supplier before dining with them the night before, the contrast of my first impression of them compared to the transferring supplier was stark. Undoubtedly, the discovery of the defective hole alignment tool at the transferring supplier was lingering. First impressions you remember, but last impressions are harder to forget, I've found. The production supervision of the new supplier exuded trust during the presentation of their transfer plan, conveying a believable commitment to transferring the production of the various cowl types. Speaking heavily accented Italian-English with hands in constant motion, the enlivened spokesman gradually garnered our confidence. His passion for the product was astounding.

Presenting a less animated pitch than the prior speaker, Emilio, a diminutive, soft-spoken man who appeared to be in his mid-fifties, had a jovial, good-natured manner of promoting trust and buy-in into the supplier's plan. There seemed an air of straight-shooting sincerity about him, I thought as he discussed the plant's capability of performing the work and complying with the schedule we provided for their agreement. He refrained from over-committing to dates that would have been beyond their capability. I liked that straightforward approach. Another thing that came across during Emilio's presentation was a sense that he was a man who had great pride in the products his company made and that he adored the processes that produced them. Emilio's presentation was a tremendous trust-building introduction to the new supplier. For someone who knew nothing about the supplier's aptness to absorb these nacelle units, I was impressed. We closed the meeting with a consensus of acceptance of the new supplier's ability to meet our needs and set a next meeting to review the plan in-depth.

While leaving the meeting, Russell and Pascal approached me to mention their flight plan back to Toulouse. "OK, what's the hitch?" I thought as Russell explained their early flight arrangements for the next morning.

"From what I've heard about the traffic in Milan, it seems impossible to go from here to the airport and make our very early flight," Russell said with a sympathy-seeking tone. Throughout his rambling pitch, I sensed a bigger question coming. "Since you're also going to Toulouse tomorrow and have an early flight, perhaps the three of us should stay at a hotel in Milan tonight and go from there to the airport in the morning," said Russell with a whining plea. Actually, my morning flight to Toulouse was scheduled for two and a half hours later than Russell and Pascal's flight. The traffic from Varese to the Milan-Linate Airport should be a lesser problem for me, I reasoned. It seemed that Russell's real issue was that I had a car, and they didn't. When arriving in Milan, they had taken a taxi to the hotel.

Neglecting to mention the dimensions of the car I had rented, I agreed to stay at a hotel closer to the airport. After Emilio's secretary canceled our last night at the Palace and booked us at a hotel in Milan, we made our way to the hotel's parking lot.

"Holy shit!" Russell wailed, peering at the car I had rented. Suddenly, we realized the enormity of the problem before us.

"How do we get our stuff in that?" Pascal asked, scratching his head.

"I don't know. Let's try," I shrugged.

Peering at our luggage, we pondered how to get the three of us and our bags into the car. On the brink of giving up after a few attempts, we finally found a way. Considering that Russell and Pascal were really big guys, piling them and our stuff into the car was an ultimate load test for a Fiat

Punta. With Russell and Pascal holding their bags on their laps and my valise sandwiched in the space between the three of us, I drove off to Milan. It was a drive of forty kilometers, I guessed, and inside the car, we were packed. It was an extreme sacrifice to gain acceptance from my Airbus counterparts.

We finally arrived in Milan, a city of over 1.4 million people. Weaving through the busy streets of the city in twilight, we entered a mega-roundabout in the center of the city, which I circled a half a dozen times before being expelled by the traffic. Looking for the hotel in darkness was frustrating in the crushed conditions. Finally, Pascal, who was wedged into the back seat, spotted a sign displaying the hotel's name. Before long, we pulled into the driveway of the red-stoned hotel. What a relief to open the door and literally fall on the pavement. When Russell opened his door, everything in the vehicle shifted. Sitting among two pieces of luggage in the back seat of the two-door sedan, Pascal had to be the most relieved when getting out. Regardless of the discomfort, Pascal laughed when exiting the car. Though it was far from the ornate palace we departed in Varese, the single-bed rooms in this hotel seemed enormous compared to the car.

The next morning, Pascal and Russell took a taxi to the airport to catch their early flight to Toulouse. I hadn't seen them since we ate a meager dinner at the hotel's café and had no idea when they left. Driving to the Linate Airport a few hours later, I recalled my adventures getting to Varese and the packed ride from Varese to Milan. For me, it was quite an adventure, but I surely wouldn't miss the car that transported me.

After the initial meetings at the new supplier's plant, we returned to Venegono three months later. Considering the circuitous route, I had taken to get to the first meetings, traveling to the second round of meetings was a breeze. The meetings started cordially, with Emilio and the supplier's quality manager, Santino, doing most of the presenting. Barring a few exceptions, most of the participants of the prior meetings returned. Emilio and Santino presented the implementation plan with contrasting styles. On the one hand, there was the calm, soft-spoken Emilio, sharing his static delivery of the manufacturing plan, followed by Santino, who presented his Quality Department plan with a wordy, gesticulatory flare. When it came to emphasizing significant features of his product integrity plan, Santino's hands were in perpetual motion. Sitting in front of him, I could feel the energy from his animation throughout his presentation.

Although Russell returned for the meeting, Pascal didn't come with him. I wondered if he was still unfolding his body from our ride to Milan. A notable addition to this meeting was Gregoire, a confidant of Jacques's who was sent to the meeting to assess the production capability of the new supplier. Sending Gregoire to the meeting was like unleashing a rabid pit bull, some had thought. Nonetheless, he had Jacques's ear and his trust, and most of the meeting attendees knew it. Sitting through the presentations of Emilio and Santino with a smirk of skepticism, Gregoire interjected with questions that appeared to irritate Santino. Having known Gregoire for three years and observing him in various meetings in the States and in France, I knew that his behavior at this meeting was true to form. He had a way of stirring the pot, particularly from an organizational standpoint. He poked at how organizations were structured and their ability to function and continually meet their commitments. To me, his style was to disrupt and watch his targets squirm and scramble to recover from his cleverly placed questions. I think Jacques liked this mode of operation, which was much like his. Despite Gregoire's referring to me as "the Savior" during our initial greetings, I actually liked him and his keen foresight. He tended to get to the root of a matter and expose the weaknesses in organizations and incompetence among those leading them.

As the meeting proceeded, it appeared Gregoire was getting under Santino's skin. Soon the emotions of Santino and Gregoire reached a boiling point. Before long, they exploded beyond the talking points of the meeting in a clash of French and Italian cultures. While snapping at each other, the fracas exposed subliminal cultural mistrust seemingly spanning well beyond Gregoire's sixty years. Finally, with the animus fully visible, Santino pointed to Gregoire, made a hitch-hiking motion towards the door, and shouted, "You leave, now," with face ablaze.

Suddenly, the room went silent. Appearing unfazed by Santino's directive, Gregoire licked his lips while scanning the room with a sheepish expression.

I had seen this expression many times after Gregoire detonated his verbal grenades. Following a moment of quiet, Gregoire resurfaced with a statement confirming his unimpressed opinion of Santino's presentation.

"I want higher-level representation at the next meeting," Gregoire demanded. Nodding his head in agreement, Emilio closed the meeting by saying he and Santino would arrange it. Considering the outcome of the meeting, the gathering had not only been an opportunity to assess the transfer plan, but also an enlightening resurrection of cultural divergence, spanning back, it seemed, to Roman times. I was struck by the intensity of the feuding and their entrenchment in this culture war. "This began well before their time," I thought while watching them battle. Following this meeting, there were subsequent meetings to monitor the supplier's compliance with their plan. Contrary to Gregoire's request for a higher-level close-out meeting, that level meeting was not held for some time.

Finally, at the blaring insistence of Jacques, the senior-level people of the supplier and our company cleared their schedules and committed to attend a close-out meeting at the new supplier's facility in early 1998. Attending the review were the organizational leaders of the new supplier, vice presidents including Jacques and Maurice from the air frame manufacturer, and Louis, the Head of Operations in our company. Although comparable levels of management from each company came to the review, the indomitable force in the meeting was as usual Jacques. Undoubtedly, he had been prepped by Gregoire's feedback.

Presenting a comprehensive transfer plan to those seated around the conference table, managers of the supplier spoke confidently about their approach to succeed. Displaying a blueprint for implementing the plan, the supplier projected ownership and accountability for the success of the transfer, something that had been less apparent with the prior supplier. Seemingly receiving buy-in from the affirmative-nodding attendees, I sensed the plans presented by Emilio and Santino were making everyone feel better about the implemented outcome. When presenting to this audience, the animated Santino seemed much more at ease than in the prior meeting attended by Gregoire. Although Gregoire was at the meeting, it wasn't an audience for performing, I observed. Besides, Jacques was present to control the meeting and ignite the room when needed.

Nodding in agreement while listening to the presentations, Jacques, as usual, asked the most pointed questions.

"How do you plan to cover us if your plan fails?" he asked a silent supplier team. Still reverberating among some attendees was Jacques's tirade during the meeting at our facility more than a year earlier. His calm, non-verbal approval of the plan appeared to be a confidence builder for the new supplier. With a contented glint in his eyes, Louis, the vice president of our delegation, seemed to like what he was hearing from the presenters. An agreeable Jacques was a powerful influencing factor, I'd noticed.

With attendees relaxed and mutually accepting of the transfer plan, the door of the conference room opened. A man walked into the room, entering like a soft breeze. Impeccably dressed in a radiant gray suit and wearing dark shoes with a new-car sheen, the man eased into a chair at the head of the table without saying a word. Sitting with a stoic erectness, he crossed a leg over a knee and surveyed the room. Gazing intently, he remained focused on the presenter speaking to the audience.

Surely, the managers of the supplier knew who the man was. Their instant shift of attention to this man indicated they were really trying to impress him. Before the man came into the room, Jacques had everyone's full attention. For those who didn't know the position of the man in the company, there was a sense that the company owner or chief executive officer had arrived. The reverence garnered by this unidentified man and the elevated respect he received signaled that he was the person who the presenters most wanted to please. Soon, all eyes were on this man—Jacques's included.

Though the man remained a mystery to me, his posture and quiet confidence projected prominence. He was an impressive example of the power of image. When the meeting ended, there was a rush of people to the silent visitor. Starting with the presenters of the supplier, one-by-one, attendees of the meeting approached the man to shake his hand. Appearing impressed by the presence of the man, Jacques coddled his hand with two hands like he was holding a precious gem. It was an extraordinary ending to a meeting that had been laden with uncertainty when it started. I gathered from the mood of the exiting attendees that the crisis we experienced at the outset of the transfer appeared to be heading in the right direction.

To celebrate the final acceptance of the transfer plan, the supplier invited the attendees to a dinner. Held at a site revered by locals, the restaurant was located in a building dating back to the Renaissance period, a former possession of the renowned Medici family. Passing through the stately gates of the grand estate was like going back in time. As we entered the venerable brick manor, we were greeted by a man dressed in formal evening wear. Before escorting us to our table, he took us to an area near the bar where food began to flow. An antipasto of numerous salamis, smoked fishes, encrusted meats, and a variety of olives prepared in different ways—from conventional to deep-fried—was placed before us. Crunchy, with soft, salty centers, I found the deep-fried olives a delectable surprise. The bar fare could have enticed the lightest of eaters to overindulge.

While standing among attendees of the meeting at the antipasto platter, I inquired about the man who had made the grand appearance at the meeting. Chatting briefly with Santino, he told me, "The man is the big boss of the company," that's all he had to say.

Approaching Jacques standing close by, I jokingly mentioned, "Jacques, in my time in Toulouse, I've learned that presenting to you is like playing Russian roulette." I'm not sure why I said this at this time, but his smiling, jovial mood had a liberating effect.

Jacques laughed. "You know, *mon ami*, the next time I come to the States, there will be no empty chambers," he said.

"Well, I guess I have something to look forward to," I grinned, knowing Jacques had another troubled program and its manager in his sights.

The dinner, with its servings of garlicky clams, pasta, and infallibly grilled steaks, was an exquisite dining experience. Soft lighting accentuating the artistic treasures above the table made the evening even more memorable. Peering upward at the frescoes painted on the ceiling, I imagined the artists lying on rickety wooden scaffolding, creating these masterpieces in semi-darkness. The ceiling consumed more of our attention than what was on our plates. I wasn't the only ceiling gazer among us. Louis and Jacques spent much of the evening with their heads tilted upward. Though centuries since they'd been painted, the red and blue colors of the skies were stunning.

As we closed out the evening, we stepped outside onto a terrazzo, where the night sky provided further entertainment. Looking upward revealed a lunar eclipse in progress. It was a storybook ending to a day during which we progressed from doubt to a mutually accepted transfer plan for producing fan cowls for large commercial aircraft.

As the transfer proceeded, execution of the plans presented by Emilio and Santino were performed with few issues. Ultimately, when the inlet, forward, and aft fan cowls were arriving consistently on schedule in Toulouse, the transfer team gained the confidence of the podding facility and the air-framer. For someone who had been skeptical when rumors of the transfer were spreading, I was impressed with the ability of the new supplier to manage the relocation of manufacturing and honor the commitments they presented. Doing what they said they would do went a long way in promoting trust with a doubtful air-framer. Even the more vocal critics like Jacques and Gregoire appreciated the accomplishment of the new supplier. So, in retrospect, when speculation was flying about the transfer, it was uncertain where fan cowl production was headed, but it's hard to argue with success. It was time to move on, and it paid off. It was undoubtedly one of the better moments of my career. The transfer revealed that nothing was impossible. The achievement inspired and propelled me in the coming days.

Jacques's remark that "There will be no empty chambers," spoken in jest at the transfer dinner, became a reality when he visited another engine organization in East Hartford, Connecticut, two weeks later.

"It was an emotional blood bath," I was told by my counterpart, who was covering the program. Apparently, that program had recommended removals of engines that were installed on aircraft. I recalled how Jacques had reacted when Joe Fine recommended thrust reverser removals from A330 aircraft. The emotional discharge was still vivid.

Fortunately, when I met with Jacques, Maurice, and Dieter in Middletown, Connecticut, Jacques's mood was again jovial. Apparently, he had fully released his venom in the morning. Plus, the cowl transfer was being executed as presented by the management of the new suppler. Neither he nor Dieter had any complaints. After all, we were now delivering our propulsion systems on time.

8

You're the Master

"Friendship either finds or makes equals."
Publilius Syrus, (1ˢᵗ c. B.C.)

As I roamed beyond the workplace, where the culture was decidedly different, my more memorable moments were etched by the locals. Admitting me into their homes and traditional lives, they allowed me to experience hospitality beyond my dreams. Exposure to other cultures and accepting them for what they are opens doors to human bonding and trusting friendships.

Initially, a relationship cannot be cleared for take-off until the parties accept each other as equals. The zone created by an accepting rapport inspires and can propel one or both parties to higher levels of esteem and achievement. These alliances flourish when both parties see value in the relationship and invest in it by extending themselves.

Following months of collaborating with managers of the air frame manufacturer, a shared sense of mission developed among us. Direct exposure to their points of view assisted in bridging cultural differences. Though I saw and met with two of the airplane company's vice presidents (Jacques and Maurice) at industrial reviews, subconsciously, we were not only developing friendships but building working partnerships.

The partnership mindset was particularly the case with Maurice. When concerns about the transfer of fan cowl production elevated to higher levels of management, industrial reviews became more frequent.

Between 1997 and 1999, Maurice and I saw each other on several occasions. Chatting briefly and sharing laughs during breaks at meetings, we discovered common interests that brought us closer. At the senior management review in 1998, when the fan cowl transfer plan and its implementation received a final blessing, Jacques and observers at the meeting noticed a friendship developing between Maurice and myself.

"I see you and Maurice are friends," said Gregoire one day when seeing me at a meeting in East Hartford.

"I'm envious of your friendship with Maurice," said Felix, the nacelle supply manager, soon after. He had a closer relationship with Gregoire than me. Unquestionably, Felix's reaction to my friendship with Maurice had been stimulated by Gregoire and his desire to stir things up.

Maurice's status as vice president in the air frame company meant he was at least two levels higher than me. Although my job title and responsibility changed when returning to the States in 1995, my level in our company hadn't. Yet the hierarchal differences in our respective companies and societies didn't matter to either of us. Our common interests of our children, zest for life, and mutual respect bound our relationship. "A friendship with me and a man in Maurice's position would be unlikely in our company," I thought. Some may have considered such a relationship a mismatch. Though it appeared to be a step down for Maurice, he showed no concern about how our friendship was being viewed. Although we weren't as close as Maurice and me, I don't think my position mattered to Jacques, either.

The evening before the final review of the fan cowl transfer, I received a call in my room not long after arriving at the Palace Hotel. Surprisingly, on the other end of the phone was an exuberant Maurice.

"Oh, you've made it. I called earlier," he gushed.

"Let's meet in the lobby, in, say, an hour?" I suggested.

An hour later, the door of the elevator opened, revealing Jacques and Maurice going down. When seeing me they appeared excited.

"I see you got here," said Jacques with a broad smile.

Sharing stories about our travel to the hotel, we joined other attendees of the meeting awaiting our arrival. Looking at the joyful expression on Maurice's face and a contented-appearing Jacques made me feel less tired.

Not long after the senior management review, Maurice invited me to his residence in a small village near Toulouse. Maurice's wife greeted me with glowing eyes. Prior to this visit, I had been in very few homes in the region. Those receptions were good, but the warmth of this greeting went deeper.

"Oh, Maurice often talks about you. Welcome to our home," said Maurice's wife, Sabine, upon introducing herself.

"*Merci, enchanter.* You speak very good English. Your English is much better than my French," I replied.

"Ah you did well. We're pleased you have come," Sabine responded.

The carefree cordiality Sabine displayed when greeting me led me to believe that she had prior exposure to people of color and different ethnicities. Moments later, when Maurice talked about his prior work in West Africa, Sabine stated that she was born in West Africa. Their exposure to other cultures extended to Greece and Saudi Arabia, where they had lived, they told me. While moving about, they raised two sons and a daughter.

The oldest child, Paul, a medical student at the university in Toulouse, came to his parents' home that evening specifically to meet me, he said. The youngest child, a school-age boy of twelve or thirteen, was curious and prevalent throughout my visit. I was struck by his attentiveness to his parents while they accommodated me. Maybe this is how French children behave when among their families, but the servitude of both sons was impressive. Their oldest child, a daughter, was married and lived in another region of France they mentioned.

Throughout the modest meal, we talked about our families. The older son departed before we sat down to eat, but the younger son joined us at the table, gazing at me in wonderment. Perhaps there was an Other Races Effect (O.R.E.) at play with the younger son. Studies show that the phenomenon has an effect on younger children of all races. I began talking about family, particularly my daughters, which inspired more chatter between us.

"I lived in the Toulouse region for fourteen months during the introduction of our propulsion systems on the A330 aircraft," I stated. Disclosing my prior exposure to the region and its culture appeared to elevate the interest of Maurice and Sabine.

"You have no problem with the language here?" Sabine asked.

"At work, I'm fine. After work, it can be difficult," I replied.

Fortunately, they spoke better *Anglais* than I could speak *Francais,* which promoted our communication. At the time, my ability to converse in their language was woefully limited and it bothered me a lot.

Like many Frenchmen, Maurice was no stranger in the kitchen. "*Oui,* Maurice loves to cook," said a gleeful Sabine when I asked about his culinary skills. Looking at each other with amorous grins, they spoke softly in French. Barely audible, their quiet manner of speaking to each other was similar to my observations of other French couples. As a token of our developing friendship, Maurice offered a jar of *foie gras* he had recently prepared. When leaving his home a few hours later, I offered to bring a treat from America for a future dinner. Listening closely to Maurice and Sabine through dinner, I tried to think of something they would like that would represent a favorite food of my region in the States. Neither of them had an idea of what I had in mind, and neither did I.

Six months later, Maurice invited me to another dinner at his home. Wanting to contribute something to the meal, I offered to bring the treat I had mentioned at our prior dinner. For my next trip to Toulouse, I purchased fourteen lobsters and had them shipped to France upon my departure from the States. When buying the lobster, I considered the out-of-pocket purchase an investment in a growing friendship with Maurice and his family.

On a sticky August evening in 1998, the *Fete d'Homard* (lobster fest), as we jokingly called it, was held at Maurice's home. For the occasion, Maurice invited a colleague from the airplane manufacturer to join us for dinner.

My wife came over from the States with me. She had come to France four times prior to this dinner. Alain, a senior engineering manager, was astounded when he saw what I brought to the dinner. Cut from the same social fabric as Maurice, Alain showed similar affability and esteem for me. Whenever I saw Alain, I was always greeted with a glowing smile and cordial words of "Ah, we see each other again." Though we never encountered each other professionally like Maurice, Jacques, and I had, Alain never appeared concerned about our differences on professional and societal levels. The calm, unpretentious genuineness of his demeanor projected acceptance wherever we were. On the evening of the lobster fest, we were three colleagues with our spouses having an enjoyable time together.

As the evening continued, our gathering became a mélange of light conversation. Before long we discovered that we had much in common.

"Do you have children?" asked Alain's wife, leaning forward with a smile.

"We have two daughters who finished college. How about you?" I asked.

"We have a twenty-year-old daughter," both Alain and his wife responded.

"No, this is not possible. You're too young," I quipped, to Alain's wife.

"I like him already," said Alain's wife with an ear-to-ear grin.

While talking, we focused on our experiences in our everyday lives, our families, and our goals for the future. Eventually, we began a discussion of retirement and life in the future.

"We want to spend our retirement in the Ivory Coast of Africa," Alain said.

"We want to retire in Senegal," said a grinning Sabine, facing Maurice.

"I'm not sure where we want to retire, but I'd love to visit you," I declared.

"Well, please come and see us. You're always welcome," they responded.

Amazed at their desire to spend a portion of their retired lives in Africa, I asked, "Why those countries in West Africa?"

"Because we find the people of these countries festive and their cultures are interesting," replied Maurice.

"What do you find interesting about the cultures?" I inquired.

"The people are nice, friendly and lively, " said Sabine.

By discussing our families, aspirations, and likenesses, we got a better sense and understanding of each other. After all, we had much in common.

Maurice, Sabine, and their guests were focused on listening and displayed an eagerness to learn more about us, which promoted our interest in sharing our lives with them.

When bringing the lobster to the table, Maurice glowed like a candle.

"You know, there were fourteen lobsters in the pot," he shrieked.

Alain appeared astounded by the quantity of lobsters in the bowl. Looking around the table, I was gladdened. Seeing how well my contribution to the dinner was received was gratifying. Peering at the tanned, radiant faces of Maurice, Alain, and their wives confirmed my investment had been worthwhile. I wasn't looking for any more than that.

In the months after our lobster fest, my friendship with Maurice continued to grow. We connected at the industrial reviews jointly held by our respective companies, and found the time to discuss how our families were doing. As I chatted with Maurice and Sabine a few months later after attending an industrial meeting in Toulouse, they invited me to stay at their home in a more rural region of France.

"You must come to our country home," said an excited Sabine.

"*Oui*, you must come," Maurice followed.

Without giving the invitation much thought, I readily accepted their offer. Before the end of the next summer, the invitation became a reality.

On a blazing Friday afternoon in August of 1999, we departed Maurice's office, not knowing where we were heading. As we left Blagnac, Maurice mentioned we were going to a region northwest of Toulouse. Eager to show us Moissac, a point of interest along the way, Maurice left the highway and drove into the aged town.

"This is interesting," he said while parking the car.

Moissac, a town overlooking a flood plain near the meeting point of the Tarn and Garonne rivers, has the *Eglise St. Pierre*, St. Peter's Church, at its core. Getting out of the car, Loretta and I followed Maurice to the site where the Benedictines founded an abbey. In the years following its seventh-century origin, the abbey was ransacked by Arabs, Normans, and Hungarians. In the year 1047, the abbey was united with the monastic foundation in Cluny, at the time among the most powerful in Europe. Consecrated in the year 1063 and growing through stages of development, the church became a masterpiece of French-Romanesque architecture. While explaining the history of the church, Maurice's voice quavered with excitement. Though he struggled, at times, to speak understandable English, his pride in the history of the grounds and joy in sharing this place with us was apparent.

"Ah, on to the cloister," said Maurice, urging us to follow him. The eleventh-century cloister was lined with alternating double and single columns of white, green, gray, and pink marble. In all, there were seventy-six decorated arches surrounding the colonnade. Flowers, beasts, and scenes from the Old and New Testaments were featured in the crowning on the columns. In fading daylight, we paused in the colonnade to absorb the courtyard and alluring gardens.

With the sun dropping below the tops of the trees, we continued our travel to Maurice's country home. Roughly a thirty-five-minute drive from Moissac, Maurice's village was among the many medieval hilltop villages in the Quercy-Périgord Region. Cut by the majestic Dordogne, Lot, and Tarn rivers, the region was noted for its pastoral green hills and sleepy villages, where distances were often calculated as the crow flies. Driving through a maze of dusty roads, Maurice arrived at his home. In darkness, it was apparent by the absence of other homes that this was a place for people seeking a slower pace of life, far from the bustle we left behind.

As we turned into a driveway, I noticed a glimmer of light through the shuttered windows. Maurice pulled up to the stone house, located a good distance from the highway we had traveled. Sabine and their youngest son came out to greet us.

"Oh, you come," said Sabine, planting a cheek on ours. Though Maurice had seen Sabine before going to work, he was awash with cheeky greetings from Sabine and their son. It was a greeting reminiscent of not seeing a loved one in a long-long time.

Inside their home, there was a sense of a farmhouse. In a room with stone walls and a massive fireplace, we sat and discussed our travel to France.

"How was your trip to France?" asked Sabine, looking at Loretta.

"Tiring," said Loretta, who had come over from the States to join me for our visit with Maurice and his family.

"Do you like France?" Sabine asked.

"We love it. There is so much to see," I replied.

"What have you seen?" Maurice asked.

"Well, Paris, of course, medieval Carcassonne, Rocamadour (a town in this region, built into the side of a cliff), Gaillac, and other small wine villages surrounding Toulouse," I told them.

Both Maurice and Sabine listened intently to my explanation. Telling them we visited Rocamadour in their region put a sparkle in their eyes. It's said that the best listeners listen even when they are eager to speak. After three prior visits with Sabine, I sensed she was burning to tell us about the region. Rather, she and Maurice restrained themselves to hear what we had to say. The focused listening sent a powerful message of their sincere engagement and desire to know us better.

Amazed at the enormity of the stone hearth of their fireplace, I imagined it being used for cooking and heating the entire house in its day. Taking us on a tour of their home, Simone began in an airy room on the other side of the fireplace. The country-style kitchen had an adjoining dining area with a communal table. Sabine next took us to a small room adjacent to the kitchen. It was typically the sleeping quarters of the hosts, but they had vacated the bedroom to accommodate our stay. Drowsy at the end of a long workday, we bade our hosts a "good night." After a reciprocal *Bonne nuit,* Maurice and Sabine uttered the most memorable words of the weekend.

"Now remember, when you're here. You are the masters!" they said.

I wasn't sure why they put it that way, but the sentiment conveyed a sensitivity to our ethnicity and presence. Those four words overshadowed any conversation we could have had about race relations or cultural differences. It was like placing a bar of chocolate on our pillows, but sweeter. If their intent was to demonstrate ultimate French hospitality, they undoubtedly succeeded. I was not only delighted but also overwhelmed.

Awakened the next morning by the scent of croissants in the oven, we joined our hosts for breakfast. The aroma of buttery croissants and brewing coffee added freshness to the new day. As I looked outside on a sun-drenched morning, I became curious about the origin of the house.

Escorting me around the outside of his home, Maurice explained what he had learned about its origin. Built about two centuries prior to Maurice's ownership, the rectangular-shaped structure was considered a long house in terms of French architecture. Made of local materials, primarily stone and clay, the farmhouse had provided a home for the family living on one end of the structure and a shelter for livestock at the other end. Humans and domesticated animals living under the same roof was not uncommon for farm life in nineteenth-century France, I was told. Maurice carried on with the history of the house, and I became more attentive when he mentioned that the room we had slept in was where the farm animals were kept.

"It was a wreck!" Maurice crowed, describing the condition of the house and surrounding area when he and Sabine bought it.

"It was exactly what we were looking for." He smiled.

As we surveyed the restored house and grounds upon which it was built, it was hard to imagine a family and their farm animals had lived under this roof. Using local contractors was an arduous, often frustrating process in France, I had heard. Maurice mentioned that he and Sabine had worked weekends and holidays to rebuild the home to their liking. I commended them for the renovation and retaining the charm of the rustic dwelling.

At a picnic table behind the house, we looked out upon the secluded backyard. At the edge of the property was a small stone building that they had also renovated. Little did I realize that Sabine's mother and their youngest son had slept in that building.

"In its day, the stone structure was used to store food for the owners and animals," Maurice stated. Other than a small area of grass and a corpulent tree in the center of it, the yard was treeless and mostly stony.

It was a Saturday morning, and like many villages in France, it was market day. Anxious to share the experience with us, Maurice gathered his wife and son and drove us to a market in a nearby village. As I peered out the window as we rode, I was struck by the sight of windmills perched on the rolling landscape. Unlike the contemporary wind-powered generators I had seen in Europe, these tattered structures were reminiscent of windmills I'd seen in older pictures of Holland.

We arrived at a small market later in the morning. It was a vibrant, convivial environment. Though most of the people had come to shop for produce, meats, and home goods, it appeared that the event was as much about mingling with fellow villagers of the region and neighbors seldom seen. For a small country market, the abundance of vendors selling farm goods and seemingly everything else was interesting to outsiders like us. Fresh vegetables and meats from local stocks were items I expected to see, but stalls selling cheeses, *foie gras*, locally made terrines of various meats, *charcouterie,* breads, pastries, clothing, antiques, and furniture made the browsing fascinating.

Viewing items for sale as we strolled through the market, Maurice stopped at a booth where a bulbous merchant was selling meats. Pointing to a ham hanging behind the man, Maurice asked for a sliver to taste. The merchant handed a sample of the meat to each of us, and I pondered what I was tasting compared to the hams I had eaten in the States.

"Do you know what you are eating?" Maurice asked with eager eyes.

"Ham for sure, but there's a gamy taste to it," I explained.

"You're eating *jambon du sanglier*. What *l'Anglais* call boar," said Maurice with a grin. After buying a piece of the rump, Maurice suggested that we leave the market to see more places in the region.

Departing the village, we traveled a serpentine road along the Lot River. Maurice stopped at sights he thought would be interesting to us. When he pulled over at a bend overlooking the river, we peered at the valley below.

"This is my favorite view of the region," said Maurice, standing before a stone wall put there for viewing the town of Agen and the adjacent Garonne River. Spellbound by the view of the river and the town of 35,000 along its shore, I could see why this view was praised by Maurice. Veering away from the Garonne river, Maurice drove through a landscape of *tournesol* (sunflowers) and fruit orchards.

"These are the trees of the famous *Pruneaux d'Agen*," Maurice said while passing groves of plum trees. "Legend has it that crusaders returning from the Middle East in the eleventh century brought the fruit to France," he told us. "Monks in the Lot Valley were the first to dry *prunes* (plums) in commercial quantities." Continuing to speak about the points of interest as he drove, Maurice said he had another treat for us. Backtracking, he drove by the market that we visited earlier.

"We go to Cahors to buy wine," he said, weaving through the countryside. Riding by fields of *tournesol* and more frequently scenic vineyards, Maurice turned into a driveway marked *Château du Brel, Vin de Cahors.* When getting out of the car, we were greeted by a woman who came through an antiquated door at the entrance of a stone structure.

"*Bonjour,*" she welcomed us with a sing-song-ash tone, recognizing Maurice and Sabine. Responding to the woman's happy reception, Simone introduced us.

"These are our friends from America," said Sabine.

The seasoned, sixty looking woman, who displayed deeply tanned skin, addressed us with a bashful glint in her eye.

"*Bienvenue, madame et monsieur. Tous les deux, vous serez toujours le bienvenu ici,*" (You both are always welcome here) she said with a sweeping smile.

The capital of the Lot Regional Department, Cahors is renowned for its dark red wines dating back to Roman times. To get a sense of how the wines tasted, we followed the woman to a rustic, paneled tasting room. I raised the sample of the wine up to an overhead light, as Maurice suggested. Tannin heavy, the wine had a smoky blackberry taste and a shadowy darkness. Knowing Maurice was coming for wine, the woman had his order ready for pickup. Placing cases of wine in the car, Maurice urged us to get in. Smiling joyfully as Maurice turned around in the driveway, the proprietress waved and bade us "*Au revoir.*"

When we returned to Maurice's home in the late afternoon, the heat was intense. While we chatted in their shuttered house, Sabine prepared a meal of chilled soup made from vegetables she had bought at the market.

"Come in, Loretta, we can talk while I prepare the dinner," Sabine said.

While the ladies talked about the children and Sabine's gazpacho recipe, Maurice and I went outside to talk under the enormous tree. Maurice sat on a chair low to the ground that appeared to be made from crisscrossing boards. He invited me to sit on a chair similar to the one he was seated on.

"Maurice, where did you get these chairs?" I asked in bewilderment.

"Sabine bought them for me when she visited Senegal," Maurice replied.

"It's the most unusual chair I have ever sat on," I said, observing our legs straddling the disk shaped cushions.

"You must go there. You would like it," Maurice advised.

"I hope to get there someday, perhaps to visit you," I replied.

"Come to the table. It's ready," said Sabine from the kitchen.

After eating the gazpacho and slices of boar with *melon au porto* (melon marinated in port wine), Maurice suggested sitting in front of the fireplace to continue talking.

"How long have you been married?" asked Sabine, looking at Loretta.

"Many years," she answered.

"What year did you get married? I asked, looking at Maurice and Sabine.

"Ah, we marry in 1970," Sabine followed.

"What month?" Loretta asked.

"August," Sabine responded.

Telling them we were married in the same year and in August opened the door to conversation ranging from education to favorite foods and pastimes.

"Do you play golf?" I asked Maurice.

"Oui, what is your handicap?" Maurice replied.

Hearing my high single-digit handicap, Maurice gasped.

"Oh, I cannot play with you!" he said with an amplified cry.

"It's not the score. It's the company that I enjoy playing with," I responded.

Maurice smiled and nodded while the ladies continued to talk about children. After speaking quietly with each other, Maurice and Sabine paused at the doorway to our room to tell us again, "When you're here, you are the masters. *Bonne nuit.*" Despite the hospitality that the words conveyed, the more memorable aspect of the weekend was Sabine and Maurice's demonstration of those words.

The weekend passed too fast for me. Following a lunch *of saucisson* (sausage) and sautéed garlic potatoes, we departed for Toulouse. Driving back to the city, I thought, "It's not unusual for a host to say cordial words at the doorway when their guests leave, but the parting pleasantries and true impression of the visitors don't always coincide." However, what made this visit resonate for me was not the words spoken by the host but the feeling of being treated like the master when with them. On top of the symbolic role reversal conveyed by Maurice and Sabine, they appeared to be sensitive to our cultural differences and wanted us to feel comfortable while staying with them. During our stay, there was a sense of equality and a desire to communicate on the same level.

Continuing to Toulouse, we stopped at every dilapidated structure I spotted along the way. As I got out of the car to look at depleted structures, I imagined how they would appear when restored. One abandoned building we came across conjured visions of a country manor, while others created images of *chambre d'hôtels*, bed-and-breakfast establishments. A closer look at these sites gave me a greater appreciation of the joy Maurice and Sabine must have felt during their search and finding of a second home. Fueled by the overwhelming acceptance we had received during the weekend; I was sky high with enthusiasm when returning to work. "What a weekend," I said to myself several days after the visit.

Three months after the journey to the Quercy region, I was stunned by news of Maurice being ill. Speculation of his condition ranged from a bad cold to more critical ailments. When hearing extreme assumptions about his health, I refused to believe them. To confirm the validity of what I was hearing, I visited Maurice in his office two months later, on my next trip to Toulouse. Maurice appeared energetic and in good health. His face lit up when I walked into his office. Hearing bad news from afar leaves a lot to the imagination, but seeing my friend in such good spirits was relieving for that moment. When leaving Maurice, I felt good about what I had seen.

I don't know how it surfaced, but during a mid-day meal with my Toulouse workmates, I expressed an interest in seeing other regions of the country. Soliciting people for their recommendations, I received a suggestion that drew my interest.

"You must go to the Loire Valley," asserted Dylan, who was seated at the table. Knowing nothing at all about the region, I referred to a *Michelin Travel*

Guide that someone on-site had given to me.

A fairy tale realm along France's longest river (1000 km, or approximately 620 miles long), the Loire Valley is a florid land of enchanting villages. The greatest attractions of the region are the luxuriant renaissance *chateaux*. Elegant architectural wonders, like the *Chateaux Chambord, Chenonceau, Villandry,* and *Saumur* are among the countless slate-roofed, castellated structures in the area possessing cone-topped towers and intricate interiors. The castles of the Loire were the darlings of the Renaissance period.

After choosing a *maison d'hôtel* (bed and breakfast) centrally located near the more renowned castles, I drove to a place near the towns of Blois and Amboise. The two-and-a-quarter-hour drive south of the Paris, Charles de Gaulle Airport gave me time to ponder the prospect of staying in a stranger's home versus checking into a hotel. I was born in the southern part of the United States in the mid-1940s and grew up during the civil rights movement in the States. There is an ingrained uneasiness among people of color when knocking on a white stranger's door. In a country like France, with a predominantly white population, it was hard not to feel uncertain when standing at the front door of our hosts. I envisioned shock on the face of whoever opened the door and was consumed with thoughts of the attitude and behavior of our hosts upon seeing us.

Upon exiting the A10 motorway in Blois, I navigated a series of roundabouts to the village of Onzain, where our lodging was arranged. Marinating in thought for several hours before getting there, I wondered how the owners would react when seeing my wife and me at their front door. When finding the place, I approached the entrance of the small white house slowly. Breathing deeply before ringing the doorbell, I imagined the feeling of the character played by Sidney Poitier in the 1967 movie *Guess Who's Coming to Dinner* when he first meets his white girlfriend's parents.

After ringing the doorbell, a second time, I heard the sound of footsteps from within and a man's voice saying, *"Je viens."* (I'm coming.) Suddenly, the door opened. Standing in the doorway was a man with salt-and-pepper hair beaming a smile as bright as the sun. As I introduced myself while extending a hand, I reminded him why we were there.

"Ah, bon. Bienvenu." (Welcome.) *"Je m'appelle George,"* he replied with a brisk handshake. Upon inviting us into his home, George called his wife. Approaching from the kitchen with a warm smile was an ample woman with her white hair tied in a bun. *"Je suis Margot,"* she said happily.

Experiencing George and Margot gladly accept us in their home was relieving. Instantly, my flashback to the 1967 Sydney Poitier movie was erased. Taking us to a small second-floor dormer room overlooking their backyard, George sought our approval.

"It's OK?" he probed with wide eyes. Tastefully furnished, the room was adorned with antique furniture, matching upholstered walls, and lamps. The room gave off a feeling of homestead comfort reminiscent of my childhood visits to Grandma's house in rural Skippers, Virginia. After a few minutes of acquainting ourselves with our surroundings, we pursued George for advice on what to see in the region.

Appearing as excited as we were, George invited us to join him in their lounge-like dining room. As we sat in large armchairs in front of the fireplace, George asked, in good English, about our interest in seeing the more notable sights of the region.

"What do you want to see first?" asked George, leaning in.

Blown away by the choices before us, we had no idea where to start.

"What do you suggest?" I asked.

"If you want feminine and romantic, I suggest the *Château Chenonceau*. If you want grandeur, see the Chambord. If you like gardens, you must see Villandry," George proposed with childlike glee. He appeared in his element while advising us and waited motionless for our decision.

"We'll start with the Chenonceau," I offered.

"Ma suggestion," he replied with a prophetic glow.

We visited the *Château Chenonceau* the next morning, with its sprawling gardens, corner towers, and bull's-eye dormer windows. The elegance of the Chenonceau was stunning. It lived up to George's hype. A gem of Renaissance architecture extending across the River Cher, the construction of the palatial edifice was marked by the personalities of aristocratic women, the last three being Catherine Briconnet, Diane de Poitier, and Catherine de

Medici, who had the greatest influence on the development of the structure and grounds. Notably, Catherine de Medici transformed the arched bridge spanning the river into an Italian-style art gallery.

Inside the castle, the grand rooms and airy bedroom chambers were decorated with paintings and tapestries that characterized the lavish living of the time. Outside, a parade of trees led to an expanse of symmetrical gardens. The beauty of the arched gallery over the river was reflected in the still water. The chapel, with vaulted ceilings and stained glass, destroyed in World War II, had been replaced in 1953, our guide mentioned. Perhaps the most amazing part of the *château* was the grand gallery over the river. With a gleaming black and white marble floor and rich wood beams spaced across the ceiling, the gallery's archway displayed incredible grandeur.

When we returned to the *maison d'hôtel* later, George was quick to open the door. He was out of breath, as though he had run to the door when seeing us pull into his driveway.

"How do you like Chenonceau?" he asked with his head tilted toward us.

"It was impressive," I responded, knowing I couldn't say anything less.

Listening with intense interest, George lit up when hearing my opinion.

"*Merveilleux*," (marvelous) he said as we shared our opinions.

Validating his superior advice appeared to give him a prideful feeling. Gratified, George ran into the kitchen to tell Margot about how much we liked the day. Moments later, Margot greeted us with a "*Bonsoir*" and cheek-bursting joy.

"George tells me you like Chenonceau," said Margot.

"It was magnificent!" I affirmed.

The next morning, we were awakened by the scent of croissants and brioche. Competing with the buttery aroma was the scent of brewing coffee so enticing it was impossible to stay in bed. Margot, upstaging euphoric George with her array of jams, explained the contents of each jar.

"Now this is *ma kiwi confiture* and that is *prune* (plum)," said Margot, pointing at the jars of jam. "I make them," she proudly continued. Following a breakfast of fruit, yogurt, and the warmed *patisseries*, we sat with George in front of the fireplace. We told George we wanted to see the *Château de*

Chambord and the Villandry, if there was time to see both, and he responded with a blissful, *"Un, bon choix"* (a good choice).

Unfolding a map of the Val de Loire as he had the day before, George launched into his run- down of the *Château de Chambord*, emphasizing its enormity. The largest of the Loire *chateaux,* Chambord has 440 rooms, 365 chimneys, and an enormous double helix staircase supposedly designed by Leonardo da Vinci.

"And the chimneys. The chimneys," Repeated a fired-up George.

Verbally walking us through the *château,* George reminded me, "Don't forget to take *beaucoup* photos. *Eh bien.* You park the car, stand in front of the water, and take picture."

Moving on to a discussion of the *Château de Villandry,* George soared when telling us about the gardens. *"Les fleurs, les couleurs,"* he declared. *"The edges, the edges,"* George crooned, alluding to the numerous rows of immaculately trimmed hedges.

"You take the picture. Enough!" he suggested while lecturing us.

Saturated in the knowledge of both *chateaux,* we set off to see them.

Said to be the Versailles of the sixteenth century, the Chambord is the most grandiose *château* in the Loire region. Among the most extraordinary structures in Europe, the Chambord, set in a royal forest, was everything George had stated. Driving on a heavily shaded roadway leading to the edifice, we spotted the *château*'s towers rising through the trees. Anticipating an unobstructed view of the castle, we eagerly awaited its unveiling. When the entire structure came into view, the sight of its grandness was jaw-dropping. "Unbelievable," I thought, while beholding its grandeur.

A colossal structure with a 420-foot façade, a multitude of rooms, and a chimney for each day of the year, the Chambord was beyond magnificent. Inside the *château,* the double-helix staircase thought to have been fashioned by Leonardo da Vinci was incredible. Seemingly a single staircase, people could ascend one spiral while another group descended the other without either of them meeting. Equally impressive were the roof terraces and numerous Italianate towers, turrets, cupolas, gables, and chimneys.

After absorbing the Chambord throughout the morning into early afternoon, we departed to the *Château de Villandry*. Said to be a green thumber's heaven on earth, Villandry was an immense estate displaying the finest example of Renaissance garden design in France. From the Villandry's cliff-side walkways, the garden terraces looked like flowered chess boards. Other notable features included an ornamental garden depicting symbols of chivalric love, the extensive *potager* (vegetable garden), vast carpets of colorful flowers, and the water garden.

Set among the arrangements of floral and ornamental vegetation was a maze of walking paths lined with meticulously trimmed box hedges. There were patchworks of coiffed shrubs and hedges of various sizes shaped into symbols of love, hearts, fans, and daggers. Oh, and "the edges, the edges," as George mentioned, lived up to his exaltation. Strolling the grounds with the *Château Villandry* in the background was spectacular, but the earlier visit to Chambord was a tough act to follow. With all due respect to the splendor of Villandry, it was, as George had described, "You take the picture, enough."

After touring both *chateaux* sites on the picture-perfect day, we departed to share our sightseeing with George and Margot. I was burning to get to his home as fast as possible. Turning into George's driveway, we noticed him in the backyard looking at something in the grass. Seeing us pull up to the house, he bolted to the front door.

"*Entrez vous*. How do you like the day?" George asked, opening the door.

"George, to put it in your words, it was *merveilleux*," I told him.

"Come, tell me about it," George said with eyes aglow.

Sitting with George in front of the fireplace, we told him about our astonishment when seeing the grandeur of Chambord and how awestruck we were when seeing and walking the sprawling gardens of Villandry.

"The chimneys, did you see them?" he asked with an ear turned to us.

"Yes. So many," I replied to a beaming George.

"The edges, the edges. Did you see them?" George inquired.

"Yes. There were lots of them, trimmed beautifully, just like you said," I told him.

"*Merveilleux*. Oh, Margot," George billowed, absorbing my comments.

Glowing like a torch, it seemed George was delighted.

The next morning, Margot again took center stage with additional fruit jams. Putting a basket of warm croissants and toasted baguettes in front of us, she introduced her melon and *poire* (pear) jams with a sweeping smile. Standing in the doorway of the kitchen, Margot peered intently as we spread her beloved *confitures* on the croissants.

"You like?" She asked, watching as we bit into the croissants.

"Margot, they're great," we answered. Suddenly Margot was aglow.

After a wonderful breakfast, we departed our hosts. Standing at the door, I thanked the delightful couple for their acceptance of us into their home and gave George a cap displaying the logo of the company I worked for. He stepped in front of a mirror in the hallway to try it on. George looked at himself with an admiring gaze.

"Oh Margot. It's so nice," he said, turning to his wife.

"*C'est tres beau, George,*" Margot responded with a fluffy smile.

"*Merci, merci beaucoup, monsieur,*" said George, shaking my hand vigorously.

"George and Margot," I said, turning to them, "we thank you for a wonderful stay. You were both marvelous."

"Will you be coming back next year?" George asked as we stood at his front door and said, "good byes!"

"I'm not sure," I responded to a suddenly saddened George.

As we drove away, I thought about the way I had felt when arriving at our host's home compared to my lofty feeling when leaving. Shortly after entering their house, my doubts about their acceptance evaporated. Showering us with hospitality and respect, both George and Margot sealed our enjoyment of the stay. As it turned out, the encounter was as beneficial to them as it was to us. George and Margot seemed as thrilled to advise us about the attractions in their region as we were to see them.

Because I was Black in the southern United States and grew up in an era when human rights and equality were the dreams of many, I'd envisioned our hosts' astonishment when they opened their front door. Instead, I was overwhelmed by their reception. Neither of them said the words "You are the masters" Maurice and Sabine echoed, but their hospitality said it for them. While staying with these people, we never had a feeling of being

African-American tourists. Rather, we were two people among many who came to the region to see the architectural treasures. Our hosts appeared genuinely appreciative of our stay with them, and our shared acceptance soared far above the differences of ethnicity and culture.

As incredibly hospitable as George and Margot had been, their warmth was repeated at other bed and breakfasts we booked. My more notable stays were with hosts in the *Bourgogne* (Burgundy) region, the Rhone Valley, and the *Cote d'Azur* (Riviera) region. Moved by the authenticity and hospitality of the hosts in the Loire Valley, the following year, we stayed with a family in the Burgundy region. Standing at the entrance of the home of our stay, I felt far more at ease than I had the prior year. When the door swung open, we were welcomed by bright-eyed proprietors, Francoise and her husband, Francois, who greeted us with hearty welcomes.

"Bienvenue chez nous," Francoise and Francois greeted us with lustrous eyes and warm smiles. Instantly, we felt like the masters. Throughout the two-day stay, they repeatedly demonstrated their acceptance by introducing us to their wine and truffle business and gleefully sharing advice about the region. We've continued to correspond for years.

Traveling south toward the *Cote d'Azur* (French Riviera) after leaving Francoise and Francois' place, we arrived in the town of Mougins, near Nice and Cannes. Not my original choice of places to stay in the region, a referral steered us to the home of our next hosts. Though the experience was reminiscent of being set up with an unforeseen date, our next hosts proved to be extraordinary people. After a protracted search for their secluded neighborhood, I eventually found them. From an intercom at the entrance gate of the community, we were greeted by the welcoming voice of woman speaking excellent French accented English.

"Come on in, kiddo," she greeted us as the gate to her community opened.

Entering the neighborhood, I continued to drive through a densely wooded section where the homes were barely visible from the street. Finding the driveway of the woman I had talked to, I parked in a courtyard in front of the house, took a deep breath, and strolled to the entrance to meet our hosts.

Having few qualms about pressing the doorbell, I waited for someone to respond. Before long, the door opened, revealing a diminutive couple of about sixty in the doorway. Smiling profusely, they greeted us with vigorous handshakes and words of welcome.

"Bienvenu mes amis," both bellowed, welcoming us as friends.

Jacqueline and André mentioned that the design of their home, a newer-appearing house, had been inspired by single-level homes they saw while visiting California. We felt accepted and comfortable with our hosts as they showed us the room they had reserved for us. Located in an isolated corner of the house, the room was surprisingly large and convenient to their patio and swimming pool. As we spent some time getting acquainted, they advised us about the attractions in the area. Getting an impassioned rundown from André about the museums in the city of Nice, it was clear where we were going the next day.

While Jacqueline and André explained the points of interest in Nice and Cannes (renowned for its international film festival) and other towns in the region, they appeared to be competing with each other to give us information. As Jacqueline spoke about the attractions she liked, André interrupted with a recommendation of his own. It appeared they were in a competition to show who had the superior know-how of the region. It was a cultural trait I had observed several times before this visit. Watching their verbal tug-of-war took me back to an encounter with young men two years earlier, when I was lost and trying to find my way back to the Paris, Charles de Gaulle Airport. The finger-wagging and "I know it all" remark by one of the men giving me directions still resonated. They were competing to be the more helpful.

The family feud of Jacqueline and André aside, over the next two days, we received a bevy of advice from both of them. From Nice, to Cannes, to Grasse (known for its perfume production) and the Gorges of Verdon, they covered the landscape. As we returned to the home of our hosts after the first day at the *Musées des Beaux-Arts* and *Art Moderne* in Nice, we were eager for their reactions to what we had seen. Both met us at the door before I pressed the doorbell, anxious to hear about our day.

"Well, *mes amis*, how do you like the museum?" asked André.

We told them about the exhibits at the museums and how much we enjoyed them, Jacqueline and André displaying radiant smiles.

"And the directions were good?" André asked.

"Perfect," I replied to an ecstatic André.

Basking in an aroma of croissants and coffee the next morning, we were greeted by our hosts in their dining room. Surprised by an unexpected item on my plate, I gazed curiously at Jacqueline.

"This is a surprise. The French eat these for breakfast?" I asked. Jacqueline responded that she had hard-boiled an egg just for me because she thought I would like it. Instantly, I felt the glow of a master. As our hosts stood in the doorway between the kitchen and dining room, we compared the cultural differences of our respective societies.

"What do you usually have for breakfast?" Jacqueline asked.

"Oh, it varies. Sometimes eggs, other times cereal," I replied.

"For us, it's normally a toasted baguette, fruit, or yogurt," said André.

Soon, our discussion shifted to children. Jacqueline and André revealed they had two working-age sons. We mentioned we had two daughters. Before we left the table, the sons arrived to check in on their parents. The older son, who I guessed was between thirty-five and forty, told us that in his younger years, he had dreamt of working in the aerospace industry. Telling him I had an association with Airbus drew his interest.

"Growing up, I wanted to work for Aerospatiale," he mentioned. (Aerospatiale was a French partner company of Airbus.) Through our conversation, we all learned a lot from each other. I was in a position of their son's dreams.

Listening to our lingering joy of visiting the museums our hosts had recommended appeared to stimulate their eagerness to advise us about other places to see. André became so engrossed in talking about the attractions in the region that he filled a cup with coffee and joined us while we ate.

"*Eh bien!* Where do you want to go today?" he asked with wide eyes.

Telling him we wanted to see Cannes and Grasse appeared to energize both of them. Soon Jacqueline joined us at the table.

"You visit *une usine de parfum* (perfume factory) in Grasse?" Jacqueline asked with a luminous smile while looking at Loretta.

"Yes, we went to one of the many perfume plants in Grasse and enjoyed it. We learned a lot from the visit," said Loretta.

Getting this feedback from Loretta, brightened Jacqueline's face.

When departing Jacqueline and André the next morning, it felt like we were leaving family. After a third visit to a *maison d'hôtel* in France, this mode of lodging became more appealing. The adventure of staying in the home of culturally different people appeared mutually beneficial and enjoyable to the hosts and us. Comparing cultural differences from an educational perspective and sharing sightseeing experiences with proprietors eager to validate their knowledge assisted in building relationships with the couples. Jacqueline and André stood out for far more than our conversations. They permitted us to enter their family. Their sons were full of advice and as accommodating as their parents. The following year, we honored our pledge upon leaving their home. We came back to stay with them again. But beyond ongoing Christmas cheer conveyed by greeting cards that continued for years, we never saw each other after that second visit. Nonetheless, memories of our friendship endure.

Reviewing the encounters with culturally different hosts, I concluded that the common thread of the relationships was a genuine, mutual acceptance—approval based on who we were as people rather than who we were expected to be (based on preconceived notions). We were fellow human beings worthy of respect and dignity. From my perspective, they showed it well. The hosts and ourselves overcame our cultural and social barriers with shared regard and mutual respect. What followed was trust founded on reciprocal propriety. Given the opportunity to be hosted them, they helped me realize that we are the masters of our relationships.

Our friendships with hosts of bed and breakfasts and others in the Toulouse region continued well past my departures from their dwellings and establishments. Viewing each other as equals created the foundations for promoting friendships where authenticity and sincerity were key. This opened the door to respectful dialogue that served to nurture our trust and promote the friendships to continue for years.

The lessons I learned from these associations propelled me into demanding workweeks and, as we'll see in the coming chapter, assisted me in building vital relationships in intense situations.

9

Air Fare

"I present myself to you in a form suitable to the relationship I wish to achieve." *Luigi Pirandello, Nobel Prize-winning dramatist, "The Pleasures of Honesty."*

I had rented cars at the Toulouse-Blagnac Airport for so long—five years—that picking one up became routine. Gone were the days of hearing, "This is not possible" when requesting to change a car. So, hearing a rental agent say, "*Monsieur*, I have a message for you," when I arrived at the rental counter in July 1999 added intrigue to the process. Upon receiving the message, I made an immediate call to our flight-line office to find out what they know. I was surprised to hear what Ian was telling me in a high-pitched voice.

"Dieter called this morning and said he had to talk to you right away. There was an aircraft problem," said Ian with a rapid cadence.

Exhausted after my trip across the Atlantic and dumbfounded about Dieter's urgency to speak with me, I called him from the rental desk. Dieter and Russell wasted no time getting to the point of their urgency.

"I need to see you right away," Dieter demanded.

"About what?" I asked.

"Korean Airlines are not happy with one of your engines and are saying they will not accept the aircraft," said Dieter. "Yah, you will come to our office now," he emphasized. Feeling drained and disappointed with the sudden command, I headed to Dieter's office.

When I arrived at his office twenty minutes later, he and Russell explained, "The on-site manager of the airline doesn't like the level of vibration seen on one of the engines on an aircraft presented to them for acceptance." When I spoke to Dylan on the phone before I left the States, he had hinted about a vibration concern that the airline raised to him. In fact, both engines were within the vibration limits in terms of amplitude (vibratory movement) and cockpit units (readings displayed in the cockpit), I mentioned.

"That's not good enough! Mr. Kim wants the limit changed," said Dieter, with an emphatic tone.

"Though the vibratory amplitude of the engine in question is slightly higher than its mating engine on the other wing, both engines were within the engineering specification when they were tested in the States," I explained.

Dieter shrugged off my justification.

"I have no authority to unilaterally change the limits," I reasoned.

Hearing my justification for not committing to change the limits, Dieter picked up the phone. He spoke with inaudible softness, sending my thoughts racing. "Is he calling Jacques?" I wondered. After listening to whomever he had called, he hung up the phone.

"We go upstairs now to talk about the aircraft," said Dieter with a sly smile.

Still puzzled about the vibration issue, I followed Dieter to the elevator. He escorted me a floor higher to an office where Jacques's boss was located.

"Go in. You're wanted inside," said Dieter, walking away.

Opening the door slowly, I walked into the office, receiving a genial smile from a towering man sitting at a desk. Seated on a beige love seat opposite him was an Asian man beaming a broad smile.

"Mr. Kim is not happy about an engine on an aircraft presented to him for acceptance," said the man behind the desk.

"The engine not acceptable to our limits," declared Mr. Kim.

Telling them I had heard about Mr. Kim's dissatisfaction earlier, I repeated what I had told Dieter. "The engine is acceptable to the same limits that all of our engines of this type are."

"Change the limit to our limit," Mr. Kim demanded.

Telling him I had no authority to change the limit but would review the issue with technical experts in our company had little effect on his position.

"Your vice president has to apologize to our vice president for being over our limit," commanded Mr. Kim.

"I will see that our vice president gets the message," I committed.

Hearing my pledge to inform someone of authority in our company about his concern drew a smile from Mr. Kim. Listening intently as I spoke, the man seated at the desk (the Senior Vice President of Industrial and Programs, I later discovered), nodded. Soon thereafter, we sealed my commitment with a handshake. Although I was corralled by the appeal of our airline customer and felt pressure from a senior level of the air-framer, I was glad I didn't over-commit when responding to Mr. Kim and the man seated at the desk. A flippant statement of appeasement may have made Mr. Kim happier and eased my discomfort, but it would have only been for the moment. The loss of our company's credibility and mine would have been more damaging.

When I walked into the flight-line office after meeting with Mr. Kim, the expressions on Dylan's and Ian's faces were telling. "Well, they didn't rip you apart," their eyes said.

"I didn't commit anything to Dieter and Russell, so they escalated the issue to their super-chief," I told them. "Not expecting an immediate change to the vibration limit, I couldn't commit anything to Mr. Kim," I continued.

Returning to the home office in the States a few days later, I discussed the matter with the vice president of the engine program. Telling Justin that the airline's on-site manager had requested an apology be given to his management with an explanation for the engine being over the airline's (internal) limit drew a wry smile from him.

"I have an upcoming trip to Korea and will discuss the situation and explain our position to the airline," said Justin.

"Thanks. I'd like to get back to Mr. Kim as quickly as possible," I replied.

When I discussed the vibration concern with the engineers responsible for setting the limits, I received a predictable response.

"We're happy with the current limits and stand behind them," they stated. Changing a limit at the request of an airline wasn't going to fly and could delay the deliveries of acceptable engines. It was apparent that Mr. Kim's request had no chance of being accepted. The existing limit was the same as applied to all engines of this type for all airline customers. Not long after meeting with the test engineers, I received a notification that Justin's trip to Korea had been canceled.

"Since the engine of concern is acceptable to our engineering limits, an apology to the airline management is not needed," Justin concluded. Truth be told, I wasn't surprised by his response. What I obtained from him that proved to be invaluable was a statement of his position with technical justification in writing. Armed with a high-level position letter and the technical backing needed to respond to Mr. Kim, I returned to Toulouse.

Having worked five years with the aircraft manufacturer and airline customers, I had learned that the most effective way of succeeding and satisfying both customers was to consider and perform the following:

1. Have a face-to-face meeting with the pursuers of technical requests.
2. Respond quickly to a customer's concerns to convey your sense of urgency.
3. Consider the underlying drivers of the concern and address the real issue.
4. Engage with in-house personnel to sensitize them to the customer's misgivings.
5. Last and most importantly, never commit to something you're uncertain of achieving. Rather, over-perform with a timely response.

Supported with the technical rationale to address Mr. Kim's true need, I arranged a meeting with him. Arriving at a building in Blagnac dedicated to on-site airline representatives, I received a gleeful greeting from Mr. Kim and two other men in his office. Acknowledging me with a bow of heads, the two men left the office immediately. With the two of us alone, I wasted no time responding to Mr. Kim's vibration concern.

"As promised, I met with our engineering group to discuss your concern about the engine vibration limits," I told him. Mr. Kim nodded approvingly.

"Our engineers have concluded that the vibration limits for the engine in question are acceptable and will not be revised," I continued.

"Can you get a letter that say that?" Mr. Kim asked.

Reaching into my briefcase, I pulled out a letter from the responsible engineering manager that stated his position. "Since our engineers agree with the current limits, there is no need for our vice president to apologize to your management," I declared.

Speechless with a slight smile, Mr. Kim listened politely to my justification for not changing the limits. Speaking well beyond the noon hour, I offered to take him and his departed colleagues to lunch. Joyfully, he accepted to join me alone. Choosing a small café near the airport, we arrived at the restaurant toward the end of the customary noon to two o'clock lunch period. Other than the two men dressed in business suits at an adjacent table, we had the place to ourselves. Restating our position about the limits to ensure Mr. Kim's understanding, I received a puzzled glance from him.

"You send letter to my vice president to explain the limits?" Mr. Kim asked with an anxious tone.

"I'll see that it's done right away," I returned.

Responding with a straight-up approach to Mr. Kim's concern and my agreement to provide his requested letter appeared to take a monstrous load off of him. Immediately, his stiffness loosened, and our conversation shifted from the engine in question to family and personal interests. Soon, a topic of mutual interest surfaced—our love of golf.

"You lucky, living in America. There are many golf courses," said Mr. Kim.

"I agree there are a lot of golf courses and people who play golf in America, but there aren't many in Korea?" I inquired.

"No, not many. Only for the privileged," uttered Mr Kim.

Apparently, golf courses in South Korea weren't readily accessible to the general public, I gathered from his disheartened reply.

"So, Mr. Kim, if I visit you in Korea and want to hit balls, where do we go?" I asked my fainter smiling lunch-mate.

"There are many driving ranges for people who can't get on golf courses. Many driving ranges are three levels because no space," said Mr. Kim.

As our discussion of golf continued, I sensed we were accepting of each other. We discovered a common passion that facilitated opening up to the other. While we talked, I offered a suggestion to promote our relationship.

"Do you mind if I westernize your name?" I asked my confounded-appearing lunch mate. "How about I call you Sonny, and you call me by my first name?" I proposed.

"Yes, OK, I like," Mr. Kim replied with a laugh.

The offer became an ice breaker and before long, we were engrossed in talking about our respective families.

"Do you have children?" Mr. Kim inquired with a more upbeat tone.

"I have two grown daughters. How about you?" I asked.

"I have daughter and son who finish university," Sonny stated.

Departing the emptied restaurant after finishing our discussion of kids, I drove Sonny back to his office. Upon dropping him off, I reconfirmed my commitment to provide the letter he had asked for. Driving to the flight-line office, I pondered Mr. Kim's initial position about the vibration limits and his reluctance to accept the aircraft. What was influencing his stubbornness? I wondered. Was there a higher authority driving his reluctance, or was there an internal limit established by the airline that he was protecting? Mr. Kim appeared far more relaxed when I committed to provide the letter. It seemed that his concern had been addressed. Considering the cultural influence on the position he had taken, it appeared that saving face with his superiors was driving his position. Appreciating now where Mr. Kim was coming from, I was happy to help him save face with his superiors.

When walking into the flight-line office, I was struck by the expressions of Ian and Dylan. I wasn't sure what they were expecting from my meeting with Mr. Kim, but the dread in their eyes was telling.

"Is he going to accept the aircraft?" Dylan asked hastily.

"He will when I give him what he wants. He wants a letter from our technical experts to his superiors that supports our limits," I replied.

"Hum, sounds like he's trying to cover his ass," Ian inferred.

Eager to get the ball rolling on the requested letter, I instantly called the program manager in the States. Summarizing the earlier meeting with Mr. Kim, I told the manager about Sonny's requested letter.

"OK, I'll ask them to write it," the program manager committed.

"Can they fax it to Seoul today?" I pushed.

Anxious to build a trusting relationship with Mr. Kim, my greatest concern was appearing reactive to his request for the letter.

"Will you let me know when the letter is sent?" I asked, ending the call.

I considered the six-hour time difference between France and the east coast of the States. It was mid-afternoon in western Europe, and I had little hope of receiving the letter before the end of my workday. Although the letter did not arrive the same day, I was elated the next morning when checking the fax machine. The letter sent to Mr. Kim's superior arrived overnight. Even more pleasing was the coordination that had taken place between our program manager and our marketing manager, which ensured that the technical explanation was directed to the appropriate people at the airline. Sharing the news of the requested letter with Mr. Kim, I mentioned the name of the person the letter had been sent to.

"I very thank you," he said, his delight resonating through the phone.

"How about a round of golf someday?" I probed.

"I would like, very much," he responded.

"I'll see if I can find something to play with," I told him.

With a few hours of sunlight remaining, two days later, Mr. Kim and I got together at a local golf course for a round of golf. Joining us from the departed Cary's office was Ken, a young, energetic replacement for Matthew. He borrowed golf clubs for me. Meeting Ken and I at the golf course, Mr. Kim arrived with a glowing smile. Appearing to have new clubs in his bag, Mr. Kim stepped onto the first tee, eager to get started. A beginner by his own admission, Mr. Kim studied every move I made, from removing a club from my golf bag to returning it after hitting the ball.

Repeating what he told me during our lunch, Mr. Kim reminded me about the luxury of being able to play on a golf course.

"When in Korea," he said, "most of my ball striking is at driving ranges, where golfers hit balls above and below me."

"I'm glad we are playing together on a real golf course," I replied.

Despite his limited golf course experience, Mr. Kim played with the intensity of a pro. Saying very little while we played, he approached each shot with deliberation. Showing extreme disappointment when he hit an errant shot, Mr. Kim would pound his club on the ground and continue playing in silence. He wasn't trying to beat Ken or me; it appeared he was solely focused on just hitting the ball. Perhaps this was the effect of playing on a real golf course, I considered. As we watched Mr. Kim hit a seldom seen airborne shot, Ken and I showered him with encouragement. Receiving the accolades transformed him into a proud golfer. Suddenly, Sonny was more talkative than he had been.

"Someday, we do this again?" he said with hopeful eyes.

"I certainly hope so," I replied.

Continuing the round to darkness, we ended after nine holes. Never mentioning the vibration issue during the round, Mr. Kim and I left the course with mutual satisfaction that the letter to his management in Seoul closed the issue, or so I thought. Providing justification for our vibration limits to Mr. Kim and his superiors served to maintain his esteem with his management back home. Essentially, we became partners in resolving his internal dilemma. Beyond the vibration limits issue raised by Mr. Kim, his culture influenced him. Considering the importance of culture on his initial position helped us to address the issue and satisfy him and others involved. It was a lesson that I continued to contemplate when working with other international airline customers. Identifying the cultural implications and acting on them was a key factor in establishing trust with Mr. Kim.

Within two months of the vibration issue, customer concerns shifted from an Asian to a European airline. Issues raised in an amusing manner by the on-site representative of an Austrian airline became the next challenge.

The operating practices of Dirk, the airline's on-site watchdog, appeared more focused on extracting recompense for his findings on the propulsion systems allocated to his aircraft. Quickly, his style of operating added another dimension to our customer service and the relationship we needed to establish with him. Dealing with his self-amusing personality became a greater challenge for me and my staff.

A likable man on the surface, Dirk's approach to working with the supplier of propulsion systems for his airline's aircraft and possibly the air-framer was to gain a psychological edge through timely innuendos and thought-provoking remarks. Call it digging or needling, it was a trait that he used effectively. While reviewing an engine or a nacelle component, Dirk showed an acute interest in identifying cosmetic issues and challenging them with vigor. Initially, I found his modus operandi difficult to understand. Was he covering his ass for a future finding that could be discovered after delivery of the aircraft, or was he looking for a concessionary agreement to put a feather in his cap before a delivery of a plane?

Despite his approach and the consternation, it caused to some members of my team, Dirk and I had an immediate liking for each other. Viewing his playful comments as harmless chatter, I found him authentic and worthy of pursuing a closer relationship. Upon approaching me about his observations of thrust reversers assigned to one of his airplanes, I listened to his concerns with keen interest. Though his issue was related to cosmetics rather than an operational problem, his finding was a visible feature that was created by an upgrade implemented on thrust reversers earlier in the program. The design modification had been added to prevent de-lamination of the carbon fiber skin. Though it appeared to be a pimple on the surface of thrust reversers, the feature had no impact on the integrity of the product, I advised Dirk.

Contrary to Mr. Kim's interest in getting technical justification for a condition he didn't like, providing a technical explanation to Dirk for a concern he raised seemed to fall on deaf ears. It appeared that he was totally focused on the appearance of his discoveries and the prospect of negotiating a settlement that would offset his perception of the blemish. Receiving requests for compensation for visual findings was new to me and something

I hadn't considered before working with him. It was analogous to buying a new car and seeing a blemish on the hood, I surmised. Nonetheless, I committed to pass Dirk's concerns on to our marketing manager to close the settlements with the airline.

Similar to Mr. Kim's dilemma, it appeared that the perception of his superiors was the stimulant for Dirk's focused observations and quests for compensation. Persistently seeking something for his findings, Dirk broke into a belly laugh the first time I informed him about our marketing department's decision for one of his discoveries.

"Your airline will be appropriately compensated," I advised him.

"Oh, thank you," he responded with booming laughter.

Similar to the Asian airline representative before him, Dirk and I established a mutually respectful relationship. Listening carefully to his concerns—regardless of agreeing—and responding quickly were key factors in building trust with him. After his initial fervor about the appearance of our thrust reversers subsided, I invited Dirk to have lunch with me and guys he knew that worked in our office.

"I'd be happy to have lunch with you," he responded with a cheek-to-cheek grin. I chose the Les Marroniers restaurant for our dining together, thinking the cozy atmosphere of the place and its accommodating proprietors would be a perfect backdrop and tone-setter for building a relationship with Dirk. Beyond the hospitality of Gilbert's establishment, Dirk and I needed an environment where we would feel comfortable opening up to each other. Neither of us had an interest in gaming or overpowering the other, I thought. Though I avoided asking his age, I sensed that Dirk was between sixty and seventy years old.

"Where in the States do you come from?" asked Dirk.

"I was born in Virginia and lived most of my life in Connecticut," I replied.

"I was born in a village in southern Austria and remember life on our farm during World War II," disclosed Dirk with a deep Germanic accent.

It was interesting to listen to Dirk's memories of life in war-torn Austria.

"We survived on apples from our orchard, bread, and bacon," said Dirk with wide eyes.

Dirk's reminiscence of his early years was fascinating to me, as I hadn't lived through such dire conditions in my life.

Additional lunches followed our ice-breaking dining experience. During each of them, I gained a greater appreciation of his subtle digs and humor.

"Not having a good day?" Dirk joked during lunch, referring to a problem we were having with an engine on another airline's aircraft.

"Rest assured, Dirk, we're fixing it," I replied to his comedic expression. Before long, I began to catch on to his self-amusing comments about issues he had with our propulsion systems. "He's setting us up for another request for compensation," I'd contemplate when listening to a joking remark. Despite his style of operating, I found nothing repugnant or even irritating about Dirk's approach to supplier relations.

"I like working with you," said Dirk when sitting next to me on a flight from Toulouse to Amsterdam, when he was going home to Vienna Austria and I was returning home to the States.

"I like working with you too, Dirk. It's always an amusing challenge," I replied to a laughing Dirk. We accepted each other for the people we were and before long developed a trusting relationship.

Although Dirk and Mr. Kim performed their duties in different ways, in the end, they were both seeking the same thing—the best propulsion systems for their money. Where they appeared to differ was their approach after raising a concern. One demanded compensation for a finding, while the other sought to change a standard to satisfy his superiors.

Engrossed in Dirk's subtle comedy and unique approach to raising issues, I failed to notice Mr. Kim's quiet departure from Toulouse. Ushering in a new set of demands, his replacement, Mr. Lee, presented an even greater challenge. With the change of on-site management, the concerns about engine vibration shifted to cosmetics. Was he wrong to raise the visual concerns? Were we wrong to provide a product in a state that stimulated his concern? The answer to the first question was a resounding no, I concluded. Considering the second question, the answer was maybe. It was something that required further insight into what was driving Mr. Lee. I would have to figure out his motivation to obtain a mutual understanding with him.

The last thing I wanted to do was to mislead Mr. Lee into thinking that we had a quick fix for his concerns. Weighing the myriad of things that could go wrong with an aircraft's propulsion systems, issues related to the cosmetic appearance of visible parts do not garner the most immediate attention of a supplier, in my opinion. Raising concerns about a propulsion system with a buff or polish mark on a casing of an engine could lead some in the manufacturing of the unit to view the finding as nitpicking. On the other hand, considering buffing or polishing had been done to remove a blemish incurred during the assembly of an engine could lead an airline customer to believe that something had damaged the product. It's a perception one should expect from a discriminating customer seeking a product that meets their visual expectations.

Meeting with Mr. Lee for the first time, we discussed the buff marks and reasons for the blending he was questioning. Upon my explanation, he handed me a document defining the airline's production policy for the aircraft engines and nacelle components delivered to them. The three-page policy covered visual items that they deemed unacceptable upon inspection of engines and nacelles. Reading the policy, the first time, I could easily have viewed it as an ass-covering document for the on-site representatives of the airline. At first, I struggled to resist viewing their guidelines that way. Rather than present a protracted defense for the items he raised, it seemed obvious that my best approach would be to establish a cooperative relationship or partnership with Mr. Lee and our in-house business units.

I conveyed Mr. Lee's policy to our folks in the States, sharing the concerns with part producers and engine assemblers who handled the units on a day-to-day basis. When suggesting eliminating the need to blend minor handling damage incurred during manufacturing, I received many rebuttals.

"Are you kidding me?" some respondents cried when hearing my requests.

"No. I'm not joking!" I'd respond to their perplexed faces.

Suggesting a change to something ingrained in the culture is the impossible dream, I lamented. Mentioning the aircraft manufacturer's displeasure with delays to their airplane deliveries gave me some leverage to get the attention of people. The concerns of the airline soon drifted across the Atlantic to higher levels in our company. Before long, the senior management of our company became roused and, in some cases, enraged by the customer dissatisfaction. As the industrial liaison between our company, the air-framer, and the airline representatives in Toulouse, the burden of the issue fell squarely on me. I became sandwiched between three inpatient forces (our upper management, Airbus, and the airline).

Raising awareness of the issue to in-house departments had a profound impact on improving the handling practices and provisioning of protective covers added at points in the machining and assembly processes where the risk of damage was greater. Soon, the improvements appeared to eliminate the need for subsequent corrective blending and polishing of visible findings. Ding marks and scratches occurring during manufacturing and assembly operations were no longer present at first. After implementing additional protective covers and improved handling procedures, a minor finding would occasionally be discovered. Rather than rejecting a costly part deep in the manufacturing process, the need to blend small imperfections surfaced.

My developing relationship with Mr. Lee resulted in establishing a mutually agreed solution for each engine delivery without scrapping functionally acceptable parts. For massive parts like titanium fan inlet cases, the costs associated with scrapping and replacing such behemoths plus the ripple effect of delivery delays due to lost time would have been costly to our company, the air-framer, and the airline.

Meeting face-to-face with Mr. Lee upon my return to Toulouse, I shared my concerns about scrapping good parts and delaying deliveries. Quickly, we acknowledged that neither of us had been given our jobs to delay aircraft deliveries. As I chatted with him in a less strained setting, Mr. Lee, with his wide eyes and soft-spoken demeanor, exuded a willingness to collaborate. Instantly, the foundation of a working partnership was established. It became apparent upon briefing him about my in-house efforts that he was feeling as confident as I was about working on a solution together. We needed each other to overcome this issue, we agreed.

Absorbed in a discussion extending beyond noon, I invited Mr. Lee to join me for lunch. I suggested a café not far from his office. We walked into a dining room filled with businessmen. The atmosphere of hushed voices was like being in a library. Taken to our table by a seemingly turgid escort, we were seated in a sunny corner of the room. Soon a waiter arrived.

"Messieurs. Vous desirez?" he asked, poised to take our orders.

Since neither Mr. Lee nor I spoke much French, we couldn't understand the discrete French being spoken around us. Advancing from reciprocal smiles, the conversation between us became about our family and personal interests. We discovered that we both had daughters and a mutual interest in golf. After spending some time conversing about our lives and pastimes, we got around to my primary reason for our dining together. Clarifying his concerns about the cosmetic appearance of our engines, Mr. Lee made a case for his uneasiness.

"Fixing handling damage on external parts of engines is a big problem," said Mr. Lee. Listening to him, it seemed that his real concern was the extent of the damage prior to a blend repair and how it would affect the airline's future repair capability. In other words, Mr. Lee's real issue was how close the correction had come to the maximum allowable repair limit. We agreed that it was a legitimate concern. If I was buying a new car, I would want to know about any existing damage. In an instant, I found myself standing squarely in his shoes.

As we lingered in the restaurant after the adjacent tables had cleared, our conversation shifted from Mr. Lee's policy to expectations for developing a joint plan to address the requirements of the airline. For starters, I committed to return to the States and sit down again with our production management, machinist, and assemblers to stress the importance of better handling of internal and external engine parts. In addition, I committed to pushing for more protective covers for parts that were more prone to damage during manufacturing and assembly. When a risk assessment identified a greater risk of damage, a protective cover would become a requirement.

Beyond the awareness and additional preventative practices, if minor damage was discovered and a blend fix was feasible, I would notify Mr. Lee in advance of shipping the engine. Upon alerting Mr. Lee, I would provide a photo of the blended area showing the dimensions of the repair.

Though it appeared cumbersome on the surface, what our agreed plan lacked in pre-ship timeliness it gained in building trust. Unsurprisingly, our agreement resulted in fewer delays after the engines were received in Toulouse. Inspections and ongoing deliberations between on-site airline personnel and our people in the podding facility were no longer necessary.

After applying this agreement for a few weeks, our mutual trust developed to a level where we were sending e-mails to each other in our versions of French. Neither of us could speak the language well, but we felt safe trying the French we were learning with each other. The more important achievement of our relationship was that we entered a zone where trust overshadowed the fear of being admonished for not saying the words correctly. We were totally accepting of one another and agreed to play a round of golf together.

Mr. Lee and I met to play a round of golf on my next trip to Toulouse, inviting a fellow countryman to join us on a warm afternoon. Completing the foursome was a young Frenchman who was paired with us. Beaming an extensive smile and speaking with pride about a Korean golfer who had recently won on the U.S. P.G.A. Tour, Mr. Lee mentioned that K.J. Choi had won a golf tournament in America. Striding to the first tee with an even broader smile, Mr. Lee's joy reminded me of how I felt when Tiger Woods won his first Masters Tournament. Mr. Lee struck the ball with a lashing blow, and it hardly left the ground. Though the ball didn't go far, Mr. Lee appeared delighted to be hitting a ball on a real golf course.

Following a protracted completion of the first hole, we strolled the fairways with light conversation. Being a college professor in Seoul, Mr. Young asked me, "Where do you go to school?"

"I got a degree from Rensselaer Polytechnic Institute," I told them.

"Ah, that good school," said Mr. Young.

"How long have you been a university professor?" I asked Mr. Young.

"Oh, maybe twenty years," he replied with a proud smile.

As we played, I noticed Mr. Lee and his friend, Mr. Young, becoming more focused on striking their balls. It was similar to what I had seen while playing with Mr. Kim. I wasn't sure if they were trying to outplay or impress me and the Frenchman playing with us, but their focus and desire for perfection did impress me. We carried on a conversation about their lives in Korea versus mine in the United States, speaking leisurely among the three of us to the completion of the round.

"Do you like Korean food?" both men asked.

"I've never eaten Korean food, but I'd like to try it," I answered.

"Well, we must eat some," Mr. Lee declared with a cheek-busting grin.

"OK, I'm game," I replied.

Back in the States two weeks later, I received a phone call from one of our guys in the podding facility. Speaking in sporadic statements, Geoff, who had been transferred from the flight line as a change of scenery and peace-keeping move, mentioned he had conducted a tour of our product line earlier in the day, accompanied by a senior-level manager from our company. Continuing to speak with nervous hesitation, he mentioned, "The visiting manager appeared appalled when hearing that Mr. Lee had not been satisfied with the cosmetic appearance of certain parts on our engines." Seemingly startled by the unexpected visit of a senior manager at a level well above his, Geoff rambled through his briefing of the questions that the visitor, who was accompanied by an occupant from the office of Cary's replacement, had asked him, including "Who do you work for?" and "Who is responsible for this process?"

When answering the query, Geoff had mentioned my name. Hearing his disclosure, the visitor hastily departed the building. Feeling a bit vulnerable and uncertain of the repercussions of his information, it appeared that Geoff had called to give me a heads up about what could impact me.

Shortly after speaking with Geoff, my boss and his boss received calls from the visitor demanding that changes be made. I was uncertain of the meaning of the visitor's request that "changes be made," and I continued to meet with our in-house managers and their people to convey Mr. Lee's concerns, emphasizing the importance of sustaining the improvements they had made to the product.

Regardless of the discussions at higher levels about the changes needed to eliminate the concerns of our customer, about a week and a half later,

I received a more encouraging call from Toulouse. It was Emile, Geoff's office mate, who called to spread the word about the results of an inspection of propulsion systems for an aircraft that he and Mr. Lee's inspector had reviewed that morning. Speaking about the results of their review, Emile was ecstatic and eager to share his joy with me.

"I am glad to tell you we inspect the two engines and nacelles and find no marks on anything," said a joyous Emile.

"Great news!" I proudly replied. I'd been wondering prior to the call if I was on the brink of being removed from a position I had cherished for years, and the results reported by Emile were lifesaving. You don't fire yourself out of problems, you fix them, was my takeaway.

Feeling uplifted by the recent update, my next order of business was to share the success. Since the in-house manufacturing and assembly business units had put a lot of effort into improving the visual appearance of our delivered engines, they were at the top of my list to inform. Not far behind them were my counterparts at Airbus, who were brutally persistent when an airline was unhappy. Finally, I sent an e-mail and followed up with a phone call to Mr. Lee to share the news of the recent deliveries. He'd heard about the results from his inspector before I had called and sounded happy to share his mirth with me.

Like a shot heard around the world, the results of the inspections of the recent propulsion systems traveled through the senior management offices in our company and at the air-framer. Collectively, their feedback and acknowledgment of the effort put into improving the manufacturing processing were comforting to hear.

As we examined our efforts to overcome the worries of the airline, we found what appeared to be three key contributors to the success. First and foremost, though we worked for different organizations and business units, we collectively embraced the common cause of satisfying our customers. Had I tried to convince Mr. Lee that blending surface indications was OK because it had no operational impact on the engine, I would have set a cornerstone for a disastrous relationship. Being accountable for the appearance of the delivered product and its future repair capability, Mr. Lee and I would have been tugging against each other.

The second key to our success was establishing relationships on both sides of the Atlantic founded on a mutual understanding of the predicament we were in with the airline customer. It opened the door to a shared sense of cooperation and ownership. Considerable improvements resulted from the collaborative efforts of in-house departments. Within a few weeks, engines were consistently arriving at the podding facility without blend marks or indications of prior handling damage.

The third and perhaps most meaningful piece of feedback from our efforts was provided by the management of the air-framer. In the business of producing and selling aircraft to airlines around the world, the airframer's attention can easily be drawn by complaints from a dissatisfied airline. Not long after hearing about the successful inspections of our propulsion systems, my Airbus counterparts responded with congratulatory comments. Soon, Mr. Lee followed with a letter praising our in-house efforts. Gratified that our customers were happy with the progress we had made, I shared their evaluations of the latest deliveries with the departments that had contributed to the success. The positive feedback from the air-framer and airline was instrumental in motivating the employees of engine parts and nacelle component producers to remain focused on sustaining the success. Suddenly, hands-on machinists and assemblers became more careful when handling their respective units. Accolades coming directly from customers made workers feel better about their contributions to the improved appearance of their delivered product. At the grassroots level, there was nothing more encouraging than knowing that the end-item users were satisfied with what they were receiving.

Although I invited Mr. Lee to come to our engine assembly facility in the States to see the implemented improvements, he declined and asked a local representative of their airline to visit us and see them. At Mr. Lee's request, Mr. Park toured our in-house departments where the improvements had been made. Although Mr. Park raised questions about the condition of some parts he had seen at the overhaul facility he was covering, he seemed content with our recent improvements shown to him. Toward the end of the tour, Mr. Park took the opportunity to resurrect the airline's concern about the engine vibration limits. I wondered if it was a second attempt to test our willingness to modify the limits. But eventually, Mr. Park acquiesced to the existing limits that had been acknowledged by Mr. Kim earlier.

I spoke to Mr. Lee a day after Mr. Park's visit. He seemed delighted with the briefing he had received from his colleague.

"Mr. Park happy with what he see," I was told. The satisfaction transmitted by Mr. Lee and the positive impression expressed by Mr. Park fueled greater enthusiasm for satisfying our customers. Undoubtedly, his recognition of our efforts augmented the vigilance of the machinists on the shop floor and the mechanics who assembled and tested our engines. Before long, extreme care in handling the product permeated the shop-floor culture. Receiving praise from celebrated and discriminating customers like Airbus and the airlines made the accomplishment even sweeter.

From a culturally distant customer-supplier relationship, a cross-cultural partnership was established. Stimulated by a willingness to listen open-mindedly to the real concerns of the customer, we were able to develop a solution that became a win-win for all parties. We were so pleased with the outcome of the improvements that Mr. Lee and I conveyed our regards in French, our mutual comfort and trust high. More importantly, I obtained a better understanding of Mr. Lee's culture and its influence on him.

Mr. Lee is thousands of miles from his superiors and fellow workers in Seoul. When a new aircraft arrives there and is reviewed by the receiving team, the appearance of the air frame and propulsion systems rests squarely on his shoulders. He was totally accountable for any visual issues discovered during the receive-in inspection. The more I got to know him, the more I could see that it was human nature driving his heightened scrutiny of our engines and nacelle components. The airline's production policy appeared to be his insurance policy for avoiding the consequences of the inspection findings at the airline's home base. Suspicions of prior damage would have come back to bite him, I had thought when standing in his shoes.

As I look back on my relationships with Mr. Lee, Mr. Kim, and Dirk, I observe a common trait—a cautious nature stemming from being at the end of the aircraft delivery stream. Accepting a condition that could be detected and challenged after delivery of an aircraft could be embarrassing to them. Amplified by the culture of the airline and the nation in which it is based, these factors had a profound influence on the oversight of all three men when reviewing and accepting an aircraft and its components. As a passenger on many flights, I appreciated their additional scrutiny.

Understanding the true motivators of the persistence of these men saved me countless hours of explaining or attempting to justify issues they couldn't readily accept. What they were really seeking was something to cover themselves for a future finding—something like written justification from someone of authority who explained and accepted the identified condition. A formal apology, tangible compensation, or, ideally, a commitment to corrective or preventative action for what they had found. Call it face-saving, or better yet, a demonstration to their superiors that they were working hard to do their jobs and satisfy them.

Working with *Messieurs* Lee, Kim, and Dirk became more enjoyable and fulfilling when I embraced their concerns and collaborated with them to develop mutually beneficial solutions. The results of the partnerships resolved the problems at hand and prevented disapprovals from our respective superiors. The experience I gained from working with these three men to resolve their aircraft acceptance issues was invaluable to me and instrumental in developing our trusting relationships.

Honesty and consistency are vital to building trusting relationships that produce mutually acclaimed results. More importantly, the way one presents oneself to others and how others perceive them ultimately determines the success of a relationship. The lessons I learned through these experiences would be further tested in the coming days.

Sam and Mr. Kim after their round of golf.

10

The Image

"If you open Pandora's box, you never know what Trojan horses will jump out."

Ernest Bevins.

Early one February morning in 2000, I received an alarming phone call at the hotel in Toulouse. Awakened from a deep sleep, I peered warily at the clock on the dresser, showing that it was 1:00 a.m. When I picked up the receiver, I thought it must be someone calling from the States. Rather, it was Ian on the phone, providing an update for an engine that had been removed from an aircraft to investigate a significant problem.

"We found what was causing the problem," said the excited Ian.

"OK. What did you find?" I asked.

"You won't believe what we found," he answered in a shrill tone.

As he described what the mechanics had removed from the engine, my reaction was, "Wow, tell me I'm dreaming."

Bidding Ian goodbye, I called the States immediately to tell our engine assembly management about what was discovered. My drowsy voice explaining what Ian told me created a stir on the other end of the phone. Going back and forth with the department manager, I committed to confirm the finding in the morning. Intrigued by Ian's revelation, I couldn't sleep. Lying in bed with my eyes wide open, I recalled the hours leading up to Ian's startling discovery.

I had arrived in Toulouse yesterday, the end of February, for what I thought was a routine visit. I met with Dylan and Ian soon after landing. While talking, they mentioned a predelivery issue on an A300 (large passenger) aircraft. During an acceptance flight of the aircraft, the cockpit gauges displayed a problem with an engine installed on the aircraft. The engine was consuming more oil than the engine installed on the other wing. Refilling the oil tank between flights revealed the same condition during the next acceptance flight.

Following the usual course of action for an oil consumption problem, the main oil strainer was removed from the engine for review. Upon inspecting the filter, threads of a reddish fibril material were discovered on the screens. Instantly, the finding raised concerns about the origin of the fibers and how far they had migrated through the engine's oil system.

Considering the urgent need to launch an investigation, Dylan and I called the States seeking advice from our Engineering Department. Isolating the problem to a bearing compartment near the front of the engine, the technical experts recommended pulling the low-pressure compressor (front rotating section) from the engine to gain access to the suspect compartment. Receiving a detailed technical recommendation from the in house experts, Dylan and I were bewildered.

"Bloody hell! This is a big job," said Dylan, scratching his head.

Discussing the complexity of the recommended task, we concluded that performing the fix on-wing of this multi-million-dollar aircraft was an undesirable option. The risk of damaging the engine and aircraft was high. Adding to our worries were the frequent calls from the air-framer's management seeking an immediate solution. Undoubtedly, their persistence was elevated by the airline's delivery team, who were on-site to accept and deliver the aircraft to their headquarters in Japan. Time was money for them and the air-framer.

Since there was no replacement engine on-site, nor tolerance for sending the engine back to the States for investigation and correcting, it was decided to remove the engine from the wing and tow it to a hanger to fix it. During the removal and transport of the engine, other issues surfaced. The specialized tooling to remove and support the low-pressure compressor after pulling it from the engine was not available in Toulouse. More importantly, there were no experienced hands on-site to perform the task. In lieu of having the tooling readily available, mechanics or returning the engine to the States, a more-timely solution was needed. As we deliberated about overcoming the predicament, Dylan and I chose to pursue a certified maintenance facility in Europe. An inter-Europe fix, with time saved from reduced travel, would serve to restore the engine quicker.

Starting with the nearest facility, we called Swiss Air for help. When we heard that the tooling we needed to perform the work was occupied in their shop, we reached out to another maintenance facility. A call to Lufthansa Technik in Hamburg, Germany, resulted in everything we had hoped for. Jubilant after hearing the response of the person on the other end of the phone, I listened intently to their terms of the agreement.

"We have the tooling and mechanics available to do the work for you," said the voice. What made the response more appealing was their commitment to gather a team of mechanics and an inspector after receiving a signed work agreement. I was eager to get the job started and can't remember ever being happier to sign any agreement. Before hanging up the phone, Dylan and I could hear the contract coming through the fax machine for our review.

It was a leap of faith to arrange assistance for such critical work with a person sight unseen, but the sincerity conveyed by the person we were speaking to and his willingness to support our urgent need created trust. Clearly, the man on the other end of the phone understood the severity of our situation, I sensed.

While the mechanics and inspector were traveling from Germany, the engine arrived at the hanger where the work would be conducted. A few hours later, the mechanics showed up, anxious to get started. Wasting little time, they unpacked and laid out the tooling like an operating room team. During the set-up of the work area, they conferred among themselves about performing the disassembly. Observing their diligence and professionalism made me confident of the outcome. Positioning the large fixture needed to support the engine's low-pressure compressor, they began removing the retaining hardware from the engine. While they continued the disassembly, I departed to the hotel. After having traveled to Toulouse that very day and encountering this mystery not long after arriving, I was physically spent. Ian remained with the German crew to witness the disassembly.

The next morning, I arrived at the hanger where the engine had been taken apart and noticed something in Dylan's hand. It didn't appear to be an engine part. I was mystified by the object. Greeting me with a wry smile, Dylan revealed the thing Ian had called about. Looking at the roughly twelve-by-eight-inch, half-inch thick object, I was confused about what I was seeing. The opaque, silver object had traces of what looked like red tape around its perimeter. We surmised that it was a connection to the discovery of red fiber seen on the screens of the engine's oil filter. Though it was unimaginable that the object had been the culprit, before long, the object's identity became apparent. It was a piece of equipment (seemingly a mirror) used by mechanics during the assembly of the front end of the engine. It appeared that the apparatus was used to facilitate assembly in an area of the engine that wasn't openly visible to a mechanic, otherwise known as a blind assembly. Standing in front of the partially disassembled engine, Dylan and I peered at the object and shook our heads. Prior to our arrival, Ian and the mechanics had departed for some well-deserved sleep.

Shortly after viewing the object, I called the air-framer to advise them of our deduction. Creating an anticipated ripple effect, the airline's delivery team was soon notified. Within minutes of ending my call to the air-framer, two representatives of the airline strolled into the hanger. Smiling cordially at Dylan and myself, the men looked around the shop and walked over to the engine. I was uncertain of how they would react when we showed them the finding, and my heart was pounding.

"We found what was causing the problem on your aircraft," I said with a hard swallow, anticipating their reaction. I took the airline representatives to a workbench to reveal the object. They approached the disfigured, rectangular implement with squinting eyes.

"Ah-ha," they observed, shaking their heads. They gazed at me, appearing to sense my embarrassment.

"I'm so sorry to show you this," was all I could muster at the time.

After hearing my commitment to share our recovery plan with them and the air-framer, within two hours, the representatives of the airline left, shaking their heads on their way out. Immediately, my team and I began putting a plan together to restore the engine. Within an hour, the air-framer's personnel at the aircraft delivery center were pushing us to resolve the problem.

In a meeting a few hours later with representatives of the airline and managers at the air-framer's aircraft delivery center, I presented what the mechanics had exposed the night before and our plan to recover the engine to an as-new condition. I struggled to control my emotions during this first session with our airline and air frame customers. It was the most difficult sixty minutes of my career. The doleful audience around the conference table seemed to recognize my discomfort. They listened without venting frustration about the situation. It was a moment of mutual acknowledgment—it was what it was. While we investigated the root cause of the problem and restored the engine concurrently, we committed to providing progress reports to the airline and air-framer at the beginning and end of each day of this ordeal.

When hearing about the object discovered in the engine, our engine assembly department became feverishly engaged in correcting the problem. Bringing the Quality and Engineering Departments together, they went about investigating the root cause. Within a day, they sent representatives of both departments to Toulouse to review the object and support the recovery of the removed engine. Upon arriving, the in-house representatives presented their understanding of the cause of the problem and how best to correct and prevent it from reoccurring. During the update sessions, the air-framer and airline attendees appeared satisfied with the attention shown by our company by sending the experts to Toulouse. Appearing comfortable with what they heard, the airline reps smiled and nodded through the explanations.

Considering that the airline was a Japanese customer, cultural differences soon surfaced during the meetings. Beyond the challenge of restoring the engine, there was a feeling expressed by the airline delivery people that their superiors would think they failed if the aircraft wasn't delivered quickly. During our initial sessions, the airline representatives conveyed an urgent need to add this aircraft to their fleet. Overshadowing the meeting was a fear by the airline reps of being viewed unfavorably by the folks back home.

Expressing a greater need to satisfy the management of the airline during the second day of meetings, the delivery team raised a concern about accepting delivery of the restored engine.

"This engine has bad history! We want another engine," declared an impeccably dressed man sitting opposite of me.

"There is no available engine in Toulouse or at our plant in the States," I replied to the solemn-looking reps. Telling them we would fix and restore the engine to an as-new condition drew an expected retort.

"We don't want the engine," repeated the team's spokesman.

Diving deeper into a discussion of the backup engine dilemma, I explained the reasons why another engine wasn't available. Though they weren't happy with the current situation, I explained the state of producing the engine type for their model of aircraft.

"The engines produced and delivered to your aircraft were the final engines of this model," I mentioned to the stoic reps. At this time, there was a gap in the production of similar engines. The next engines of the model family were scheduled to be a different configuration and were several months away from production. The next versions of the same engine model were designed for freighters. Presenting my best account of our production situation had no influence on the airline reps.

"We don't want the engine," said the man sitting across from me while the others of of the team looked upon him admirably.

"The only thing I can offer is the engine restored to new condition," I said. Peering at his colleagues, the spokesman made a big request.

"You must write an apology to our company about the engine and your findings," he proposed softly. He appeared to be requesting a face-saving document for the airline's delivery team, and I agreed to his plea.

"We want a letter of apology to us, also," he continued.

Agreeing to provide the requested letter to the management of the airline was absolutely the right thing to do, but considering the pressure we were facing, I committed to writing the second letter myself. Like how I had felt when working through dilemmas with Mr. Kim and Mr. Lee, I found myself standing in the shoes of another airline customer. With a better understanding of their cultural need, I accepted their request for the letter. Before closing the meeting for a second day, the topic of compensation was raised. Though it was far beyond my authority to decide how an airline would be made whole after a problem, I committed to pursuing the question with higher authorities in our company. Immediately after the meeting, Abe, who had replaced Cary, and I pursued the high-level letter and the compensation suggested by the airline's delivery team.

While composing a letter of apology to the airline's delivery team, I included an explanation of the remedial action we were taking to restore the engine. I gave it to them, and the team appeared to be delighted with the documented solution. It was something tangible to show their efforts to get the aircraft delivered, I surmised. After finishing our appeal to management in the States, Chris walked into Abe's office to alert him and me about a call she had received from the airline's delivery team. We phoned them right away and were told that the head of the delivery team wanted a separate meeting to discuss their requested compensation, and he wanted it now.

We met in an office at the air-framer's delivery center. Abe and I were joined by two men from the airline's delivery team. Before us was the airline's inspection manager and the dapperly dressed spokesman of the delivery team who attended our daily meetings. Displaying a lawyerly façade, the spokesman opened our discussion with an anticipated demand.

"We want compensation. We want new engine!" the man said.

"There is no engine available at this time," I replied.

"We want lease engine," he commanded sharply.

Having reviewed the availability of a replacement engine before the meeting, I reminded them that there were none available. Turning to his colleague momentarily with a shrug of a shoulder and a few words in Japanese, the spokesman continued to pursue compensation.

"We want more compensation," he said, leaning forward in his chair.

With the restoration of the engine proceeding as planned and no replacement available to offer, Abe looked at me and turned to the spokesman.

"What did you have in mind?" Abe asked cautiously.

Pausing for a moment, the spokesman stated a financial amount. Stunned by his muttered seven-figure demand, Abe and I peered at each other.

"He wants that?" we whispered. Neither of us had the authority to commit to the lofty appeal and told the men so. After about half an hour, we closed the meeting by committing to convey their demand to a higher authority in our company. After providing momentary relief to a delivery team feeling the heat from their superiors, we shook hands and walked away.

In Abe's office the next morning, I was greeted by a blissful Abe.

"We got the letter," said Abe, waving it with joy. What a relief, I thought.

Overnight, a letter of apology had been written by a senior vice president in our company and sent to an executive at the airline. In addition to the apology, there was a commitment to compensate the airline for the incident. Elated about the timely response and contrition conveyed by the offer, I drove to the flight-line office to write a personal letter of apology to the airline's delivery team. Though the monetary compensation requested by the delivery team's spokesman had not been accommodated, they received a satisfactory alternative in the end, I had thought.

At the daily update meeting a few hours later, we presented the delivery team's letters to them. Nodding approvingly, the spokesman of the group raised additional concerns about the engine being fixed.

"We want another engine," he said, scanning his teammates at the table.

"There is no other engine—new or in the lease pool," I reminded them.

Instantly, the conversation moved to the delivery of the aircraft. They stated that their superiors wanted the aircraft as soon as possible. It seemed their priority had shifted to the urgent needs of their bosses. Implying they had to comply with the wishes of their superiors, they became accepting of having the engine restored to a new condition, with a full warranty.

"It's a new engine and fully covered," I reminded them. After agreeing to a re-installation of the engine, the airline reps became more focused on the progress of the engine being restored.

While the daily meetings with the airline reps and delivery management of the air-framer continued through the weekend, the Lufthansa Technik mechanics removed and disassembled the front of the engine, cleaned internal passages, and flushed the bearing compartments. The team reassembled the engine by the end of Monday, restoring it to an as-new condition. Working with unimaginable professionalism, the mechanics performed the task with the precision of surgeons. I was particularly impressed with their constant checking and double-checking of each step of the task. Getting confirmation from fellow mechanics after completing each sequence of the recovery was reassuring from my airline passenger's perspective. They lived up to the billing conveyed by their manager when we agreed to their services.

From my standpoint, there was an immediate connection with the German mechanics. We were mindful of the urgency of our mission and shared a mutually accepting relationship. Before turning their wrenches, I felt their trustworthiness. There was something about their respectful introduction and the way they presented themselves during our initial greeting that made me comfortable with them. After we corrected and restored the engine on short notice over a three-day period, it was returned to the aircraft for re-installation. Before long, the engine and aircraft were readied for an on-wing test and acceptance flight.

After going up with the aircraft on its acceptance flight, the airline's delivery team returned with glowing smiles. With the oil consumption problem corrected and confirmed by the flight crew, the airline reps accepted the aircraft. Eager to see the reaction of the delivery team upon their return with the aircraft, I waited for their arrival at the delivery center. Standing near the stairway after the plane had taxied to a halt, I was greeted by each member of the delivery team exiting the aircraft. Showing broad smiles as they descended the stairs, they shook my hand briskly when seeing me. The lead rep and compensation negotiator personally thanked me for the help in getting the aircraft recovered. It was gratifying for our team and me to have the delivery team accept the engine and aircraft. It was a tremendous relief for the airline's delivery team, the air-framer, the German mechanics, and our on-site team in Toulouse. That day has stayed with me since then.

As I waited in the airport the next morning for my flight from Toulouse to Paris, I noticed the aircraft with the fixed engine taxiing near the terminal. At this time, in early March 2000, I was going back and forth from the States to Toulouse three to four times a year. Peering through the window as the plane rolled by, I waved at the onboard delivery team, who likely couldn't recognize me. As it continued to the runway, I watched the airplane take off and disappear over the horizon. Seeing it fly away into revenue service was an incredibly satisfying feeling.

I transferred in Paris for my flight to the States and was seated next to a woman who told me that she was traveling from Istanbul, Turkey. She was the first person I knowingly had met from Turkey. While we talked during the flight, she revealed her affinity for swimming and skiing. Neither of them were sports of my interest, nor what I expected her to say. Nonetheless, her enthusiasm for both sports was convincing. Though she showed no hints of her religion through the clothes she wore, she talked about her Muslim faith. But I was still thinking about the aircraft that was flying into service, her religious beliefs weren't on my mind.

After enduring the hectic ordeal over the weekend, the conversation served as a reset to a more normal life. Culturally, I found the conversation with the woman beneficial in understanding how someone from a very different place lives and enjoys their life. When we arrived in New York hours later, our goodbyes were brief. At that time, any thought of ever seeing her again was far from my mind.

Within a week after briefing our company's management about the recovery of the engine, I found myself back at New York's J.F.K. Airport for a flight to France. Before leaving the States, a meeting had been arranged with the air-framer's management to discuss the engine incident and the action we had taken to prevent a reoccurrence. The meeting had also been viewed as an opportunity to mend our relationship with the air-framer. Prior to boarding the flight to Paris, my eyes were drawn to a person who appeared to be the woman seated next to me on my prior flight to the States. I walked over to where she was sitting and greeted her. As she raised her head, her eyes widened when seeing me.

"Where are you seated?" I asked.

Checking her boarding pass, she stated the row and seat number. Scanning mine, I was astonished to see that we were seated next to each other again.

"You're joking," she replied with a gleeful gaze upon hearing my seat.

"It's true," I nodded.

"Unbelievable," she said.

It was the first time I had traveled on round-trip flights seated next to the same stranger from a prior flight.

Delayed by an early March snow-squall, we boarded our flight to Paris three hours after its scheduled departure. We chatted about education, religion, and our cultural differences, talking ourselves to sleep, only to be awakened by the wheels of the aircraft pounding the runway in Paris. It was revealed before deplaning that we had missed our transfer flights— my flight to Toulouse and her flight to Turkey. Before long, our flights were rescheduled, taking us separate ways. Although we never saw each other again, the memory of our encounter and the cultural enlightenment imparted by her made a lasting impact. Regardless of our racial and cultural differences, our conversation was free-flowing and uninhibited by preconceived notions. Absent of tell-tale restraints or patronizing, the discussion paved the way to bridging our cultural differences. For me, it was an educational experience.

I departed Paris an hour after her flight and arrived in Toulouse absorbed in thoughts of the forthcoming close-out meeting with management of the air-framer. A post-mortem of the engine incident had been scheduled to review the cause and actions taken by our company. Expected to attend the meeting were our new vice presidents of the Operations and Quality Departments. For the air-framer's management team, it was expected that Jacques, Maurice and someone from the Procurement Department would attend the meeting. Considering the visibility of the incident and the uncertainty of Jacques's reaction to its occurrence, the intensity prior to the meeting was electrifying. Our team would shower Jacques with a ton of apologies, I anticipated.

Picking up our senior managers at the Toulouse Airport, I escorted them directly to the room where the meeting was to be held. Walking into the conference room together, Jacques and Maurice appeared to be in good spirits. Displaying a friendly smile, Jacques bounded over to us, greeting each attendee of our delegation with a vigorous handshake. After an affable clasp from Maurice, the meeting began. Jacques kicked off the review.

"Allor messieurs, what do you tell us about the engine problem on 797?" Jacques asked, referring to the A300 aircraft affected by the problem. Scanning our team of managers, Jacques folded his arms and awaited a reply. Presentations of actions taken began with Bob, the new Head of the Operations Department in our company, who provided a bountiful mea culpa to Jacques and the air frame management in the room. Listening with astute interest, Jacques and Maurice repeatedly nodded during the confessional of our management.

The presentations proceeded in a low-key manner, progressing from the root cause of the engine problem to the actions taken by our company. The steps we had taken to restore our relationship with the airline were also presented. Sharing this information seemed to please Jacques and other attendees of the air-framer.

All appeared to be going well until a presenter strayed to a restructuring plan associated with transitioning engine parts produced in-house to the supply base and vice-versa. Included in the presentation was a plan for managing the resourcing of parts and the benefits to product quality and delivery performance. Indisputably, the benefits were substantial and impressive. While presenting the Overview of Suppliers segment of his pitch, the presenter inadvertently stated, "We are working closely with our foreign partners and suppliers to implement this plan." As he proceeded to discuss the role of our international partners and suppliers in assuring success, he continually referred to them as "our foreign partners and suppliers."

After hearing the statement repeatedly, Jacques exploded. His jaw protruded, and his face became flaming red. It appeared that the presenter was using the word as a contextual reference to our international suppliers and partner companies, but Jacques didn't see it that way. His reaction was well beyond the emotional blips that I had witnessed in prior meetings. It seemed that it was the way the word was said and the frequency with which it was said that got under his skin. Livid, Jacques verbally flogged the manager with emphasis on the word "foreign." Around the room, every meeting attendee dropped their head.

Sitting next to me with a distressed smile and a clenched fist, the manager who had made the volatile utterances listened. He turned to me briefly, and I put my hand over his hand and shook my head. No. Let Jacques go, I said to myself. As quickly as the front blew into the meeting, it departed, leaving a suddenly calmer Jacques. It seemed that Jacques was offended by the way the manager had said the word "foreign." He had seen it as a barrier between the speaker and our international vendors and partners, I thought. He also may have sensed a distancing attitude by the speaker toward suppliers of other countries—an "us versus those people" mindset.

At this time, I, too, was sensitive to the word "foreign." It seemed a bit much. It raised thoughts about the way people of color feel when someone says, "You people," or "Those people," referring to people not like them. It appeared that Jacques, with his intuitive nature, may have sensed an attitudinal wall between us and our international suppliers. Perhaps another contributor to Jacques's agitation was his interpretation of the apology preceding the comment. Was the speaker attempting to downplay the incident? Whatever Jacques ingested; it surely fueled his rage.

Designed to improve the management and control of parts and processes in the supply base, the initiative, created by our company, was embraced by key overseas suppliers and partners. During the sharing of this information, the presenter mentioned the word "foreign" several times. The intent of stating this initiative was to convey the action our company was taking to improve our management of and relationships with the suppliers. However, at this time, the information wasn't relevant to the engine incident. The timing and setting of the announcement had clearly missed its mark. Considering Jacques's reaction, it appeared that mixing discussions of the corrective and preventative action for an engine problem and unrelated supply chain improvements was a *faux pas*.

Later, when discussing the disclosure of the supply chain initiative with attendees of the air-framer, the frowns on their faces conveyed their thoughts of the timing of the revelation. If there was one lesson I learned from this meeting, it was that when presenting a close-out of a crisis, stick to the topic. Explain how the incident happened, what was done to correct the problem, and how it would be prevented in the future. In other words, focus on the reason for the meeting. Sharing how a solution will be executed provides great value to a customer.

One of the things that stood out when I first arrived in Toulouse was the multitude of restaurants in the region and the diverse cuisines they offered. In the center of the city, there was an eatery on every street corner and backstreet alley. For assistance in finding more noted dining establishments, there were countless books. The renowned Michelin Guide and Hubert's *Tous les Plaisirs de la Table* listed and rated *bonne tables* in each region of the country. Normally, locals didn't use such high-end references when seeking a local place to eat, I noticed. With a bounty of good restaurants within close proximity, who needs a book? Undoubtedly, word of mouth prevailed. Just enter one of the many fine restaurants in the city, enjoy the meal, and be amazed at the modest bill when finished.

On the evening of the engine meeting, I chose an active restaurant near the center of Toulouse to have dinner with managers of our company who attended the meeting. It wasn't posh or fancy, but its red meat menu was well received by everyone. It's hard to go wrong with any restaurant in Toulouse's center, I'd discovered after dining here for six years. However, presenting one's thoughts about the tenor of a meeting while having dinner with managers at levels higher than your boss could be risky, I thought before opening my mouth. Nonetheless, I opened up and shared my feelings with the managers at the table.

"Who was that (expletive) nut at the meeting?" asked one manager, referring to Jacques, I gathered.

"Oh, he was just the customer. I think the nut was more interested in the solution to the engine problem rather than our foreign suppliers and partners," I replied. "Saying 'international' rather than 'foreign' suppliers may have prevented Jacques's eruption," I told them. While I shared my opinion, the others at the table nodded wryly.

"It was Ben's idea to present the new initiative," said one manager. Ben was the boss of the senior manager who had felt the wrath of Jacques after making his foreign comment in the meeting. Throughout dinner, we continued to discuss the value of presenting the new initiative. As we debated the merit of bringing up the initiative during the meeting, our discussion petered to an unagreeable halt. Leaving the restaurant, I sensed my opinion and interpretation of what I thought had ignited Jacques had not sunk in with the others. For me, the engine crisis and close-out meeting provided lessons about sensitivity to cultural perspectives and a great opportunity to build relationships with the airline and air-framer.

Looking back at the episode, I had valuable takeaways from the crisis, beginning with a fundamental premise I learned from extremely discerning customers: customer trust begins with communicating a vision of how you are going to help them, rather than peddling excuses for the findings. Since alibies are often transparent to customers, they do not want to hear them. Secondly, you don't have to be the loudest voice in the room to make a difference. Being the best listener and reactor to the needs of those affected is far more useful to a customer impacted by a crisis. It's best to listen with an open mind to a customer issue and be prepared to spring into action.

One thing that struck me about the maintenance team's finding was that when a significant issue arises out of the blue, there is a crossroad of exposure of the finding and full disclosure to those affected by what had been found. In this case, the air-framer and airline customer were the victims of the finding. As a result, an irate representative of the air-framer paid a hasty visit to our flight-line office upon hearing about the problem. Feeling the temperature rise when Bernard walked into the office, we became engulfed in sonorous venting. Hey, what else could one do at a moment like that but hear him out and commit to quickly fix the problem? Regardless of the flack we knew would come under these circumstances, our swift disclosure of the finding established credibility and trust with both the air-framer and airline. From a front-line perspective, waiting another day or even a few more hours to create a more politically correct revelation may have impeded our ability to be trusted by both customers.

During the process of contracting the maintenance crew, I was amazed at how quickly trust was established with the management of Lufthansa Technik AG. When we called the repair facility for help, they didn't know us, nor did we know them. However, after explaining our need, a common understanding and sense of urgency led to a partnership. There was no panic or pitch to convince the voice on the other end of the phone about the immediacy of our request. We just stated what we knew about the problem and our desire to resolve it quickly. They grasped our predicament and responded instantly with mechanics and the required tooling. You couldn't ask for better reactivity. With mutual trust between distant parties, sending the signed contract to the maintenance manager was a no-brainer.

Recognizing the urgency of our predicament and eager to begin the work upon arriving in Toulouse, the mechanics exhibited regimental workmanship while positioning their tools around the engine. Every tool and person had its exact place. Even more impressive was the confidence exhibited by the mechanics while performing the critical disassembly and reassembly outside of their normal shop environment. Delving into the bowels (internal oil systems) of a sophisticated jet engine and reassembling it over a weekend was an astounding achievement by the mechanics.

Adverse situations have a way of revealing fortitude and building character, spurring some to greatness while sending others to despair. Under extreme circumstances, adversity becomes the glue that bonds groups of people. Case in point, the American and Allied cohesion during both World Wars. Such was the case with the engine incident. As the mechanics went about removing the fan and low-pressure compressor (the front section of the engine, where the air is drawn in and compressed) and went further into adjacent compartments to identify the source of the problem, the intensity of the situation produced camaraderie of mutual acceptance and respect. In the end, a trusting relationship developed. Everyone involved in recovering the engine played a role in creating the congenial environment.

Throughout the daily update meetings, no one vented or said disparaging words about our company or anyone participating in the recovery. Standing twice daily before the representatives of the airline and air-framer, I was inspired and motivated to speak truthfully about the problem without feeling dread of being the target of finger-pointing, cynicism, or criticism. Sure, the airline asked for another engine, but why not ask? At that time, providing a replacement engine would have been the shortest route to getting the aircraft delivered, but let's face it, adversity doesn't work that way.

Once the airline's delivery team accepted that there was no replacement engine available and trusted our efforts to fix the engine to a new condition, their focus shifted to the timeliness of the recovery and their standing with superiors in Japan. Receiving multiple apologies and compensation for the ordeal seemed to elevate their esteem with superiors. If the team had chosen to vent frustration rather than seeing the incident for what it was, the air-framer would have weighed in. In retrospect, disparagement by the airline would have impeded our focus on recovering the engine and diverted the attention we showed them to help them save face. Focusing on a win-win solution rather than surviving to the next briefing was my objective.

Comparing the less voluble yet attentive airline delivery team with the emotions of Jacques at the close-out review revealed an interesting contrast of styles and demeanors in a crisis. While neither of them liked the situation they were in, they displayed their despair in vastly different ways. The airline representatives appeared to focus on the engine recovery and progress being made to accomplish it. Getting the aircraft accepted and delivered in the shortest amount of time was their primary objective for image and face-saving. Undoubtedly, they provided daily updates to colleagues awaiting the delivery of the aircraft.

On the other hand, there was Jacques, whose intent was seizing the attention of the key people in his presence and using a tinge of posturing to convey his message. Jacques's reaction to the repeated emphasis on the word "foreign" at the close-out meeting was his way of telling the speaker that they had departed from the relevant discussion. Perhaps introducing the initiative was an attempt to mask the problem, he may have thought. In the end, the approaches of Jacques and the airline's delivery team were equally effective. Jacques garnered the attention of our senior manager when he erupted. Within our company, there was a greater top-down emphasis on ensuring that the problem had been corrected and would not resurface.

It's said that overcoming adversity shapes the character of a person as well as distinguishes a group. Surely, this moment shaped me and my perspective of working with an intercultural team. It's further alleged that your most painful experiences present the greatest opportunities for growth. We all grew through this experience. Through intense moments and when encountering the unexpected, one gains a more acute perspective of their surroundings and a better understanding of themselves. Under excruciating pressure, one may feel alone at times, as I had. But in those moments, one must remain focused on the task at hand and persevere to closure. Beyond the on-site air frame and airline personnel, it seemed that the eyes of the industry were on us. Seeing me on the flight line in the midst of our recovery, Dirk, from the Austrian airline had a comment.

"Not such a good a day yesterday," he mentioned with a chuckle after the object was found and identified. Bad news travels at warp speed, Dirk revealed. But regardless of his untimely humor, I still liked him. The image of our company was on the line, we imagined. From the president of our company down, we needed confidence in our efforts. During the ordeal, we received reassurance from many of them. Conveying that "The problem is under control and is in good hands" without saying it helped our cause. Collectively, those involved on-site had concluded that the things we had in common (fixing the engine quickly and delivering the aircraft soon thereafter) were more important than making excuses and pointing fingers at folks in-house. Taking that route would have increased the divide between us and delayed delivery of the aircraft.

Considering the incredible effort put forth to correct the problem and project a benevolent image to our customers, perhaps an old English proverb describes the collective effort best: *"A good name keeps its luster in the dark."*

Below the eagle on our company's logo that we affix to every delivered engine, the team of on-site and in-house company folks added a motto of "Cohesive and Dependable Support" to this aircraft.

Though I didn't have an opportunity to talk to Maurice at the close-out review, the magnitude of the problem and Jacques's dominance at the meeting overshadowed everything on that day. However, it was great to see my friend fit and appearing well. I looked forward to a time when we would get together to chat about our lives and families.

11

The Flame Outs

"Sickness often comes on horseback and departs on foot."
A Dutch axiom.

Though there was little opportunity to speak with Maurice at the engine recovery meeting, three months later, we found some time to talk. We chatted in his office during my next trip to Toulouse. Despite having less hair on his head, Maurice was his usual jovial self. We spent more time together in January 2001, at a post-holiday reception in Toulouse. I was happy to see him in greater spirits. When returning to the hotel that night, the glow on Maurice's face was vivid.

Surprised by a phone call the next evening, Maurice called the hotel to invite me to his home.

"Would you like to come to a Russian New Year's party?" he asked.

Pondering this far-fetched notion, I considered his seriousness.

"Sabine will be disappointed and won't take no," pleaded Maurice.

"OK. I'm coming," I replied.

When arriving at Maurice's home the next evening, I was showered with greetings from him and Sabine. Unbeknownst to me, their observance of the Russian New Year coincided with the celebration of Three Kings Day. The holiday commemorated the arrival of the three wise men (Balthazar, Caspar, and Melchior), bearing gifts for newborn Jesus and marked the end of the Christmas season. Traditionally observed on January 6th, Three Kings Day is widely celebrated in France and other Christian nations. However, Maurice and Sabine chose to celebrate both events a week later than usual. Being the first person to arrive at the party, I was soon followed by a couple who were close friends of my hosts. Before long, a man living across the street appeared at the door. Considering the closeness of the invitees to Maurice and Sabine, I felt grateful to have been included.

Although French, as expected, was predominantly spoken during the evening, I was able to grasp some words being said. My inability to speak the language was obvious to all who attended, but using the little I had learned over six years, I tried to participate in the conversation. To include me in the discussion, everyone went out of their way to speak English and paused when speaking French to translate what they were saying. I was struck by their social intelligence and inclusion throughout the party. As the evening continued, the couple, Albert and Claire, appeared fascinated with my presence. A scholarly man with a gray beard and a seasoned woman with a mane of silver-dark hair, the couple displayed wondrous eyes and inclusive smiles whenever I spoke.

Regardless of my lack of knowledge of French politics, through the evening, politics consumed much of the discussion. With the recent election of George W. Bush to the presidency of the United States and his inauguration a week away, I soon became the center of attention. Despite having nothing to say for or against Mr. Bush, it was then that I realized how politically inclined the French are. Apparently, they were following the U.S. presidential election. While Maurice and his guests showed interest in the American leadership, they strayed into a discussion of the French right-wing National Front advocate, Jean-Marie Le-Pen. Early in my enlightenment of the opinions of Mr. Le Pen, the focus suddenly shifted back to me.

I was inundated with questions about myself that, I surmised, were driven by curiosity. I was asked customary queries like, "Where in the States are you from?" and "How long will you be in France?" by Albert, Claire, and the inquisitive neighbor, Laurent. Seemingly more curious than the others, Laurent asked questions repeatedly. He and the other two guests were amazed upon hearing that I had lived in the region for fourteen months when beginning my assignment.

Albert was astounded that someone with such a meager ability to speak the language could become so acquainted with the region. Seizing on the language deficiency, Laurent asked with his head skewed, "How do you get along so well without being able to speak the language?" The question stimulated deep thought about what I believed was the key to developing relationships where language barriers exist.

"Acceptance is not exclusive to language skills or cultural ties, but rather is conveyed and received by the projection of one's inner self," I responded. As I met locals in the region, I found that showing a willingness to adapt and connect with them by listening to their stories of the past and present projected a desire to be seen as a traveler rather than a tourist who is just there to view the attractions.

Having exhausted our conversation about my presence in the region, Maurice called us to his dining room. On the table were shot-sized glasses filled with vodka. Proclaiming a brief toast, Maurice raised his glass. Promptly we clinked our glasses with the words, *"A votre santé"* (to your health). The party had begun.

While continuing our discussion of politics in France and America, a fragrance of stewing vegetables came from the kitchen. Coupled with the recent vodka, my appetite was fully awakened. As we waited for the food to be brought to the table, the discussion of Le Pen, the fiery leader of the National Front Party in France since its founding in 1972, resurfaced. The mere mention of him aroused everyone. Maurice paused from the heated debate to tell me about their upcoming election in April when Jacques Chirac would seek another term as the president of France. Expressing controversial views shared by many of his followers, Le Pen appeared to affect the opinions of everyone at the table. Focused on topics related to immigration, abandoning the European Union, maintaining the traditional French culture, and reducing high unemployment, Le Pen was widely discussed and extremely polarizing. I'd read a news article about him on my flight from the states, but I hadn't realized the emotions he stirred among the people of France.

With Sabine's arrival at the table, the political chatter subsided. Beaming a broad smile, Sabine announced what she had prepared for dinner.

"This is a traditional Russian meal," she said, ladling the steaming, creamy borscht (beet and potato soup) into the bowls before us. Completing the meal was a colossal, domed crusted bread, dense and chewy. It was my first-time eating borscht soup, and regardless of the vodka before the meal, the taste lived up to its aroma. With more eating than talking, we proceeded through the meal without a word of politics. When the dining ended and the table was cleared, vodka was again brought to the table.

Considered the youngest person at the table by a consensus of opinion, I was asked to sit under the table until a cake was brought in. This was a tradition of the Three Kings Day observance, I was told. As Sabine walked toward the table, I was asked to return to my seat. Sabine sliced the pound cake into thick portions and distributed them among us. Plunging my fork into the slice I was given, I struck something hard. Instantly, everyone's eyes were on me. Removing the object with my fork, I discovered a minuscule figurine of baby Jesus.

"Oh, you got it! Do you know what this means?" Sabine asked.

Truth be told, I had no idea what my finding meant.

"You are the king," said Sabine, putting a gold paper crown on my head.

Puzzled about the game we were playing and the process by which the players were selected, I was told that Claire, the wife of Albert, had been selected to be my queen. Claire was a charming, sophisticated, full-figured woman. I gladly accepted her as my queen. By tradition, the king is expected to kiss the queen. Following some mock amorous gestures, we touched cheeks. With everyone clapping, Claire blushed and began laughing.

When the game ended, the conversation returned to politics and the differing opinions of Le Pen's sociopolitical ideology. Having drained the debate about Le Pen, before long the focus returned to me. Everyone seemed concerned about my perception of the game we had played, the experience of celebrating the Russian New Year, and my impression of the region. Their pride in the region and desire to hear an outsider's opinion was apparent.

"It's a wonderful region!" I affirmed to the attentive listeners.

While sharing my impression of the region, inquiries turned again to my limited ability to speak the language.

"How were you able to get by without speaking French?" they asked.

Plain and simple, I told them, "I was able to get along because my working relationships were with people who could speak English. Working with the highly complex components that make up a commercial aircraft, we communicated in a common language (English). For the sake of our companies and customers, we have to clearly understand each other. When I encountered people who didn't speak English, we resorted to unspoken ways of communicating," I continued. Being alert to another person's body language can make a difference in relationships. Words matter, but the way others carry themselves can tell you a lot about their feelings. It's said that "The mouth of a wise man is guided by his heart." Undeterred by concerns of ethnicity and social standing, using a few words of the other's language and gesturing, we were able to share our feelings and understand each other.

Relationships with people like Marc, the owner of Vecchio Pizzeria, blossomed into friendship from scant beginnings. While I shared my thoughts about adapting to the region, a sea of moony eyes looked upon me. Leaning forward with a glint in his eyes, Maurice appeared to accept my reasoning, while Laurent, shaking his head, seemed not fully on board.

As curiosity about me ground to a halt, the party ended. I enjoyed the cultural exposure and the opportunity to participate in a different celebration. The evening was unforgettable and one that I carry with me to this day. As I walked to my car in the chilled January air, I thought about the game we had played and the coincidental, or perhaps not so coincidental, selection of me as the king. Maybe I was picked to allow me to obtain the full experience of the game, I considered. Nonetheless, I appreciated the interest in exposing me to their culture. Thoughts of such events sparked my motivation and propelled me through adverse times.

As the winter of 2001 departed, rumors of Maurice's ill health became more frequent. By the fall, speculation about his declining health was rampant. Because I received the news from far away and didn't hear about his condition from him or his family, I refused to believe what some people were saying. To their credit, Maurice's family kept the state of his health to themselves. Whatever was known was sparingly released. I understood the family's interest in protecting a private matter, but it also told me that the situation was serious. I heard that before long, the people he worked with were seeing less of him. Yet throughout the ordeal, Maurice's family protected his privacy.

While on a business trip to Toulouse in the early spring of 2002, I called Maurice's family to inquire about his health. Someone who worked closely with him mentioned that it may be a brain ailment. Hoping to hear he was improving, Sabine permitted me to see him at their home. I entered Maurice's house unsure about what was awaiting me. At the door, Sabine was her usual bubbly self, greeting me with a radiant smile and a vibrant, "Well, *bonjour.* He has been waiting for you."

I followed her to a small room on the first floor of their home. Sabine continued into the room to announce my arrival.

"He's excited you are here," she said, stepping out of the room.

Maurice was sitting erect in the bed with a broad smile and broke into laughter when he saw me. Hairless and appearing physically diminished, Maurice's eyes were glowing. Upon hearing his laughter, Sabine joined us.

"He's so happy to see you," said a cheerful Sabine. Holding Maurice's hand and putting an arm around Sabine's shoulders, I felt like another member of their family. Soon, their teenage son came into the room.

"This is the happiest he's been in weeks," said a joyful Sabine.

Maurice's face was lit up like a Christmas tree. Contented with his momentary well-being, Sabine and their son left Maurice and me alone. Maurice spoke faintly, and I put my ear closer to his mouth to hear him. I understood that it was up to me to carry the conversation, and I talked about anything that popped into my head—my family, and the latest issues at work. "Whatever it takes to keep him engaged," I thought while talking. Smiling incessantly through my non-stop blather, Maurice shook my hand and closed his eyes. After telling Maurice, "I love you," I left the room and sat with his son in their living room.

Sitting on the sofa with his head on his chest, Maurice's son was sullen. I talked to him about how I had felt when my dad was ill and fighting for his life, mentioning how hopeful I had been that my dad would miraculously recover and that I was expecting Maurice to get better, too. It was the best I could come up with to ease our pain. Understandably not in a talkative mood, Maurice's son peered at me with a sorrowful smile. I felt gloomy when leaving Maurice's home. It seemed that it would be the last time we'd talk or see each other again.

As I waded through dozens of e-mails six weeks later, I noticed a message from Sabine. I opened it immediately. Her April 15, 2002 message conveyed the dreaded yet inevitable news.

"Your dear friend died just after midnight. He is now at peace," she wrote. Deeply saddened by the e-mail, I replied, "I feel fortunate to have spent some time with him in his final days. Thanks so much for giving me the opportunity!" The news of Maurice's passing was the saddest day I had since my dad passed away twenty years earlier. Since Maurice's funeral had taken place while I was away on vacation, I was unable to attend. In my mind, our friendship exemplified mutual acceptance and demonstrated how cross-cultural barriers of language, ethnicity, and societal status can be bridged by those who are willing to disregard the differences between them.

On future trips to Toulouse, I made a point to call Sabine when I was in town. Maurice would have liked that, I imagined. If she was up to seeing me, I would visit her, and we would gab about her knowledge of Africa. As a friend, I felt obligated to check on his family when in France.

Despite the loss of a working partner and a personal friend, issues continued to surface at work. With the A318 and A380 aircraft programs on the horizon, there was no shortage of things to plan for. The A318 aircraft, the smallest member of the popular A320 aircraft family, required a totally new engine and nacelle. It was a smaller turbofan engine than the engines we were delivering to Airbus, and so it was determined that the engines would be assembled and shipped to the Airbus assembly facility near Hamburg, Germany. A plan had to be put together to get the engines assembled and shipped to a podding facility for integrating with the nacelle prior to installation on the aircraft. The situation presented an additional coordination and logistics chore.

The A380 aircraft program, developed concurrently with the A318 aircraft, presented a much greater challenge. A four-engine, double-decker airplane with a seating capacity of 500 to 600 passengers, it would be the largest commercial aircraft in the world. Five years earlier, while having a beer with a young Airbus engineer, we discussed the prospects of launching the A3XX program. At that time, I scoffed at the size of the massive plane.

"A double-deck aircraft? It's not possible," I teased my drinking companion. Speaking to the euphoric engineer about his involvement in the program, I went out of my way to not appear negative about my thoughts. Little did I realize that in a few years, the A380 would literally be spreading its massive wings and traversing continents.

Among the largest commercial jet engines ever produced, the size of the A380 engines presented many issues. Because they had been developed and produced by an alliance of two rival jet engine makers (General Electric and Pratt and Whitney), the program required extreme coordination. Organizationally, a producing company was formed and appropriately named "The Engine Alliance." Once the collaboration was established, details of the divisions of work between the two partner companies had to be settled for engine development, part producing, and the location for final assembly and testing of the engines. Behind the scenes, battles between the competing partner companies undoubtedly took place, but from my perspective, the joint venture of decades-old adversaries appeared to come together well. One important decision of the divisions of work was whether all the engines would be assembled and tested at our Middletown, Connecticut facility.

Despite my joy about where the engines would be assembled, there were many issues associated with the enormity of them. The fact that the engines were too large to ship intact created a need for additional coordination. With a fan inlet diameter greater than the width of the doorways of most freighter aircraft, the engines had to be split at the front fan sections and shipped to a certified assembly facility, like the Aerostructures Division of the former Goodrich-Europe, located near the air-framer. At that plant, the fan sections would be reassembled to their respective engines and delivered to a podding facility. For this engine model, it was decided that the integration of engines and nacelles would be performed by Aircelle, a joint venture of Airbus S. E. and the Safran Group. With the planning and point of delivery of these colossal engines settled, the next challenge was establishing relationships with our counterparts at General Electric and the managers of the newly formed Engine Alliance.

As issues mounted on the planning and introductions of the new engines and propulsion system programs, there was no shortage of other worries. One day in June of 2002, I was visited by Jacques and two other managers from the air-framer. They had come to the States for Industrial and Quality meetings with our organization in Middletown and the International Aero Engines (I.A.E.) organization in East Hartford. Although both meetings with the engine producers were scheduled for the following day, Jacques, Bernard (a quality manager), and Jean-Francois (an industrial manager) arrived at my office a day earlier than our planned industrial meeting.

As I met the three men in the main lobby of our Middletown plant and escorted them to my office near the engine assembly floor, our cordial greetings quickly became an onslaught of questions from Jacques.

"So, you've fixed the oil problem on the A300 engines?" asked Jacques with a penetrating gaze.

"Yes Jacques, we fixed the problem long ago and reported it to you. I'd be happy to take you to the assembly floor and show you the fix," I offered.

"No, that's not necessary, I trust you." Jacques responded.

"Are you having problems with I.A.E. engines? Tell me, tell me, or I will break everything in this office, starting with your computer!" demanded Jacques, pointing a finger at the computer on my desk.

"Whoa, where did this come from?" I thought while looking at Bernard and Jean-Francois. The suddenness was like being whacked in the head.

"OK Jacques, here it is," I replied, handing the computer monitor to him.

Placing the monitor back on the computer, Jacques laughed like I had never seen him laugh before. Soon, we all joined in the laughter. When the joy ended, I offered to take them out to dinner after stopping at my house. As we entered my home about thirty miles from Middletown, Jacques's good nature was subjected to the Jasper test. Jasper was our dog, a Miniature Schnauzer we obtained from the Humane Society six years earlier. He had the demeanor of a Jacques. He growled and barked at strangers and was slow to warm up to people. Jasper displayed the same traits to my guests when we walked into my house.

As Jacques sat outside, enjoying a cocktail in my wooded backyard, Jasper leaped into his lap.

"Get down, Jasper," I commanded.

"No, it's OK, I like dogs" Jacques replied in a soft tone.

Jacques and Jasper appeared to be in love, with Jacques coddling Jasper and stroking his ears and Jasper's head resting on Jacques's belly. Upon leaving my home, Jacques and Jasper reluctantly separated. The next day, the meeting with our management went well, with Jacques smiling cordially throughout the review and acting agreeable to everything the management team presented. Later in the year, at Christmas time, I received a wonderful note from Jacques, thanking me and wishing my family and our *chien* (dog) a Happy Holidays. After working with Jacques and his people for eight years, it was a side of him I had not seen before.

Amid planning and preparing for the launch of the engines for A318 and A380 aircraft, I was awakened one June night in 2004 by a severe headache. Consumed by excruciating pain, I hoped aspirin and a few more hours of sleep would provide relief. That night, we had attended an event near home, and I thought that I was paying the price for over merriment. But when I woke hours later, the pain hadn't subsided. Facing a day off from work to play in a charity golf event, I left home, expecting the pain would disappear. At the golf course, a short drive from home, I parked in a remote corner of the parking lot, hoping to sleep off the pain before teeing off. Within seconds of closing my eyes, my lights went out. A flame-out, one might say in our industry, when referring to an unintended cessation of operation of an operating jet engine.

Hours later, I opened my eyes and found myself in bed in a hospital in Hartford. Little did I know how I had gotten there or when the tubes attached to my hands had been inserted. Recognizing Loretta and a golfing buddy standing near the doorway to the room gave me comfort. The friend, Alfred, who I had planned to play golf with, explained what had happened to me after getting out of my car.

"Welcome back," he said, beaming like the sun through the window. "I woke you up when it was time to tee off."

Beyond the first swing of the day, I couldn't remember anything. Driving me to where my tee shot landed, Alfred and the others in our foursome had urged me to get off the cart to hit my ball. Seeing me in an unresponsive state, Alfred had driven me to the clubhouse to get some help. I appeared listless, and the clubhouse personnel had called an ambulance to take me to the hospital. As Alfred revealed what had befallen me, I remained bewildered about how long I had been in the hospital and what had been done to revive me from my prior state.

While talking with Alfred, a man walked into the room wearing a white shirt and smart-looking tie. Displaying a friendly smile, he extended a hand.

"Hi, I'm Dr. Langford. I examined you yesterday when they brought you in," he said. He said that he was continuing to assess my condition and subtly mentioned that he was a neurosurgeon.

Hearing "neurosurgeon" sent chills through my body. I thought of Maurice's demise. The doctor's comments about a tumor putting pressure on a segment of my brain were even more disturbing. Apparently, as he told me, "Your severe headache was caused by a tumor, putting extreme pressure on your brain that made you unconscious." Hearing the doctor assert, "I think you have a common form of brain tumor that can be removed with moderate risk," left me speechless. It was frightening to hear that someone would be going into my head to remove a mass of something from the inner lining of my skull. Knowing nothing about the credentials or reputation of the doctor, I asked to call my primary physician. During my talk with Dr. Keating, my family doctor, he cited his discussion with Dr. Langford about my condition.

"You shouldn't wait. You should go ahead with the operation," he advised.

Returning with an energetic stride, Dr. Langford told me what he needed to do to perform the operation, which was far beyond my comprehension. Proposing a date to perform the surgery seven days away, he left the room. Moments later, I was discharged from the hospital to marinate in anticipation of the operation.

Returning to the office the next day, I worked on closing pressing issues before my departure in a week. Talking to Dylan about the things happening in Toulouse was therapeutic in diverting my mind from the surgery. Despite being back on the job, the week between my discharge from the hospital and re-entry for the operation was the shortest of my lifetime.

As I walked into the hospital, the reality of the operation set in. During an agonizing forty- five minutes in the waiting room, my mind raced with thoughts of the outcome of an operation I knew little about. I was told that I had, in medical terms, a meningioma—a slow-growing, noncancerous tumor that forms in the membranes that surround the brain inside of the skull. People with meningiomas have a good prognosis, provided the tumor is completely removed. If not completely removed, the tumor can grow back and become problematic, even life threatening, I learned after the operation.

Finally, I was called into a room for the surgery. Not long thereafter, the lights went out again. When I was awakened in the recovery room several hours later, I was told that the operation had been successful. Engulfed in pain, I could barely see the nurse or hear what she was saying. Meningiomas occur along the inner lining of the skull, I was told. The specific location of the tumor (near a major artery, or at the base of the skull), can add complexity to the surgery. Treatment of the condition is typically performed by M.R.I.-guided micro neurosurgery, or stereo-tactic radiosurgery. Though I had localized hair removal and stitches in my head, it was my understanding that the surgeon had conducted the surgery without opening my skull. However, before a discussion with the doctor, I remained fearful of a malignant tumor.

After being subjected to several neurological tests over the next two days, the medical staff decided to transfer me to a rehabilitation hospital. Upon leaving the room, I was told that a person in the room next to mine had gone through a similar operation. Coincidentally, the man worked for the same company that I did, someone mentioned. Knowing this raised thoughts of publicized complaints of brain-related issues from other employees of our company. At this time, a study was being conducted by an independent research party contracted by our company.

At the rehab hospital, I was assigned to a room with a patient appearing twenty-five to thirty years older than me, who I was told had suffered a stroke. Looking around, it appeared I was on a sub-ground level, with a casement window near the ceiling. The room was like being inside a cabin on a cruise ship. As daylight retreated to darkness, my two daughters, who had come up from North Carolina, walked into the room. The sight of Rachael and Aprell boosted my spirits and optimism of a full recovery.

During the first night at the rehab hospital, I felt a sharp pain in the calf area of my leg. Despite having pulsating rings around my calves to stimulate blood circulation, something had developed. Later that evening, I was in agony in my lower torso and upper back. I lay in bed and tossed from side to side, but I couldn't find relief. I got out of bed and walked back and forth in the hallway. Observing me wandering in the corridor, a nurse asked, "Where is your room?"

After telling her where I had come from, I described my agony.

"It could be a gas pain," she replied, walking me back to my room.

As I returned to my bed in unyielding pain, I thought about my daughters, who hours earlier had brought me food. Perhaps there was a connection between the food and speculated gas, I hoped. "This should be gone by the morning," I thought as I stacked pillows behind my back. "God punished me for enjoying the food my daughters brought me," I thought when morning came, pulling the cord beside me for assistance.

"Good morning. Feeling better?" asked the nurse answering my call.

"I'm feeling a sharp pain here," I replied, pointing to my ribs. I told the nurse about the migration of the pain from my leg to my ribs, and she departed to find a doctor. Soon, she returned with a youthful, clean-shaven man wearing thick-rimmed eyeglasses.

"Hi, I'm Doctor Miller. You had quite a night," he said, shaking my hand.

Appearing fresh out of medical school and maybe thirty-five to forty years old, Dr. Miller discussed my night of anguish while touching my ribs. Although I was feeling severe pain in my torso, the doctor departed to consider how to treat it.

Later in the morning, a physical therapist came into the room. Perky and athletic with a bright smile, she introduced herself as Donna. Seemingly an avid sports fan, she talked about the National Basketball Association finals. Soon, we entered a discussion of golf. It was great therapy for my agony.

Donna invited me to take a walk, and I rolled out of bed to join her. Putting her arm around my waist, she walked me through hallways I had paced during the night. Stopping at a service elevator, we went down a floor. As we stepped through a doorway leading to a courtyard, we were awash in hazy June sunshine. Strolling around the stone patio, I paused and took a deep breath. Immediately, I felt a congestive clunk in my lungs, followed by sharper pain. It seemed I had inhaled a chunk of air. At that point, I was experiencing pain with every breath. Noticing my distress, Donna rushed me back to my room.

She returned a short while later with Doctor Miller. The doctor appeared perplexed as he stood at my bedside. After a few questions about the location of the pain and its intensity, he departed the room with no remedy or relief. Watching him and Donna walk away, I was mystified about what was causing the pain and if it was even curable. Going through another night of pain, I again slept in an upright position, hoping to ease the torment.

The next morning, a nurse and a grim Doctor Miller came into the room. Saying that he was at his wit's end about what was ailing me, he decided to send me back to the hospital where my brain operation had been performed. He gave no hint about the tests I would be subjected to, or what he thought could be causing my pain. Perhaps it was best, I didn't know. My mind was racing like a Formula-One race car through sinuous European streets.

That afternoon, I was ambulanced back to where my medical journey began. Though I was still sporting a partially shaven head and scars from the operation, I was so agonized by the pain in my rib section that I had forgotten about the prior surgery. Nurses wheeled me to a place in the hospital, where testing was conducted, and I was given a CAT scan. When the technician found nothing relating to my pain, I was taken to another room. In the next room, an ultra-sonic test was performed. I found the ultra-sonic test interesting to watch. Leaning toward the screen being studied by a technician, I could see the super-highways of arteries within me. I noticed joy on the face of the man performing the test. I could see he was getting a kick out of what he was looking at.

"Ah-ha," he uttered, nodding at his assistant. It was seemingly a eureka moment; it appeared he had discovered something significant. I had no idea what they were looking at, but if it meant they discovered the source of my pain, I was game. Leaving the room, the technician ran to report his finding.

While I waited to hear what the tech had discovered, a compact man with a balding hairline approached me. Hearing "A blood clot, originating in your leg, traveled through your blood stream to a lung" was scary. According to the doctor's explanation, it seemed the migration of the clot correlated to the journey of my pain. In order to prevent subsequent clots traveling through me, the doctor proposed implanting a filter in an artery. Shortly thereafter, I was wheeled to an operating room, where the procedure was performed. Although the operation was successful, there continued to be pain in my chest.

I was taken to the emergency room and put in a bed in an area near an entrance to the hospital, joining other patients awaiting their next destinations. The emergency room was a mad house. If you're looking for a good night's sleep, an emergency room isn't the place to be. Throughout the night, a steady stream of people came through the entrance. Before long, I realized that there were others in this open area in greater pain than me. Every hour, a woman in a bed behind me brayed like a distressed calf. At times, the room sounded like an ill barnyard.

After a night of interrupted sleep, I awakened to a room bustling with hospital staff. Appearing in the midst of a shift change, the influx of staff went about settling into their daytime duties. Brightening the room was a nurse with red hair. She mentioned that she would be taking care of me for the day. "If one could bottle personality, she'd be on the label," I thought as she spewed hospitality. I had no idea what the doctors were planning or what the day would bring, but for a moment, the pain subsided.

Soon, a doctor came to me with a grave expression. "You had a pulmonary embolism," he said.

"Wow, I don't know what that means, but it sounds serious," I gasped.

Apparently, as the doctor told me, I had an obstruction of a blood vessel, where the embolus (clot), traveled from my leg to a lung. As I listened to the doctor's revelation, my first thought was, where could it go from there? Reading my grieving expression, the doctor answered before I asked.

"We want to get to the clot before it continues to somewhere like the brain," he said with a hushed tone. Suddenly I gasped with pain.

With deep concern written on his face, the doctor informed me of the options he had for removing the clot. Listening to his rundown of the procedural alternatives, I concluded that none of the options were desirable. Because of my recent surgery, blood thinners to dissolve the clot were eliminated as an option. The second option was to cut me open to remove the clot in my lung.

"No way! I'd rather live with the pain," I responded.

Finally, the doctor gave me a third option.

"You're lucky," he said, with an up-beat tone. "Within the past year, a process has been developed to remove vascular clots without resorting to traditional surgery." The doctor went on to caution that I would feel drained after the procedure, but a few hours later, I would feel better. Hearing this, I gladly accepted this option.

My effervescent nurse guided my mobile bed through corridors until we reached the operating room. Riding in the bed was like being in a demolition derby. During the bumpy ride, my mind was filled with thoughts of, "Am I going to survive this?" and, "Will my life be the same again?"

Upon arriving at the operating room, I was put in a sitting position in the same bed that brought me there. Soon, assistants prepped me for a catheter-directed thrombolysis, or CDT, as they called it. Prior to starting the operation, the radiologist explained its painlessness to ease my anxiety.

"Great," I replied, feeling a sharp pain in my lung. Un-sedated, I witnessed the entire process as it unfolded.

To my recollection, the procedure involved placing a catheter in a vein in my groin area. Guiding it through the vein using fluoroscopic imaging, the medical staff transported it to a location near the embolism in my lung. A red substance used to break up the clot was released through the catheter such that its highest concentration was at the embolus. In addition, as I recall, a probe type device was inserted into my chest. The operation, performed in a specially designed room, required people in an adjacent room to assist with the procedure. The people in the adjacent room were being directed by the doctor in mine. When the doctor gave instructions, a voice coming from another room was heard.

During the operation, it seemed as though I was being subjected to an electrical charge. At one point, I imagined seeing sparks near my lips. Perhaps the charge was coming through the probe inserted in my chest, I wondered. Each time the doctor requested the charge, I felt a penetrating jolt. Gradually, my energy was sapped. The operation wasn't painful, but draining as predicted. It appeared that the doctor peering at a screen liked what he was seeing.

"That's it," he said, removing the probe and catheter from me.

"Great. We got it," said a cheerful voice in the other room.

Instantly, I felt the success of the operation. Miraculously, the pain had vanished. Not long after returning to the emergency room lobby, I noticed my skin color had changed to a burnt crimson. It appeared that the effect of the medication injected prior to the operation had lingered.

The next day, I was sent back to the rehab hospital, hopeful that my medical woes were behind me. But within a day of re-admittance, other ailments surfaced, starting with a bladder infection and followed by extreme swelling of my legs. Though I was cured quickly of the bladder discomfort, controlling the swelling, and preventing additional clotting wasn't so simple.

Still healing from the brain operation, using traditional blood thinners to dissolve the clotting was determined unacceptable by my primary physician and the neurosurgeon. To decrease the risk to my brain, a lower strength blood thinner was prescribed. A routine duty that up until then had been performed by a nurse, I could never imagine injecting myself with the thinner. But following a crash course given by the nurse, I plunged needles filled with medication into my gut daily. After the nurse's demonstration, my injections became the most dreaded time of my day. On top of that, my legs had become so inflated that I couldn't walk without help.

When hospitalized with a life-threatening affliction one recognizes how vulnerable they really are. Bedridden with virtually nothing to do but think, I became reflective and introspective about the events and encounters during my time in France. While submerged in solitary thoughts, I concluded that feeling accepted by those who matter—like family, cherished friends both near and far, and trusted colleagues—has a great healing effect. Whether they were conveyed by e-mails, phone calls, or kindness shown by the hospital staff, the people by my side kept me optimistic that I would soon recover.

During my time in the hospital, two men visited me several times a week. They were close friends who I had known for twenty-five years. Upon first seeing me in a bedridden state, they appeared shocked. One of them said, "You were the last person I would expect to see here." A few years later, illnesses galloped in and whisked both of them away to the hereafter.

As I pondered the quality of my relationships with Maurice and diligent hospital visitors like John and Buddy, I found that the true test of a well-wisher is their empathy with the pain of the afflicted as the person physically declines. The investment in an-other's well-being is evident without words.

Feeling better albeit wobbly on my feet, my happiest day in five weeks came when I was released to go home. After weeks of confinement, the sun seemed brighter than ever. I took a deep breath outside of my home. It was great to be away from the hospital and its medicinal smell. I stepped into my home, walking the ground floor with a wheeled walker. It was invigorating to be in my house.

Through physical therapy sessions three days a week and a will to walk normally again, I was determined to return to a normal life. At first it was like turning the clock back five decades to when I was a toddler. Within the first day or two, walking one revolution around my modest-sized family room seemed like a marathon. Soon, one revolution became two, then three, and so on, until after two weeks, I was able to shed the walking apparatus.

In a month, I progressed to adding other rooms and a staircase to the round trips. Soon, I added walks around the outside of my house. The road to recovery took longer than I expected. After nearly four months of enduring the ordeal in the hospital and recovering at home, the doctor authorized my return to work. During the time at home, many well-wishers conveyed their encouragement. That much of the sentiment came from France inspired me to work harder to recover. The phone conversations and e-mails from Sabine and counterparts at Airbus kept me hopeful for a complete recovery.

Returning to work after being away all summer was like going back thirty years to when I started working for the company. Although all the players in the home office were still there, I had a detached feeling when walking into the office. Perhaps a biding mistrust in the organization was contributing to the feeling. I strolled gingerly down the aisle to my office. There was nothing out of the ordinary about me being back. It seemed my office mates were avoiding a discussion of what I had been through. I found it understandable.

Reading the countless e-mails that had accumulated in my absence, I came upon a message that was sent by my boss. Announcing my anticipated extended absence to a wide audience had undoubtedly been the right thing to do. However, I was alarmed when reading the content of what had been shared with others. Upon discussing the operation with my boss weeks earlier, I had asked that he not mention details. To my dismay, the e-mail included explicit reasons for my absence. At a time when I was overjoyed to be back at work and confident that my parting request had been honored, I found the e-mail deflating. Discoveries of such unnecessary disclosures tend to impede trust. Undoubtedly, this event soured our relationship and my impression of the trustworthiness of my boss. Although we didn't discuss my misgivings at length, in the end, I wasn't surprised by how he handled the situation. It was his nature.

A week after returning to work, there was a quarterly review of managers in our organization. Quarterly meetings were held to update our vice president of Operations about the progress of initiatives in his organization. The vice president, I noticed, was on the distribution list of the announcement of my absence. When I passed him prior to the start of the meeting, he pointed a finger at me to acknowledge my presence. Moments later, the meeting started. Despite my thoughts about the subtle greeting, I realized an important lesson from this finger-pointing gesture.

Relationship building and trust begin with situational acknowledgment, recognition, and displays of empathy. Words alone are often more valuable than a financial reward. In the workplace, innumerable things can be done to inspire and motivate individuals without spending a dime. For example, he could have said, "Welcome back. Nice to have you back." "Thank you. It's great to be back," the employee might reply.

Such an exchange would have gone a long way in promoting the image of the senior manager in the eyes of a returning subordinate and others in the room. If change comes from the bottom up, the inspiration and promotion of motivation to embrace change has to come from above. Otherwise, neither change nor trust among various levels will be likely. When the quarterly review meeting ended, I watched a dispirited group of managers file out of the room. I felt dejected myself. Nonetheless, in the months that followed, I focused on making up for lost time.

In November of 2004, two months after the operations review meeting, I returned to France. I was thrilled to be back in a working environment I had truly missed. As I reentered the workplace in Toulouse, I was greeted warmly by Airbus counterparts and the folks on my team. Upon walking into the flight-line office, I received a reception like I was coming home. "Welcome back stranger," Dylan greeted me with a sweeping smile. Before long, it felt like I had come home. The trip had been intended to reconnect me with my group in France and air frame counterparts, and I found the three-day visit great psychotherapy to the weeks I'd endured in solitude.

Upon traveling back to the States via the transfer in Paris, the elevated, post-9/11 security really hit home. Flights to the United States were being subjected to much more scrutiny than I had previously experienced. I wove through barriers in Charles De Gaulle Airport that lead to the passport control booths. Beyond them awaited metal detectors and belts for X-raying carry-on bags, as usual. Getting through the X-ray detectors was uneventful, but when exiting the area, I was confronted with another check point. Security officers conducting physical pat-downs of passengers headed to boarding gates, patted legs, arms, and torsos.

As an officer patted me down on both legs, he observed that my left calf was considerably larger than the right calf.

Detecting the difference, the officer ushered me out of the line and asked me to follow him to an area away from the security check point.

"Wait here," he said while calling another security official. With all eyes in security lines on me, I became self-conscious of being singled out. Appearing to be a security risk, I became an object of the rubber-necking travelers; those in lines and those who had been cleared.

As I waited a long time at the surveillance booth wondering about my fate, the airport police arrived. They instructed me to step into the tiny booth and drop my pants and I complied, worrying about missing my flight. Not convinced after dropping my pants, the officer asked me to pull my socks down. Observing my fully exposed legs, the police concluded that the bulge was a swollen leg. Giving me an OK to leave, the blushing officer apologized profusely. Though I was fully aware of the swelling when my legs were inactive, I hadn't thought about the condition being a security concern.

Proceeding to the departure gate for my flight to New York, I boarded the aircraft in the nick of time, consumed by self-consciousness. As I looked around the cabin in the section where I was sitting, it seemed all eyes were on me. After take-off, a woman who looked about sixty in an adjacent row watched every move I made. Though I was tempted to look across the aisle and say, "Boo," I decided it'd be best to keep my mouth shut. She had a grimaced, awe-struck expression when looking at me, and I didn't want to scare her or anyone who may have seen me at the security checkpoint. When getting out of my seat to walk to the bathroom, the keen eyes of the woman followed me there and back. As we exited the plane in New York, I helped the watchful women remove a carry-on from an overhead bin.

"It's so good to be back on the ground," she said thanking me.

"I totally agree, ma'am," I smiled.

A month after returning to Connecticut, I received an invitation to an event that was one of the most memorable of my lifetime. A personalized e-mail invitation from the president and CEO of Airbus was sent to prospective attendees to witness the unveiling of the jumbo A380 aircraft to the world—the A380 Reveal, the event was called. Honored to have received the invitation, I later discovered that some of my closer counterparts of the air-framer weren't invited.

Thoughts of the upcoming event seemed to stimulate my physical recovery. The aircraft had been undergoing development for several years and it was time to show the results to the world. Gushing with pride, I shared my good fortune with friends and family. I refrained from sharing the news with my boss and some stateside colleagues due to concerns of envious reprisal. Intuitively, there was mistrust between my boss, certain others, and myself. Regardless of our differences, I returned to France in January 2005 to attend the celebrated Reveal ceremony on the 18th.

Filled with excitement, I could hardly sleep the night before the event. Upon waking the next morning, I immediately turned on the television in my hotel room to view the announcement. On CNN, the announcer claimed with a profound British accent that "Today, a who's who of commercial aviation will converge in Toulouse, France to celebrate the reveal of the super jumbo A380 aircraft." "Really, a who's who of commercial aviation?" I thought. The announcer continued, naming the dignitaries that were invited. Most notable were the heads of state of the four partnering countries that produced the aircraft. The distinguished leaders included the president of France, Jacques Chirac, the Right Honorable Tony Blair of Great Britain, German Chancellor Gerhard Schroder, and the prime minister of Spain, Jose Luis Rodriguez Zapatero. Propelled by the top news of the day, I rushed to get dressed and join others from our company.

Upon arriving at the Jean-Luc Lagardere aircraft assembly site where the

Reveal was being held, I observed a multitude of invited guests accumulating and being screened for entry. Thinking about my prior security encounter in the Paris airport, I was nervous when approaching the security checker. I was relieved that there was no detectable accumulation of fluid in my leg and I was permitted to pass through the check point. Entering the event without being singled out took a tremendous load off my mind.

Proceeding to an area arranged for pre-event networking, I took the opportunity to connect with people in the industry that I would have never had the chance to meet. People representing airlines that ordered the plane and prospective buyers reviewing the aircraft for a future purchase were among the invitees. Aircraft part manufacturers were also there.

Speaking with airline executives, ground staff, and crews of prestigious international airlines was an incredible experience and opportunity to share impressions of the yet to be unveiled aircraft. While walking among the mass of people, something became glaringly apparent. Other than a sturdy, gregarious guy who mentioned he was a professor of engineering at the Massachusetts Institute of Technology, it appeared that we were the only people of color at the ceremony. At such an event where the attraction was colossal and the invitees represented much of the world, should the color of one's skin matter? Following a warm reception by the people of Airbus and attendees in the room, I followed the assemblage to an area on the assembly line that had been set up like an arena.

After being escorted to a seat in the front central section of the arena, I settled into a chair about forty feet from the stage. I peered at higher sections of the audience behind me. There appeared to be several thousand people in the building. Located among delegations of people representing airlines of China, a man seated next to me mentioned that he was a representative of China Southern Airlines. At that time, they hadn't ordered the aircraft, I recalled him saying, but he too sat on the edge of his seat, awaiting the unveiling of the jumbo plane. On the other side of me was a manager of a German company that supplied the miles of wiring for the aircraft. As the three of us chatted about our respective interest in viewing the airplane, the heads of state of the nations associated with partnering to produce the aircraft were escorted to their seats.

Commencing in a dramatic fashion, the ceremony began with a luminous introduction to Airbus, its history, and families of aircraft since the inception of the Airbus Industries GIE consortium in December 1970. Displaying images of artwork, the program continued with flashes of multicolored strobe lighting synchronized with classical music. A semblance of the aircraft behind a sheer curtain had the audience sitting up in their seats. A chorus of "oohs" and "ahs" was heard throughout the darkened arena until act one of the tribute to the producers of the aircraft had ended.

The lights were turned up one by one as each head of state came to the podium at center stage and spoke to the viewers. The men conveyed their pride in the efforts of the multi-national collaboration that had produced the aircraft. Following the inspiring remarks of the heads of state, the curtain hiding the aircraft was slowly raised. Gradually, the A380 aircraft, highlighted in blue lighting, was revealed to the audience. A buzz erupted throughout the crowd. Some attendees came out of their seats when seeing the plane. Soon, the dignitaries and audience were invited to walk around the fully revealed airplane.

Walking among the hundreds of people viewing the A380, I came upon a familiar face. Unsurprisingly, it was a close friend of Maurice who had played a role in creating the aircraft. Exuding pride in the technical features of the airplane, Alain (my former fellow lobster fest diner) invited me to walk with him. As we reviewed the unique features of the airplane, Alain showed a particular interest in the fuselage, under-carriage, and massive landing gear. While he lectured me about his involvement with the airplane, I felt blessed to be among the first to see this roll-out aircraft and to have someone so close to the creation of the plane share his accomplishment with me. When departing the ceremony, Alain mentioned he had recently become a grandfather. I was honored that he had chosen to share his joy with me, and his excitement became a part of the aura I felt about the entire event. "It would be glorious if Maurice was sharing this moment with us," I thought while looking at the elation on Alain's face.

Witnessing this extraordinary happening was something far beyond my imagination. Seven months earlier, my physical condition had been in a place where attending such an event would have been unfathomable. Experiencing the traumatic ordeal in the hospital had erased my sense of invincibility and deepened my appreciation of acceptance. Nothing can be taken for granted, I thought while recovering. I've heard "What doesn't kill you makes you stronger."

Physically and mentally fitter after an arduous six months, I was eager to continue my journey.

12

The Departure

Hearing rumors of a retirement offer, I thought deeply about accepting or rejecting it. The valuable relationships I developed during the prior eleven years of this duty made my decision extremely difficult. Looking back at the period between the spring of 1994 to the end of 2005, when our country and the world were riding a wave of economic prosperity, I thought about how fortunate I had been to be given the chance to participate in this multi-cultural arena.

During this era, I worked for six different bosses, from Norm, relieved from his position shortly after giving me the assignment, to Tim, who had been in the position less than a year. Tim, who I assumed had been with the company for twenty years, mentioned that he had traveled to Boeing (in Seattle) several times but never visited Airbus in Toulouse. To accommodate his desire to visit Airbus, I arranged a tour of their assembly facility in January of 2006.

On the evening of Tim's arrival in Toulouse, we dined in a noisy restaurant in the center of the city. It was a place known for its *steak-frites* ensembles (steak and fries), which I imagined Tim would like. I waited until we finished eating before broaching the topic of retirement.

"I'd like to retire later this year," I brought up, eager to hear Tim's response.

Appearing stunned by my disclosure, Tim shrugged a shoulder.

"OK. When do you want to leave?" Tim asked with raised eyebrows.

"Not sure, but my guess would be between the end of October and the end of December," I replied.

After disclosing my thoughts about retirement, I shifted the topic to my immediate concern. During the winter of 2005 to 2006, my scope of responsibility had expanded from the south of France to Hamburg, Germany. Considering the launch of the A318 aircraft and our imminent PW6000 engines, I was buried in working on the details of setting up an engine support office in Germany. As my visits to the Hamburg assembly site increased, the differences between the cultures of Germany and France became more apparent. In terms of the acceptance I received, I found the people in the facilities of both nations courteous and respectful.

Observations of the work-forces in French and German assembly locations revealed definite differences in the people. Perhaps it was me, but there appeared to be differences in demeanors. Workers in the northern German plant seemed to mirror the cloudy, drizzly climate of the region with their staid soberness, compared to the zesty folks I was accustomed to in Toulouse. In Hamburg, the people appeared more structured in the way they went about assembling aircraft, with assiduity written on their faces. At the Hamburg plant, final assembly of certain models of the A320 aircraft family and cabin furnishing of A300 airplanes had been performed for years. I would gaze at the angled aircraft assembly workstations as I walked through the facility, impressed with the layout. Simple in design, the work bays were arranged in a congruous manner for the precise and efficient workforce. Every tool and person had its place, it seemed.

Despite my initial perception of the stoic culture in Hamburg, my working relationships developed quickly in the plant. I worked with people like Reinhold, who was reminiscent of Sargent Schultz from the television show *Hogan's Heroes*, and Andreas, another regimental person. Before long, we were given an office and shop floor space in a convenient location in the assembly building. We entered negotiating discussions with a clear plan of how we would use the space, showing the management of the facility that we had created an operational plan that not only covered our needs but also supported their operation. We weren't just asking for floor space for our on-site operation ; we were justifying it.

Before seeking space for my Hamburg operating unit, I learned that our program management for the engine model determined that the final assembly of the A318 engines would be performed by a sub-contractor (MTU) in Hanover, Germany. Accordingly, a relationship for engine delivery from MTU-Hanover had to be established with their industrial management. Located about an hour-and-a-half drive south of Hamburg, the MTU plant had assembly experience with certain models of our engines, conducting overhaul and maintenance work on them and engines of our competitors.

During the first meeting with the shop management of MTU, we initiated a plan to coordinate the transporting of assembled engines from Hanover to the podding facility in Toulouse. In the meeting was Helmut, a stocky, gray-haired production manager, and his staff. I found myself working with incredibly mechanized people who were acutely focused on the work they performed in the building. With deadpan yet accepting demeanors, they mirrored the men I had been working with at the airplane facility in Hamburg. Although I departed the first Hanover visit with guarded skepticism, on the next visit, we warmed up to each other and were able to forge a working arrangement that satisfied our needs.

Both Dylan and Horace came up from Toulouse to join me in meetings with the production teams in Hamburg and Hanover. During one of our visits to the MTU plant, the city of Hanover was hosting matches of the 2006 Football World Cup (or soccer, as we call it). Coincidentally, the national teams of some of the participating nations were staying in the same hotel as us. Located a short walk from the Hanover Airport, the hotel appeared convenient for the teams and their fans. The lobby and lounge areas were extremely festive. Team members and their avid followers sang verses of their national anthems. Among the teams in the lounge area was a large delegation of people from an African nation who danced incessantly to the beat of conga drums. The gaiety of the colorfully robed men and women celebrating a victory, waving batons with streamers of animal hair, captivated onlookers in the lobby and lounge area of the hotel.

While the spectacle continued, one of the men who had come to Hanover for our MTU meeting asked me a strange question.

"Have you traced your ancestry to Africa?" he asked with a wry smile.

"No," I replied. "It hadn't crossed my mind. Surely, not currently."

Perplexed by the query, I pondered why the hell he was asking me this now. It was the second time I had been asked a racially curious question since taking this assignment. Given the stained racial history in America, it was obvious that the inquirer was not an American. In America, a question like this from a white person would likely be considered inappropriate—an insensitive or bigoted wisecrack. From a person from a faraway continent, I preferred to believe that the question surfaced from naivety, ignorance, or simply a lack of self-awareness. His cultural sensitivity was lacking. In retrospect, the question was telling me more about the questioner than the response he was seeking.

That the man had raised the question during the celebration of the African delegation brought back memories of a question I had been asked ten years earlier. Similarly, the man asking the question then was from a faraway region like the man asking the question in the lobby of the hotel. After he arrived in the States on business, the man and I got together for an afternoon of social enjoyment. As we rode in my car on a country road in Connecticut, suddenly, the man asked a question.

"Have you experienced prejudice in America?" he inquired.

Struck by the out-of-the-blue question, I paused to consider where he was coming from. I responded "No," to his probe but thought, "That's not true." From there, my mind wandered from thoughts of whether this was a wise-ass search for future happy-hour chatter, to the kind of impression the outside world had of America, its history, and its inhabitants of color. Trying to be tolerant, I considered the person asking the question and surmised his query may not have been intended to be derogatory but may have been asked to satisfy his burning, albeit untimely curiosity. It was the first time someone asked a racial question while I was in this position. Beyond its untimeliness, what disturbed me most about the question was that, considering the shameful history of race relations in America, I saw no value to me in satisfying his curiosity. In retrospect, perhaps a more palpable question would have been, "Does racial prejudice still exist in America?" Such a question is direct and avoids misunderstandings. Better yet, why even raise the concern? The history is known around the world.

The tumultuous time of the American civil rights era has been well documented. Over the years, I've found that if two or more parties in an encounter are not on the same cultural plane, questions about ancestry and societal oppression tend to inhibit the development of trust. It's like picking a scab off an old wound.

Following our chat in the hotel lobby, Dylan, Horace, and I met the next morning with the production management of the MTU facility. During the meeting, we continued our delivery planning and discussions of logistics for the engines allocated to the A318 aircraft. On this trip, as with prior travel to Germany, when our discussions were completed, I continued to Toulouse to meet with my colleagues of the airplane manufacturer and members of my on-site staff. Although most stopovers in Toulouse were uneventful, on this June 2006 stopover, I scheduled a meeting with my entire Toulouse staff. Prior to meeting with them, I met with a trusted colleague of the aircraft manufacturer to disclose my intended retirement. Muriel responded with disbelief and an obvious concern.

"Has a replacement been named?"

"No, but your company will be advised when I know," I committed.

Not long after the meeting with Muriel, I met with my on-site office and labor staff over lunch. Advertised as a celebration for achieving the highest level of quality excellence awarded by our company's continuous improvement department, the luncheon proceeded with low-key conversation like prior group lunches. When side discussions faded to a single voice, I informed the group about my anticipated departure from the company. They were engulfed in silence for a moment, and there appeared uncertainty among them. I wasn't sure they heard me. Soon, a person broke the silence, by saying, "We knew this day would come. We weren't expecting it so soon."

After lunch, we dispersed and converged at the entrance of our office building. By consensus, the staff chose to take a group picture. While we arranged ourselves for the photo, I scanned those among us to see if someone was missing. Though he had attended the luncheon, somehow Horace wasn't present. I asked someone to go find him. Considering where he may have gone, Ian offered to look for him. Minutes later, he returned with Horace. Arranged like a school graduating class, we posed for our final group photo.

An old Chinese proverb tells us, *"A lifestyle is what you pay for and it's life that pays you."* As I advanced a decade in my career and experienced the life of this region, the significance of the adage became more vivid. In life, it's the things we remember and the incidents we're inclined to forget that define us and our perspective. That evening I dined alone in Toulouse and contemplated what would be needed to clear my exit from the company.

My restaurant of choice for the evening was La Pizzeria Vecchio, as usual. While dining alone, I gained an appreciation for the camaraderie I had developed with diners at adjacent tables. Many times, the conversations were as enjoyable as the meals I ate. Typically, discussions with patrons at neighboring tables were spontaneous, the first words being, *"D'ou venez vous?"* (Where do you come from?) Upon observing my Yankee accent and my clothes, most people concluded I was an American. The color of my skin increased the curiosity of many, it seemed. Regardless of the status of a restaurant or the neighborhood in which it was located, I found people accommodating, unpretentious, and extraordinarily accepting of me.

There are certain foods one remembers when eating out, but food alone never dominated my opinions of the places I dined. Rather, the more impressionable factor was the overall dining experience. What makes a restaurant memorable? It's how it makes its customers feel, from the time they're received at the entrance through the time they leave. Establishments that became my favorites had the same formula for customer value. Be it a homey clunk of a pot or pan in an open kitchen, genuine words of welcome from a proprietor, or wait staff serving with military precision, these establishments and experiences made me feel important.

The next day I returned to the States to continue clearing the issues that needed closure before my departure. While phasing out of the less active A300 and A330 aircraft engine programs, I approached my daily duties with the same vigor I adopted when accepting the assignment. I wouldn't expect anything less from myself, or those we depended on, to support our propulsion systems deliveries.

As my time in the position grew shorter, deliveries of components from some suppliers were increasingly delinquent. Although engine deliveries were on schedule, or close to it, I pushed harder on producers of parts and engines to keep them focused on our customer commitments. In some instances, I experienced resistance to my appeals. When delivery issues persisted, I went directly to the hands-on workers on the shop floor, pleading for their support. At this time, nacelle component suppliers were struggling to deliver their units on time. Though there were four suppliers producing various nacelle components, all of them were having difficulty delivering on schedule. After delivery, some units were questioned by the airplane maker for what they saw as quality issues. With dwindling orders of aircraft powered by our propulsion systems, it appeared that the nacelle manufacturers were being affected by the shrinking production. After the shocking events on September 11, 2001, orders of aircraft declined, and the supply chain struggled to rebound to levels seen in prior years.

Within our company, Felix, the procurement manager who managed contracts with the nacelle suppliers, was suddenly replaced after working with those suppliers for more than ten years. His replacement, Nelson, seemed overwhelmed with the task of convincing the suppliers to maintain their commitments. Despite my continual reminders about the impact of the late deliveries to the air-framer, Nelson chose the defiant route. Nonetheless,

I continued to implore him to honor his commitments.

At loggerheads, the disagreement between Nelson and myself gradually became a war of **e**-mails—my push for delivery performance and his shove to ignore my request. The responses I received were riddled with innuendos and insolence. Managers of the air-framer noticed the obstinacy and were vocal about their dismay. The disagreement continued to intensify.

In the months before my exit from the company, there were countless issues to be closed. Still open was implementation of the plan for setting up the field office in Hamburg. In addition, arrangements were needed to staff the organization with personnel to support the engines for A318 aircraft. Five years earlier, in 2001, planning for the Hamburg office had begun. At that time, optimism about having more airline customers was greater. Unexpectedly, performance issues were revealed during engine development, resulting in a delay of the engine program. The program was postponed for a short while, and there were rumors that it would be canceled altogether. I anticipated the performance issues would soon be resolved. Expecting an eventually fully recovered program, I continued to pursue people for the Hamburg office.

Through the industry grapevine, prospective candidates surfaced for the manager position in Hamburg. Unable to come to an agreement with any of the recommended people, I continued to search for a leader. Several months passed before receiving a call from a man I had met years earlier. Coincidentally, he had been my air-framer interface when I visited the Hamburg facility in December of 1994. Unemployed and with no specific position in mind, Horace called to inquire about job opportunities. Residing somewhere in Sweden, he drove to Hamburg for an interview. As I interviewed him for the manager's position, I considered Horace's familiarity with the airframer's Hamburg operation, which was an advantage. Upon completing our discussion, I felt good about his ability to handle the task. But despite my initial confidence in Horace's capability, I had a lingering concern about why he left his prior position.

My uncertainty about the longevity of Horace's commitment to the location of the task continued to fester. When I shared my reservations with Horace, he assured me of his interest in the job. Accepting his words, I pursued hiring him. Although Horace came on board soon thereafter, I took him on much earlier than the launch of the program. Starting at least two years prior to the assembly of the first production engines, Horace was trained and oriented to our company's policies and procedures to prepare him for the future task.

As the months went by, the early hire began raising concerns. I considered the occasional dreary climate in the Hamburg area compared to sunnier Toulouse. The longer Horace lived in the south of France, the more he became rooted in the region. When a person is contemplating a purchase of property where they are living, they are raising a flag, I thought. Upon seeing signs of him tapping into the region, I reminded Horace of our prior understanding and where he would be working. Horace recited his intent to move to Germany.

For some reason, the reassurance wasn't penetrating my skepticism. Feeding my uncertainty was his growing affinity for a woman he had met in the region. Despite hints of his diminishing interest in relocating to Hamburg and the urging of some of his advocates in Toulouse, I remained resolute to our prior agreement. Since taking on this task, I had heard many people on both sides of the Atlantic say, "A commitment is a commitment." Hearing it for twelve years, the meaning of the words had truly sunk in.

To administer the expenses incurred by a future group in Hamburg, I needed a service agreement with a company registered in Germany. Our sister company, Otis Elevator, was well established in the country, and I pursued the assistance of people in the financial and human resources departments of Otis-Germany. After speaking to representatives of both departments for years without seeing them, we agreed to have a meeting at the Otis-Germany office in Berlin.

I traveled to the German capital in August of 2006 to meet with Bjorn, a manager in the financial department of Otis, and Lars, representing the H.R. department. It felt like preparing for a blind date. Before meeting the soft-spoken Bjorn at the Berlin Airport, I had been expecting a much shorter man. He was taller (six feet) than I expected. When I was greeted by Lars the next morning, I was shocked to see him appear smaller than the booming voice I had heard on the phone. I can imagine what they were thinking when they met me, but their body language revealed nothing. In fact, it was comforting to have these guys greet me in such a nonchalant manner. They introduced themselves with vigorous handshakes and broad smiles, conveying genuine acceptance of my presence. Meeting face to face with these faceless voices was incredible.

Later in the day, we drafted a service agreement and an employment contract for the manager and imminent staff of our Hamburg office. Beyond establishing the support agreement, which we came to faster than I had expected, the true highlight of our union was the dinner that evening at the renowned Reich-stag in Berlin. The meal of fish and other specialties of the sea contributed to my memory of the evening, but what captivated me most was the parliamentary ambiance of the building and its history dating back to its completion in 1894, and its more recent cultural history before and after World War II. After dinner, we left the building and strolled the enormous square in front of Brandenburg Gate. Before long, we came upon remnants of the Berlin Wall. Dismantled in the early 1990s, markers on the pavement identified its location before the reunification of Germany.

As Bjorn, Lars, and I departed for the evening, we summarized our earlier agreement to ensure a common understanding. In a cordial, mutually respectful one-day meeting, we were able to develop a service plan with ease. Based on our phone conversations and the trust established through them, Bjorn and Lars prepared the required documents in advance of our meeting. Their proactive preparation played a vital role in the success of our agreement. For that, I was extremely grateful.

Toward the end of September, I traveled to Toulouse to continue the phase-out of my duties. While there, I received additional appeals on behalf of Horace to conduct his Hamburg duties remotely from Toulouse. Considering the pleas and where they were coming from, I concluded that the appeals had been contrived with these advocates. Though I thought about it for a moment, the attempt fell on deaf ears. Regardless of being less than two months from leaving the company, I could not imagine introducing a new propulsion system program without an on-site manager to oversee the start-up activity.

Within a week, Horace traveled to the States for training on the new engine. Near the end of his first day of training, I stopped by the class to say hello to him and his instructor. Following an exchange of cordial greetings, I handed a contract to Horace for his employment in Germany. Lars had finalized and sent our Berlin agreement so fast that it arrived at my stateside office before I had. Horace appeared miffed when I gave him the envelope and requested to take it back to his hotel for a closer review. As I left the training facility, I expected Horace's review would result in some concerns and questions, but ultimately we would come to an agreement.

I returned to the training class the next morning expecting to field questions from Horace and was surprised to find what was awaiting me. Contrary to the amicable greeting of the day before, a grim-faced Horace handed me a letter. Drafted by him the night before, the letter asked for consideration of an alternative to sending him to Hamburg. I was stunned by his request and rejected his last-ditch demand. Between a manager and a subordinate, discussions of money are always debatable, but justifying an absentee manager at the start of a new program was beyond my acceptance.

I stated my position to the sullen Horace, and we faced each other in silence. Before long, Horace handed me the signed contract. Relieved that he had signed the document, I extended my hand.

"I can't shake your hand," he uttered, peering at my hand. I continued to stand next to Horace with my outstretched hand, and moments later, he clasped it and apologized.

"You've been through so much," he said in closing. Though he had expressed an initial reluctance to signing the contract and shaking my hand, I felt there was a moment of mutual acceptance in the end.

After saying goodbye to Horace, I remained worried about sending someone to a place where they seemingly did not want to go. Seeking a remedy for my inhibitions, I visited the manager of the engine program for the A318 aircraft. Briefing Jason on my conversation with Horace, I shared my thoughts and misgivings about his reluctance to go to Hamburg.

"Perhaps you should consider a backup candidate from your group for Hamburg. I'm not sure where I stand with my current choice," I suggested.

"After taking him on so early?" replied Jason, with a puzzled glance.

Hearing Jason's response, I had a flash of regret for taking Horace on early. Disturbed about the situation and still concerned about the leader of the office, I ended the briefing.

Looking back, perhaps I had taken him on too early, but his reasons for not wanting to go to Hamburg had nothing to do with time. Nonetheless, I accepted Horace's signed contract and newfound willingness to relocate.

As I closed the Hamburg staffing issue, my focus shifted to other items in the path of my departure. A major contributor to my uneasiness was that with three weeks remaining before my end of October departure, my replacement hadn't been named. Considering the many issues on my plate, the last twenty-one days of my tenure were frustrating. One issue that continued to drag to the end was the closure of the service agreements covering Horace and the support staff in Hamburg.

The slippage of the engine and nacelle deliveries continued for months leading up to my departure. Reminding me about the delays of our deliveries, my air-framer counterparts called daily to share their grief.

"We're waiting for propulsion systems for aircraft on the final assembly line," They'd sonorously remind me.

By this time, Dieter had retired, and Russell had been transferred to a new military aircraft program, but the message was still the same: "We need the propulsion systems now!"

Despite an occasional hiccup during the engine assembly and testing phase, engines were being shipped within days of the commitment dates. Through extraordinary expediting at the podding facility in Toulouse, we were able to deliver propulsion systems on or within a day of the contract dates. By contrast, some nacelle components slipped to a point where meeting the dates became a constant struggle. The decline of nacelle delivery performance amplified the consternation of my colleagues at the air-framer. As usual, they weren't bashful about asserting their dismay. To understand what was causing the delays, the air-framer requested a meeting.

Held in Toulouse two weeks prior to my departure from the company, the meeting was marked by the absence of the nacelle procurement manager, who was responsible for the nacelle suppliers' delivery performance. Instead, he chose to conference in by phone. During the meeting, which was attended by me and some of my on-site folks, representatives of the air-framer asked unequivocal questions about reasons for delays from the suppliers. Upon reading the faces of the airframer's attendees while listening to the procurement manager explain the reasons, I could tell they were not buying what they were hearing. It was reminiscent of what I had heard when I came over in 1994. Falling short of their expectations, the air-framer abruptly adjourned the meeting. Upon terminating the call, unpleasantness were voiced on both ends of the line.

Leaving the conference room, I was stopped by an air frame attendee who I had met a year earlier. During my prior trip to Toulouse, she had expressed an interest in giving me a parting gift.

"Can you come to my office?" Karine asked with a broad smile. Curious about what she had in mind, I followed her. In her office, Karine opened a drawer of a filing cabinet and removed a wooden box.

"A friend of my family made this," she said, handing it to me. As I peered at the inscription on the box bearing my name, its contents became clearer. "A bottle of something?" I guessed. Upon opening the box and seeing my name printed on the label of the contents, I was stunned. Karine was aglow. Not only was her gift a pleasant surprise, but my greater gift was seeing how happy she was when handing it to me. The moment erased my thoughts of the prior regrettable meeting. Following a heartfelt "thank you," I left Karine's office thinking how acceptance had prevailed over conflict.

Returning to the States the next day, I continued to pursue closure of staffing concerns for the Hamburg office and the declining reliability of propulsion systems deliveries. To close out my tenure in the position and the professional relationship with my air frame partners, I set a meeting for the end of October 2006. Scheduled days before my retirement date, the meeting was expected to convey our Hamburg organization's readiness and to present solutions for the troublesome engine and nacelle component delivery issues. In addition, it was thought to be the appropriate time for me to pass the baton to my yet-to-be-announced successor. As I came closer to my departure, the replacement remained unknown to me. Nonetheless, I continued to march toward a final get-together with counterparts in Toulouse. If nothing else, I wanted harmony on both sides of the Atlantic after my exit.

For the close-out review with Airbus, the agenda included a discussion of the plan for introducing our new engine for A318 aircraft in Hamburg and the recovery plan for the nacelle manufacturer's delivery issues. To execute the plan, I needed buy-in and support from the responsible engine and nacelle managers. Part producers and relevant engine assembly managers communicated their support instantly. However, the nacelle supply management was not as conciliatory. Unwilling to accept the situation, I continued to prepare for my departure from the company, feeling the contractual commitments to the air-framer would soon be restored. Although I had no idea who my replacement would be, for some reason, I sensed a person had been identified and communicated to a select few people. Finally, on the morning of my final trip to the air-framer, Tim, came to my office with news of the person he had selected to replace me.

"I want you to know, Barney will be replacing you," Tim disclosed.

I wasn't surprised when Tim said the name but was bewildered hearing it two hours before heading to the airport. Barney and I knew each other, though not well. We had worked in the same organization in the company for many years but had never worked together. As Tim walked out of my office, I reminded him that I was a few hours away from leaving for my close-out meeting with Airbus. The transition between me and Barney would be limited to my remaining two days after returning from Toulouse, I told him. Better yet, it could begin on this trip to Toulouse, I offered. Minutes later, I sent my travel itinerary to Barney to coordinate our connecting at the air-framer. Since a formal introduction to my group and colleagues in France would facilitate a better transition, I thought I should be the one to introduce Barney.

Soft-spoken and clean-cut, Barney had previously worked on an engine program that provided smaller propulsion systems to Airbus. He was no newcomer to managers of the air-framer and the podding facility. From my perspective, he was a model of what our senior management would be looking for in terms of the image of one in this position. Outward persona notwithstanding, I had observed during my twelve-year tenure working with the air-framer and on-site airline representatives that the most valuable attribute of a person in my position was their trustworthiness and ability to navigate through issues in adverse times. It's not a position for someone seeking something to hide behind. I had no reason to doubt Barney's ability to confront the inevitable challenges of the future. What remained to be seen was whether he could face unexpected issues without being overly reliant on the support of people who weren't on-site. All too often, many decisions needed to be made on the spot. The need to take immediate action often dictated the options to rectify issues.

Feeling isolated and alone during adverse situations gave me a greater appreciation of the power of acceptance. The influence of valued cross-cultural relationships had often fueled the inspiration that propelled me through difficult situations. Appearing solitary during some highly visible situations had not gone unnoticed. I had received written feedback from my air frame colleagues that expressed that they sensed a lack of in-house support for me. While looking out for industrial matters between our company and the air-framer, I had a feeling from my counterparts, both air frame and airline, that our mutual respect was deeply seeded.

In Toulouse for my final visit of the assignment, I disembarked the aircraft absorbed in thought. Walking through the Toulouse-Blagnac Airport to the baggage carousel, I considered the prior twelve years and how the terminal had expanded over my time of coming here. As I pursued my baggage, I thought about how much I had learned about intercultural acceptance and how it changed my perspective of other nationalities. Over a dozen years, my eyes had been opened to new parts of the world.

During my time in this position, I thrived on trusting relationships. As I built valuable partnerships with culturally different customers and suppliers, I was hopeful that the accumulated experience would lead me to a higher plateau in my career. Through this period, the aerospace industry was riding a wave of prosperity. The ripple effect of the economic up-turn was felt around the world, with increased long-range travel resulting in the need for larger, more efficient aircraft like the Airbus A330 and A340 series aircraft, the jumbo A380, and Boeing's 747, 777, and 787 aircraft.

Opportunities for career advancement were prevalent in many companies in the industry. Several people in our company were elevated at meteoric speeds. Categories of people who in prior years appeared to be on the outside looking in, including women, African Americans, Hispanics, and Asian-Americans, were more visible in higher positions. For those who were lucky to be in the right place at the right time, like I had, it became an opportunity to demonstrate their capability. For those like myself who had been waiting for opportunity to come knocking, seeing the upward mobility of others fostered hope. There were times when I was dispirited by some around me after comparing my credentials and experience to theirs. Regardless of what was happening around me, I liked what I was doing and tried to focus on my day-to-day duties. Perhaps I was too satisfied, I sometimes thought, but there were no regrets with my pursuit of advancement to a higher level.

When I considered my relationships with French managers at much higher levels than I, a common thread was apparent. First and foremost was our acceptance of each other. Surely it overshadowed second thoughts about the positions we held in our companies. Where we originated from was never a factor in our relationships. Feedback from Gregoire, a man who knew Jacques and Maurice well, revealed both men thought I was or should have been at a higher level than I was.

While engaged in last-minute preparation for my final meeting with Airbus, I received an e-mail from the nacelle supply manager, Nelson, and Gus, the manager of the A330 engine program. It appeared they collaborated on a position regarding the nacelle delivery issues. The gist of the e-mail was to inform me that no one would be coming to the meeting to present a recovery plan for the deliveries of engines or nacelles. In addition, they stated that they would not be conferencing into the meeting. I was struck by the scornful tone of the message. At a time when the relationship between our company and the air-framer was tenuous, I felt the position they had taken would appear arrogant to our air frame counterparts.

In completing the planning for the coming meeting, I met with Russell, a colleague from my earlier years in the assignment. By now, Dieter was back in Germany enjoying his retirement, Russell mentioned. We hadn't worked together or seen each other in three years, but I had a strong desire to see him before I departed. We met at a café near the airport and reminisced about our years together, my introduction to the A330 program, and the perplexity that existed when I was summoned to France. It was an evening of pure merriment. Russell stirred my memories of the uncertain world I had entered. We reminisced about the persistent calls from Dieter and him and the frat-house culture it seemed I had entered with non-Airbus people on-site. We talked about the changing of people and organizations in his company. Sadly, Jacques had been moved to a position where we saw far too little of him. He was an asset to the air-framer and our company, I had thought, and the chief promoter of honoring our commitments for propulsion system deliveries. As we discussed how we had grown since my skeptical acceptance of the assignment, we extended a final toast to each other. Raising a glass, Russell patted me on the back with a "Good luck, mate," and departed the cafe'.

Russell, who twelve years earlier had appeared steeped in the fraternal on-site culture, had grown personally and professionally. "He is a good guy and I will miss him," I thought when leaving the café.

The next day, the close-out with Airbus was held. Joining me at the meeting was Pierre, a Canadian national working on the A318 aircraft engine program, Barney, and Dylan. Representing the air-framer was Karine, who presided over the meeting, and other managers of their Quality and Industrial Departments. Though we started in a business-as-usual manner, before long, a blemish surfaced. The absence of representation from the nacelle supply management group was blatant and didn't escape the eyes of the air frame attendees. Though I delayed bringing up the topic of nacelle delivery performance, the air-framer looked unfavorably upon the lack of a spokesperson for the nacelle suppliers. Attendees from the airplane manufacturer appeared to interpret the no-show as a lack of interest. Barring further comments about the nacelle delivery issues, there was mutual agreement for the plans we presented for covering the air-framer's aircraft deliveries.

Soon thereafter, the meeting progressed to an exchange of gratuitous recognition and statements of appreciation for my years of involvement with the air-framer. As a memento, the Airbus attendees gave me a scale model of an A330 aircraft. They couldn't have chosen a more symbolic offering to encapsulate my years of servitude. It was a touching moment. My twelve years of involvement with Airbus ended as quietly as it began. The meeting came to an unceremonious closing. It was a fitting bookend to my inaugural visit to Toulouse in 1994.

To end my stewardship the next day with my team in Toulouse, we sat down for a final lunch at the Les Marroniers restaurant. Gone were Gilbert and Janine, who provided fond memories of good meals and the hospitality there. Special people, I would have loved to see them before my departure. Regardless of the change of proprietorship, the last lunch with the group was beyond special. Following a contented meal among the twelve or so people in the group, they presented a token of the team's appreciation.

Peering at the artistry of Emile's crafted weather-vane, I was overwhelmed by the thought that had gone into making it. Instead of a traditional rooster on the top of the vane, there was an image of a black golfer with a French flag in his golf bag. The uniqueness of the group's gift captured my two greatest passions at that time—golf and the south of France. While holding the present, I realized that my journey was ending. Consumed by atypical emotion, I bade my great team a heartfelt goodbye.

Standing at the cash register to pay the bill for lunch, I handed a credit card to the chef and got my second surprise of the day. Appearing distraught after several swipes of the card, the proprietor told me, "The card has been rejected." Hearing the nightmarish comment, I was lost for words. Puzzled by the muddle, I chose an undesirable means of paying —another person's card.

I phoned our accounting department in the States to discuss my credit card dilemma. In a matter of seconds, they advised, "Your card has been terminated." Dumbfounded, I explained my problem. "I'm currently on a business trip out of country where expenses have been incurred. I have to settle my bills before I leave tomorrow. I don't have enough cash to cover the hotel or the car rental," I continued. After enduring a multitude of hand-offs from our accounting department, the credit card was reactivated later.

Relieved about the outcome of the card issue, my thoughts drifted back to the prior meeting with the air-framer. Still vivid was the absence of responsible players from our company. More bothersome was the condoning of the manager's absence by higher authorities in his department. With the no-shows fresh in my mind, I drafted a letter summarizing my takeaways from the meeting. Conveying a metaphorical theme of the good, the bad, and the ugly, I scribed a parody of the amiable spirit of the attendees of the meeting and the impact of not having the responsible manager present to explain what was causing the delays and the remedies to fix them. Not attending the meeting had sent a message of defiance.

Returning to the States the next day, I struggled to erase the thoughts of the ugly side of the meeting. Despite the horrible image that had been projected, I departed with gratitude for the opportunity of the twelve-year experience and the memorable moments of that time. I spent my last three days with the company mulling over the priceless encounters and trusting relationships I developed during the twelve-year period. Summarizing my departing thoughts in an e-mail message, I bade the recipients an *adieu*.

I began this adventure by accepting an impossible task in a place renowned for its food, wine, unique language, and culture. Long before that day in April 1994 when I accepted the assignment, my fortitude and drive to succeed were cemented by my dad's tough love. After being denied entry into the company's manufacturing core experience program in the mid 80s (a program touted as a developmental stepping stone for promising leaders), I came to accept that the two rejections had been a blessing. After a devastating second rejection by the administrators of the program, I pursued an understanding of what I needed to improve to be accepted. Taking my concern to the president of the company, I received a cordial response but no answers to the question. I could have given up and drifted through my career in obscurity, but I chose to persevere. Despite the warnings of naysayers and the adversity they predicted, I agreed to accept Norm's challenge and succeeded with five straight years (1995 through 2000) of flawless on-time deliveries of all models of propulsion systems to Airbus. It was a benchmark for delivery performance in our company and in the industry for years.

For the less fortuitous of our society, life's highway is paved with adverse moments, cynics, and skepticism. Nevertheless, through it all, it's the memories of the meaningful encounters, unique experiences, and the relationships we develop from them that power us through adversity. I could have taken a defensive posture when starting the task, but rather, I evolved to thinking of myself as the quarterback of my team.

I look back at my tenure in the assignment without regret. I wouldn't swap the experience or the enrichment provided by the intercultural relationships for anything. Perhaps my greatest takeaway from this wonderful experience is that broadening cultural exposure expands one's perception of others in the world. And that mutual acceptance is the mortar of bridges that span cultural, racial, and societal divides. With an open mind, personal extension, and uninhibited regard, we can achieve cross-cultural acceptance and bridge most of our divides.

So, to my international friends, colleagues, and valued partners, a grateful caress of each cheek. *Merci beaucoup.* Thanks for the enlightenment and lasting memories.

Fin

Conclusion

I started this unexpected journey plunged into an uncertain, intense working environment in a foreign land. A twelve-year connection with a locale and its culture would likely change anyone. It certainly changed me and my perceptions of other parts of the world. Granted, the food and wine of France were magnificent, but my fondest memories of the era were founded in the exposure to vastly different people, their cultures, and the trusting alliances that developed. We're not responsible for the hand life deals to us, but we are accountable for our willingness to extend ourselves to others not like us.

When wading into my appointed task, I had a feeling that my success would be judged by the duration of the recovery and how soon on-time deliveries of propulsion systems would be resumed and sustained. Fortunately, with the help of people on both sides of the Atlantic, the milestone was accomplished in little more than a year. But there is much more to this story than the delivery achievement. Departing our company twelve years after beginning this voyage, the focus of my earlier skeptical notion transformed to a greater understanding of the value of acceptance and the relationships created by it. Seemingly distant acquaintances became trustworthy, inspiring propellants.

Entering a new world eager to assist in recovering an ailing aircraft propulsion program, I left discovering something more powerful than the thrust of the engines, it was the sensation and influence of mutual acceptance.

Acknowledgments

This book would not have been possible had it not been for the support of many encouraging people. I would like to thank those who provided inspiration, advice, guidance, and assistance to me in completing this book.

I would not be where I am today without the love and guidance of my mother and father, Mary, and Samuel Pair Sr. Hardworking parents, they strove to make a better life for their children than it had been for them.

Thanks to jet engine maker Pratt and Whitney and their upper management team, notably Mark Coran, former Vice President of Operations, Dick Leonard, Vice President of the Product Delivery Center, and Marshall Yudin, Head of Engine Assembly and Test, for choosing me to address a crisis in France. Their faith and confidence in my ability to succeed in this critical assignment provided an enormous incentive to succeed. I will forever be grateful to them.

Many thanks to my patient and supportive counterparts at Airbus, who I partnered with for twelve years to resolve propulsion systems and aircraft delivery issues. They were persistent motivators. I'd be remiss if I didn't thank the Airbus Industrial Programs and Quality Vice Presidents, Jacques Mousson, and Michel Platonoff, for their faith and trust in me. They had a tremendous inspirational influence on the writing of this book. A special thanks to Madame Karine Franz, a former Airbus colleague and true friend, for her assistance with the writing and translations of French language stated in the book.

Thank you to the on-site airline representatives I worked with to resolve problems associated with their aircraft. Mr. Kim and Mr. Lee of Korean Airlines had a profound influence on the writing of this book. Through our collaboration, they awakened me to stand in their shoes when considering their aircraft concerns and those of other airline customers.

I am extremely grateful to the men and women of my Toulouse team and the folks at the podding facility. Their dedication and allegiance lifted me up during adverse times and helped us to succeed as a team.

I would like to thank the people of Toulouse and other regions I visited in France, who embraced me, shared laughs, and were the propellants that powered me through countless issues. You will always be in my memories.

Finally, there is no way I could have completed this book to a publishable state without the wonderful collaborators who provided advice and guidance through the writing and publishing process. A hearty thanks to the people of the critique groups I participated in who read my writing and offered helpful recommendations for improvements.

Last, but not least, thanks so much to editors Jacqueline Congro and Lia Ottaviano whose coaching and editorial insight further developed, shaped and honed the writing of this book. The sharp-eyes and spot on questions of Susan Gaigher during her proof reading of this work were a god sent. These women were invaluable in guiding me through the completion of this book.

For those who inspired, and supported me during my duty in France and the writing of this book, a very grateful thank you for giving me reasons to be hopeful and optimistic to succeed.

About the Author

Born in Norfolk, Virginia, Samuel E. Pair lived most of his life in Connecticut. Working his way up from an entry level engineering aide at jet engine maker, Pratt and Whitney, his education and years of experience in project engineering, quality assurance, manufacturing, and engine assembly engineering, helped him progress to higher levels in his career.

Sam, a.k.a., *Yankee Noir*, has a bachelor's degree in Mechanical Engineering and advanced studies in Environmental Engineering from the University of Hartford, as well as a master's degree in Management from Rensselaer Polytechnic Institute. He is a four-time nominee and finalist of the Black Engineer of the Year Award, presented by the Council of Engineering Deans of Historical Black Colleges and Universities, the Lockheed Martin Company, and the Mobil Corporation.

Sam is an inspirational leader with a zest for life and an ardent interest in cultural awareness and cross-cultural relationship building. An acclaimed aerospace engineer, international operations manager, industrial specialist, and speaker, he has extensive brand expertise in building relational bridges with people of different cultures.

Since retiring from Pratt and Whitney in 2006 after thirty-eight years of service, he has been an industrial consultant serving local manufacturers. He has also spent time developing the skills leading to the writing and publishing of his debut book, *Le Yankee Noir – The Power of Acceptance*. He is working on his next writing project. A sequel titled *Le Yankee Noir – The Color of Acceptance,* the next volume of his acceptance experiences, is underway. He has two grown daughters and continues to live in Connecticut.

Sam with hosts Jacqueline and Andre'

Sam with weather vane.